D1607853

Dark Tongues

Liber Vagatorum, Der Betler Orden (Augsburg, 1512).

Dark Tongues

The Art of Rogues and Riddlers

Daniel Heller-Roazen

ZONE BOOKS · NEW YORK

2013

© 2013 Daniel Heller-Roazen

ZONE BOOKS

1226 Prospect Avenue

Brooklyn, NY 11218

Printed in the United States of America.

Distributed by The MIT Press,
Cambridge, Massachusetts, and London, England

Library of Congress Cataloging-in-Publication Data

Heller-Roazen, Daniel.
    Dark tongues / Daniel Heller-Roazen.
        pages cm.
    ISBN 978-1-935408-33-8
        1. Jargon (Terminology) 2. Cant. 3. Languages, Secret.
4. Poetics. 5. Historical linguistics. 6. Anthropological
linguistics. I. Title.

        P409H35 2013
        417–dc23
                                        2012047271

Contents

The howtosayto itiswhatitis humustwhomust worder schall.
A darktongues, kunning.

James Joyce, *Finnegans Wake*

CHAPTER ONE

Forkings

That human beings are speaking beings is an old and oft-stated belief. Aristotle was perhaps the first to make of it the basis of a definition when, in a famous passage of the *Politics*, he declared that among all animals, "man is the only one that has language" (*logon de monon anthrōpos ekhei tōn zōōn*).[1] "Language," however, was and remains an obscure word. The fact that the Greek philosopher's animal that has language could have been renamed, in Latin translation, the "rational animal" (*animal rationale*), affords one example of how a term for the fact of speaking can lend itself to several interpretations. Aristotle's *logos*, in Greek, signified a thicket of notions usually distinguished today: "word," "speech," and "discourse," to be sure, but also "reason," more generally, and more specifically, arithmetical "ratio" and musical "interval."[2] The Aristotelian argument, therefore, can be recast in more ways than one. Yet its grammar is also significant in itself. Aristotle's words suggest that what human beings possess in contrast to all others is an ability that may be named by a singular noun. It is the faculty of speaking. However self-evident it may seem today, that claim runs up against a reality more perplexing than the ancient philosopher and many of his successors seem to have been willing to admit. It can be simply stated: speaking beings never speak language, except in speaking languages.

English has one word for two linguistic beings that may clearly be distinguished: on the one hand, "language," insofar as it designates the generic fact of speaking, and on the other, "language," insofar as it points to a variety of speech, such as Armenian, Japanese, or

Arabic. Some foreign tongues are more perspicuous. The Romance languages, for example, regularly admit a lexical distinction between an abstract term for speech (such as *lenguaje, linguagem, langage,* or *linguaggio*) and a specific term for a language, with its words and rules (*idioma, lengua, langue, lingua*). That there is a relation between the ideas expressed by these two sets of terms, of course, can hardly be doubted. It points to an epistemological circle that, explicitly or implicitly, sustains a practice of definition by abstraction. The single faculty of language can be found nowhere but in languages, which are plural by definition; yet languages, for their part, cannot be considered as the members of a class unless one has presupposed this concept: language.[3] Depending on one's interests and one's perspective, one may wish to consider the notion or its instantiations, the faculty in general or its varieties. Yet the point of departure, among speaking beings, remains this first forking. Whenever there is language, in the definite singular, there are, in truth, languages, in indefinite and indeed innumerable multiplicity; whenever there are languages, in the plural, one may detect the shadow of a speaking faculty, no less perceptible for remaining distinct, by definition, from every tongue. The predicament may be extolled or decried, but it cannot be denied. "Languages," Mallarmé observed: "imperfect in that, being many, the highest of them is lacking."[4]

If one considers the history of investigations into the nature of speech, it is difficult to avoid the impression that more often than not, the discourse on language, in its simplicity, has left little room for the multiplicity of tongues. That human beings are speaking beings has been interpreted as implying that, by nature, they confer with one another about the good and the bad, and do not only signal the pleasant and the unpleasant; that they aim to impart to each other, as best they can, their ideas and conceptions, for whatever ends; that they designate, act, reason, calculate, or communicate. The possibilities are many. The "theory of language," in any case, has tended to consider its object as a single being.

This much may be an inheritance from antiquity, at least with regard to those forms of knowledge, such as philosophy and grammar, that claim their roots in the disciplines of Greece and Rome. More than once, it has been observed that the Greeks and Romans displayed relatively little interest in the idioms that, as they knew well, surrounded them. Scholars have advanced several hypotheses in explanation of this omission. Perhaps the Greeks and Romans did not trouble themselves with foreign tongues because they held the peoples they called "barbarians" to speak idioms absolutely unlike their own, being both unknown and essentially unknowable. Perhaps, instead, the Greeks and Romans deemed foreign languages unworthy objects of study because they held them to be essentially like their own, differing only in their vocabularies.[5] It is remarkable, in any case, that the great exponents of classical disciplines as diverse and sophisticated as philosophy, geography, historiography, and grammar all concurred in seeing no need to treat the plurality of languages as a fact in need of special comment.

The Homeric epics, the earliest monuments of Greek literature, portray a world that hardly requires interpreters, and in which important speaking subjects, whether Achaean or Trojan, all converse freely in one tongue. Certain passages, to be sure, indicate that the Homeric poet was well aware of some foreign idioms: thus the *Iliad* evokes the Carians, "barbarian" (*barbarophōnoi*) on account of their tongue, and the *Odyssey* dwells briefly on the Cretans, said to be "of many roots and tongues."[6] But such non-Greek languages would seem, in the Homeric world, to be signs of distant marvels. The philosophers said little more. There is no doubt that Plato, for example, was familiar with the fact of linguistic diversity. Yet when he dedicated a dialogue to the nature and formation of names, he wasted no words on the differences between Greek and other tongues, nor did his Socrates see fit to investigate the reasons why forms of speech clearly differed among the parts of Greece, to say nothing of different peoples. The world of the *Cratylus* is one of a single language, in every sense. Aristotle, who defined the human peoples as the sole possessor of *logos*, proposed an elaborate theory of language and logic, which he developed in treatises bearing on numerous subjects, such as signification, deduction, poetry, rhetoric, politics, and biology. Yet everywhere Aristotle proceeds as if his *logos* could be treated as one.

One might expect the classical historians to have had a livelier interest in differences of speech, and to a certain degree, this is indeed the case. Herodotus, the first in the tradition, noted with curiosity that in different regions, the earth bears not one but three names, each of which appears to evoke a woman: Europe, Asia, Libya.[7] He observed, moreover, that the same divinities seem to reappear from culture to culture, named each time differently.[8] Yet despite his commitment to studying the testaments to human diversity, Herodotus saw no need to wager any explanation for them, nor did he offer a commentary on the proliferation of apparent synonyms among the peoples of the world. One might well have wondered why it is that different communities call the same things by so many different names, even if one did not go so far as to pose this fundamental and unavoidable question: What sense may one give to the fact that the human capacity to speak finds expression only in a multiplicity of tongues?

It would be untrue, of course, to maintain that the thinkers of the classical world simply ignored the problem of linguistic difference. References to variation in dialect and language are never hard to find, and occasionally, the question of plurality even emerged in philosophical form. Democritus, the early atomist, seems, for example, to have treated the multiplicity of languages as a phenomenon in need of scientific analysis. According to Diodorus, the materialist addressed the question in a book now lost to us, arguing that variations in speech result from distinctions of geography and climate.[9] Yet his discussion, if it did exist, would have represented more the exception than the rule. The evidence suggests that the classical Greek and Roman thinkers, by and large, believed speech to be a thing from which multiplicity could be, as it were, subtracted, if not in reality, then certainly for the purposes of theoretical speculation. They accorded only slight importance to the fact that language is always distributed in languages. To this degree, at least, their view was not inconsonant with that of the Bible, which was to exert such

an influence on later thinking about the nature of the speaking animal. According to the author of the Book of Genesis, there was an
age in which "the whole earth was of one tongue." In sacred time,
if not in history, language could, therefore, be purified of the difference of languages. Confusion could come later.[10]

Today, there is, of course, a form of inquiry and knowledge that
takes the diversity of languages to be fundamental. It is the science of language. Linguistics must admit, as an axiom, that there
is not only a distinction between language and nonlanguage but
also that there is a distinction between one language and another.
Admittedly, linguists may define this distinction in several ways,
accepting, for example, existing sociological determinations, such
as labels of national language and dialect, or seeking to ground this
distinction in the consciousness of groups of speaking subjects.
But linguistics must admit this much: there are systematic formal
differences between languages. Any grammatical analysis, in the
traditional sense, will illustrate this fact.

Yet if linguistics differs from grammar in the old sense, it is in
passing from the diversity of such idioms to more general considerations. Presupposing that there are various languages that share
properties that, once abstracted and combined, define the faculty
of speaking, linguists may, for example, establish historical and
genetic relations between languages: derivations and divergences,
resemblances and dissimilarities. At times, linguistics can thus offer
a clear historical answer to the riddle of linguistic diversity: multiple
tongues may be shown to derive from a single language. Indo-European philology presents perhaps the most powerful example of this
kind. Through close examination of the distinctive properties of a
host of European and Asian languages, the scholars of the nineteenth
century succeeded in revealing a series of striking correlations that
suggested a common source now lost to us: "Indo-German," as it
was once named, or "Proto-Indo-European," as its current practi-
tioners in English choose to call it.

The rigor of such scientific inquiry, however, derives from the
limits it sets itself. No serious comparative linguist ever sought to

argue that all tongues emerged from a single source, for reasons both methodological and material. Comparative linguistic analysis rests on the supposition that languages, in general, are distinct in their rules and in their elements. From this perspective alone are correlations and analogies significant. For example, if the characteristics uniting Greek and Sanskrit, or Old Irish and Latin, are remarkable and in need of explanation, this is because they are, in principle, unexpected. Only where the natural diversity of idioms seems lacking will one think to argue for a single source. And, it should be added, some languages alone seem to be related in such a form. There are many European and Indian tongues, such as Basque, Hungarian, and the multiple Dravidic languages, that appear clearly irreducible to the "Indo-European" set. There are, more importantly, entire groups and "families" of idioms that seem to bear no substantial genetic links among each other. The Afro-Asiatic or "Hamito-Semitic" languages, for example, do not appear to derive from the same "protolanguage" as the Indo-European, nor can one establish that they derive from the same roots as the Altaic, the Sino-Tibetan, or the Iroquoian tongues, to choose only some from many possible examples. In linguistic investigation, grammatical diversity remains a fact that must be presupposed. Only exceptionally can it be explained.

If it is to possess a single object, the science of language, therefore, must pass by abstraction from languages to language: the faculty of speech. That transition may well recall the inference by which the philosophers of antiquity moved from a single language, such as Greek, to a general principle, such as *logos*. Yet linguistics has made of this procedure a first step in the constitution of a new mode of inquiry, which has led to a major discovery concerning the fact of speaking. It is worth recalling today, if only because it seems to be increasingly forgotten. Since the emergence of comparative grammar in the nineteenth century, the science of language has established, with increasing precision, that the utterances of speaking subjects, as a whole, systematically respect a limited set of formal rules of grammar, even where speaking subjects themselves have no conscious knowledge of them: rules of syntax, which dictate the arrangement of phrase structures, independently of their content; rules of morphology, which determine the possible shapes that expressions can acquire within sequences of discourse; rules, finally, of phonology, which bear on a restricted set of sounds that possess no meaning in themselves but that every speaker of a language somehow knows to order, combine, and understand.

This much, however, is no less enigmatic today than it was in antiquity: speaking subjects speak only languages, and their basic element is opacity. Of course, for an individual, study and acquaintance can dispel, in part, the obscurity of unknown tongues, but in general, foreign languages appear to speaking subjects as those that are resistant to comprehension and appropriation. One may even find in the fundamental perception of unintelligibility the simplest index of the difference of languages. Two tongues can be considered distinct when their respective speakers, each employing their own idioms, fail systematically to understand each other. One may well hold, therefore, in accordance with an old tradition in philosophy, that there is language from the moment in which there is signification, reasoning, and articulated intention. One may also concede, granting the validity of linguistic research, that there is language from the moment in which one may detect, in a single idiom, a finite grammatical system that speaking subjects unknowingly respect in producing an infinity of utterances. Nonetheless, one may be certain that there are languages, in the plural, if such modes of understanding can come systematically to a halt, as rules of forming correct utterances in one tongue run up against those in another. Language, in its singularity, may be grasped as a mode of intelligibility common to human beings as a rational species, or to communities united in following the rules of grammars. Languages, in their plurality, point to impenetrability and incommensurability, which incessantly sow division among those who speak.

The most obvious illustrations of the fracture produced by languages are to be found whenever speaking communities, coming into contact with each other, discover that their idioms, otherwise fairly reliable means of communication, forbid all understanding. It has always been known that in such circumstances, little is less eloquent than discourse; little is more obstinately unintelligible—less, in short, like language—than *a* language. What could be more unfathomable, in itself, than the significations enclosed in an unknown tongue, in sentences, words, or even such small soundings as a change in vowel quantity, a heightening or lowering of a pitch, an addition, to a string of consonants and vowels, of an aspiration, such as that of the letter *h*? Those who speak a language somehow know that such elements can all decide meanings that are irreducible to the physical properties of speech. Authorities of various kinds have always recommended, for this reason, that, when confronted with the plurality of tongues, one set languages aside. It is wiser, then, to turn to forms of expression unencumbered by the subtleties of grammar: forms such as gesture, "the discourse common to all men" (*omnium hominum communis sermo*),[11] as Quintilian once wrote, "pantomime," which Rousseau held to be older than and prior to individual tongues,[12] dance, which can convey meanings without words, as Lucian believed,[13] or music, so often extolled as a universal means of expression.

Yet the truth is that one need not look to encounters between different linguistic communities for evidence of the impenetrability brought upon speaking subjects by their tongues. There are occasions when the confounding force of languages exerts itself within the limits of what would, in all other respects, appear to be a single grammatical system. A new and unexpected divisiveness then can be perceived.

This is not merely a consequence of the continuous nature of linguistic change, which dictates that in speech, as Dante wrote, "every variation varies in itself,"[14] such that from one time to another, a single language grows ever more opaque to those who would make use of it. One must also take into account a fundamental aspect of the power to speak that has not received the attention it deserves from philosophers or linguists. Among the capacities implicit in the faculty of language there is the ability, possessed by all speaking

16

subjects, albeit within limits, to take apart and rebuild a single tongue. One language, in itself, can form a fork, not only by nature, but also by will and art. In private or in public, those who speak a language retain the capacity to draw from their knowledge of its grammar the elements of a new and cryptic variety of speech. Such an idiom may be playful or serious, a secret shared by children in their games or by adults in their work. It may affect individual words or phrases, phonemes or flexions, formulae or sentences, whether taken in isolation or in coordination. It may appear to be as alien as a foreign language, only slightly different from the idiom from which it springs, or almost indistinct from the language from which it has been made, its traits as imperceptible as its hidden sense. At the limit, the existence of such an occult idiom may itself become a doubtful thing, a hypothesis of a hidden object that one might affirm or deny. The ways of splitting speech are many, surely no fewer than their occasions. Yet each time a tongue, by effort and by skill, divides or even merely appears to divide in two, the same perplexing fact may be discerned. It seems that human beings not only speak and speak languages. They also break and scatter them, with all their reason, in the sounds and letters of tongues made multiple and dark.

CHAPTER TWO

Coquillars

In 1890, there appeared in the *Mémoires de la Société Linguistique de Paris* an article by the twenty-three-year-old Marcel Schwob, who had yet to publish the works of poetry and prose for which he would one day be known. The essay was a study of a medieval manuscript belonging to the Archives of Dijon that Schwob had transcribed, introduced, and annotated. He had learned of the existence of the codex from a bibliographical note that Joseph Garnier, archivist of the Côte-d'Or in Burgundy, had devoted to it in 1848. Garnier himself had chosen not to comment in detail on the materials he had made known, and the eminent French philologist Francisque Michel, to whom Garnier mailed one of the forty fascicles of the manuscript, had also not seen fit to discuss it. Schwob thus became the first to investigate a set of documents that had most likely remained unstudied since the time of their redaction in the fifteenth century, and it was his essay that revealed their curious contents to the public.

The manuscript contained a legal dossier, drawn from the records of the Burgundian capital, concerning a company of bandits arrested, tried, and condemned in the year 1455. The deeds the wrongdoers were accused of having committed seem, at first glance, unremarkable in themselves. The authorities alleged that in Dijon and the neighboring countryside, the vagabonds had committed various acts of violent depredation: picking and breaking locks, plundering coffers, holding up hapless travelers on their way, robbing unsuspecting merchants who shared rooms in inns. It was said that some of the idlers were skilled in the arts of petty cheats and swindlers; it was claimed that others would not hesitate to murder to bring themselves profit. There was no doubt that the company of rogues possessed no wealth of its own. But poverty being the mother of invention, the brigands had devised an ingenious technique that enabled them to appropriate one thing that they and their countrymen otherwise possessed in common. This fact lent their many crimes some originality. Before seizing any precious goods from the burghers, clerics, and aristocrats among whom they lived, the fifteenth-century Burgundian bandits had taken hold of the language. They had made of the common speech of their time a jargon, "an exquisite language," as the city authorities relate, "that other people cannot understand" (*un langaige exquis, que aultres gens ne scevent entendre*).[1]

Chief among the expressions of obscure meaning that the vagabonds had forged was the name by which they were known to each other: "Coquillars," "People of the Shell," or, as one might also say today, "Shellsters."[2] The extracts from the manuscript published by Schwob opened with a note on this one term. "It is true that the aforementioned persons have among themselves a certain language in jargon [*certain langaige de jargon*] and other signs by which they come to recognize each other; and these bandits call themselves Coquillars, which should be understood in the sense that they are 'the Companions of the Shell,' who, it is said, have among them a King, called 'the King of the Shell.'"[3] Only after establishing this preliminary identification did the manuscript relate in detail the various crimes for which the Coquillars had been condemned:

> It is also true, as has been said, that some of the aforementioned Coquillars are breakers of locks, cases, and coffers. Others are tricksters and rob people by exchanging coins for gold, or gold for coins, or by buying items of merchandise. Others make, bear, and sell false threads and goldlike chains. Others bear and sell or make false stones, claiming they are diamonds, rubies, and other precious stones. Others sleep in an inn with a merchant, steal from themselves and from the

merchant, bemoan their misfortune with the robbed merchant, while having a man working for them with whom they then share the booty. Others cheat at dice games, and they win all the money of those with whom they play. They know subtleties such as card games and hop-scotch, and no one can win against them. And what is worse, many of them are spies, and attack people in the woods and on the roads, being thieves and murderers. One may presume that it is there that they lead their dissolute life. When they have spent all their money, they go away without anything at all; sometimes they abandon even their clothes, and they return soon afterward, mounted, dressed, and full of gold and silver, as has been said.[4]

It may be safely supposed that all these vicious acts had been repeatedly attested before the appearance of the depredators tried in 1455. Doubtless for this reason, the municipal papers dwelled less on the fact of the Coquillars' crimes than on the special means that they employed to commit them. The legal documents leave no doubt that this means was linguistic and, more exactly, nominal in char-acter. Jean Rabustel, public prosecutor and clerk of the court of the viscountcy of Dijon, made this much clear at the opening of his sum-mary of the trial: "Every trickery of which they make use has its name in their jargon, and no one could understand it, were he not of their number and compact, or if one of them did not reveal it to another."[5]

As a source of evidence, Jean Rabustel cited "Perrenet le Fournier, barber dwelling in Dijon, of the age of thirty-four years, more or less." Perrenet testified that he willingly sought out the People of the Shell, not, of course, to join their perfidious company in earnest, but to "see certain secrets, so as to guard against deception were he to find himself where evil seed was sowed."[6] Thus the barber could bear witness to the fact that the Coquillars "name properly, in their language, all the matters of their sect, which matters were revealed to him by many of them, who did not distrust him, since he feigned to be as subtle as they."[7] His findings were confirmed by other sources, such as "Jean Vote, known as 'the Auvergnac,' quar-ryman dwelling in Dijon, of thirty-six years of age, more or less."[8]

21

The Auvergnac testified to the fact that to each of the customary names for their tricks and crimes there corresponded, in the special language of the Coquillars, a hidden name, whose sense the brigands took pains to keep to themselves.

As a rule, the sources relate, "when they speak in their afore-mentioned jargon, and one of them says a bit too much in a place where it seems that there might be people who could harm them or who could betray them, the first among them who takes notice will start to spit, in the manner of a man who suffers from a cold, unable to call forth his saliva." As one act of expression turns to another, "each of the Companions of the Shell then falls silent, and changes the subject, and speaks of something else."[9]

Yet at times, their precious terms did nonetheless escape them, and then onlookers and eavesdroppers could penetrate into their secret tongue. The Burgundian manuscript lavished the greatest attention on the lexical information that could then be gleaned. After a summary description of the idlers and their violent ways, Jean Rabustel offered a veritable glossary of hidden terms and phrases, filling folio after folio with definitions of the expressions that the Coquillars had sought to conceal. He conceded that his efforts were of a synthetic nature and issued in a compendium of terms that no single Companion of the Shell, strictly speaking, would have employed. "The aforementioned and other men, who are of the company of the Coquillars," he explained, "have in their language many names, and they do not know all the sciences or trickeries of which mention has been made," for while some are "skilled in doing one thing," others are trained in doing another.

First the prosecutor offered an enumeration of the professional activities into which the class of rogues could be divided: a catalogue of *noms de métier* of the most obscure and iniquitous sort. Then he furnished a lengthy key, proceeding to explain phrases as well as names:

> A *crocheteur* is someone who picks locks. A *vendegeur* is a snatcher of bags. A *beffleur* is a thief who draws fools into the game. An *envoyeur* is

a murderer. A *desrocheur* is someone who leaves nothing to the person he robs.... A *blanc coulon* is someone who sleeps with a merchant or someone else and robs him of his money, his clothes and everything he has, and throws it from the window to his companion, who waits below. A *baladeur* is someone who rushes ahead to speak to a churchman or someone else to whom he wants to offer a fake golden chain or a fraudulent stone. A *pipeur* is a player of dice and other games in which there are tricks and treachery.... *Fustiller* is to change the dice. They call the court of any place the *marine* or the *rouhe*. They call the sergeant the *gaffres*.... A simple man who knows nothing of their ways is a *sire* or a *duppe* or a *blanc*.... A bag is a *fellouse*.... To do a *roy David* is to open a lock, a door, a coffer, and to close it again.... To *bazir* someone is to kill him.... *Jour* is torture.... When one of them says, "*Estoffe!*" it means that he is asking for his booty from some earnings made somehow from the knowledge of the Shell. And when he says, "*Estoffe, ou je faugerey!*" it means that he will betray whoever does not pay his part.[10]

This list, while selective, suffices to suggest one fundamental fact about the Coquillars' hidden speech: namely, that it constituted a willful deformation of the language generally in use in late medieval northern France. The words contained in the legal documents would have been known in large part to the inhabitants of Burgundy, but not in the meanings lent to them by the Companions of the Shell. The rogues, in other words, had selected certain words and phrases, withdrawn their usual sense from them, and conferred upon them a new and impenetrable significance. The procedures by which they altered the meanings of terms were multiple. Several ties might link a Middle French expression to its homonym in jargon. In certain cases, one may detect a direct lexical tie, as when the *crocheteur*, or "picker," comes to name "celluy qui sait crocheter serrures," "he who knows how to pick locks." In other cases, the Coquillars forged their terms by subtler rhetorical means. Sometimes they proceeded by metonymy, as when they named the court of justice the "wheel" (*rouhe*), alluding to the tool that, if not avoided, might well prove the ultimate instrument of their punishment. Elsewhere, they worked by metaphor, as when they called the innocent victim of their deceptive arts a *dupe*, or in other words, an *huppe*, or "pigeon," that is, a bird to be killed and consumed with relish.[11] Yet in many cases, the connection between the ordinary meaning of a term and its technical sense, while comprehensible in hindsight, could not be anticipated by any given rule. The possibilities of suggestion, substitution, and abbreviation were too numerous. Consider the exclamatory utterance "*Estoffe!*" in the sense provided by Rabustel. To hear that single word as shorthand for a proposition, as well as a demand, one would need to apply to it principles of allusion and truncation, according to a pattern that it would difficult, if not impossible, to divine.

The medieval legal dossier, to be sure, did not take pains to analyze the various mechanisms that the Coquillars had exploited in their inventions. Yet it named the type of speech to which they gave rise in no uncertain terms, for it designated the bandits' tongue as a *langaige exquis*, a discourse literally *recherché* (the verb *exquerre* meaning originally "to seek out") and, by extension, "noteworthy," "refined," and "cultivated." More repeatedly, the manuscript referred to the idiom of the Company of the Shell by a richly ambiguous noun: "jargon." That medieval French term and its related forms (*jargoun, gargon, ghargun, gergon, gorgon*) had long designated not so much meaningful speech as the making of sounds resembling it, from animal noises to babble, prattle, and chatter.[12] In the earliest attestation of the word, which dates to the end of the twelfth century, *gargun*, for example, names an act of intelligible, yet inhuman communication: chirping. In a fable, Marie de France evokes the counsel at which birds "all spoke in their jargon, affirming with reason" (*Tuit diseient en lur gargun / e afermoënt par resun*).[13] Three centuries later, Charles d'Orléans still employed the noun in a related sense, writing that "there is no beast or bird that does not sing and cry out in its jargon, once the season has cast off its mantle of wind, cold and rain" (*Il n'y a ne beste n'oyseau / Qu'en son jargon ne chante et crie: / Le tems a laissié son manteau / De vent, de froidure et de pluye*).[14] Later, in a secondary sense, the term came to denote a foreign and

24

incomprehensible tongue.[15] In *Richard li biaus*, an anonymous Old French romance dating from the thirteenth or fourteenth century, the word appears in a meaning close to that in which the Burgundian officials employ it, indicating a language that is proper to thieves and accessible only to those skilled in their deceitful arts.[16]

That Marcel Schwob was drawn to the Burgundian brigands above all for the speech that they devised may be inferred from the title he gave to his essay of 1890: "The Jargon of the Coquillars in 1455." A year earlier, in collaboration with his friend Georges Guieysse, he had contributed to the *Mémoires de la Société Linguistique de Paris* one of the first works to bring the methods of modern linguistics to bear on the peculiar idioms cultivated by society's dangerous classes: a paper titled "Reflections on French Argot."[17] Schwob presented his study of the medieval manuscript from the archives in Dijon as a natural sequel to that essay. In his introductory remarks, he observed that historians of French argot possessed only a small number of fundamental texts. "Until now, the sources of jargon" consisted essentially of a few sets of literary and historical texts containing isolated words or phrases, such as the term *marié*, found in medieval chronicles, "which has been incorrectly interpreted, and which means *hanged*"; the word *dupe*, recorded and glossed, in a police document from 1426, as the name of the prey of scoundrels' tricks; formulae contained in late medieval farces, songs, and ballads by such writers as Eustache Deschamps and Charles d'Orléans; and works by the didactic humorists who preceded Rabelais, such as Jean Molinet. In his brief account of the old founts of jargon, Schwob then named three exceptional sets of texts: the manuscripts copied by Raoul Tainguy before 1425, which contain works by Deschamps, Jacques de Cessoles, and Froissard; six ballads in jargon long attributed to François Villon; and five ballads in jargon copied in a manuscript belonging to the Royal Library of Stockholm, recently published by Auguste Vitu, who believed them to be also by Villon.[18]

When compared with the legal papers concerning the Coquillars, however, all the documentary sources receded into relative insignificance, as Schwob himself was the first to observe. "Thanks to a criminal trial preserved in the regional archives of the Côte-d'Or," he declared in his preface, "I can now publish an independent source, the most important of all those of the fifteenth century (with the exception of the ballads), both for the number of the terms treated and for the details given over the course of the proceedings."[19] The legal records were unrivalled in their linguistic wealth and, as Schwob indicated, they were comparable only to the six ballads traditionally attributed to Villon. Those Middle French poems certainly contained at least as many evocations of the obscure language of idlers as the Burgundian court papers. But it was Jean Rabustel, the prosecutor of Dijon, who had taken the trouble to gloss each obscure name and phrase, providing commentaries and reformulations of the bandits' expressions. The prosecutor's grammatical scruples, in this sense, were unmatched, even by the author who possessed the skill to set the secret words of jargon in line and stanza.

Schwob did not remark upon the unmistakable, if surprising, coincidence between the interests of the prosecutor and the philologist, the lawyer and the linguist. It would seem that for him, it was the link between the poet and the bandits that mattered most. Editing the papers concerning the trial of the Coquillars, Schwob insisted above all on these two points: the antiquity of this source of jargon and the fact that it cast a new light on the one poet who, for him, "achieved the greatest poetic glory in his century."[20] Yet the truth was that Schwob's findings bore above all on the works by Villon that had traditionally been considered the least glorious of all: not the *Testament*, the *Lais*, or any of the memorable single lyric pieces for which Villon was so loved, but the six (and perhaps eleven) ballads set in the strange and apparently hermetic tongue of malefactors.

Already in 1489, in the first printed edition of the poet's works, Pierre Levet had separated these texts from the others, dubbing them "Ballades en jargon et jobelin." It was apparent that they were all addressed to criminals of different kinds and specialties, not least the second of their number, which opened with an opaque, if unmistakable, apostrophe to the Company of the Shell: "Coquillars enruans à ruel."[21] And for centuries, few had doubted that the strange idiom of these six ballads meant to evoke the calculatedly impenetrable jargon of ruffians. Yet the status of this curious poetic language had been the subject of considerable debate.

Villon's early readers appear to have been inclined to treat the discourse of the ballads as a faithful rendering of the speech of medieval rogues, despite the possibly troublesome consequences that such a reading implied for the biography of the poet. When he undertook to produce a comprehensive edition of Villon's works in the sixteenth century, Clément Marot, for one, praised the "antique and noble language" of Villon's great poems, while taking exception, for this reason, to the six ballads, which he refused to edit. "Concerning the jargon," he commented, "I leave all corrections and commentaries to Villon's successors in the art of the claw and crowbar" (*Touchant le jargon, je le laisse à corriger et exposer aux successeurs de Villon en l'art de la pinse et du croq*).[22] Geoffroy Tory, in the same generation, was no less severe. On the opening page of his treatise *Le champ fleury*, he condemned "three types of men who struggle and compete to corrupt and deform language": "skinners of Latin, jokesters, and *jargonneurs*." Yet he immediately conceded that among the third variety, there had been one poet: "When *jargonneurs* hold forth in their malicious jargon and nasty language," he wrote, "it seems to me that they show only that they are destined for the gallows, yet it would be better were they never born. I admit that Master François Villon, in his time, was wonderfully ingenious; yet he would have done better had he attended to doing some better thing."[23] Villon's subsequent readers often expressed a similar dissatisfaction with the unruly ballads, which few editors deigned to translate into more standard French. Some denied that these poems were, in fact, the genuine work of the author of the *Lais* and the *Testament*. Others held that their language was less the record of any historically attested form of speech than a bizarre and Baroque invention: "some imagining of the poet," as Lucien Schöne argued in 1888, "rather than the unique monument of a vanished language."[24]

Schwob's edition and study of the records of 1455 settled that debate. In a lecture given before the Académie des Inscriptions et Belles-Lettres in 1890, he produced a strictly philological demonstration that the idiom of the ballads was, in large part, that of the Coquillars condemned in Dijon. One might, of course, continue to interpret historical and biographical indices in the poet's work, hypothesizing about the dealings that Villon himself may have had with the Company of the Shell. Schwob himself sought to do as much in his "imaginary life" of the fifteenth-century poet. But this much would henceforth be certain: a fact of linguistic identity could be ascertained. Schwob showed that no fewer than twenty-four of the obscure terms in the poems had been recorded in the Burgundian proceedings, where they had been explained, translated from one region of the language into another. "These words," Schwob continued, bringing his proof by lexical units to a higher sum, "being repeated many times, form a total of fifty-eight terms, with respect to which, from now on, discussion can concern only matters of nuance and etymology, the meanings having been established."[25] "The fact that such a large number of words are common to the language of Villon and those of the Coquillars," he concluded, "suffices to show that these pieces were truly written in the jargon of malefactors."[26]

There now arose, however, one fundamental question, which strictly historical and philological forms of evidence, on their own, could not resolve. Schwob had unearthed the oldest major witness to the secret idiom of rogues; he had shown, moreover, that it was to become the medium of a poet's work. From his research, one could conclude that "the art of the claw and crowbar" and the art of verse had become strictly inseparable, not slowly or gradually, but almost immediately and within the first years in which, it seems, thieves' cant was born. That marriage of the two arts could hardly have been more rapid. Yet what sense might one give to it? One could, of course, consider the meeting of the idioms of the poet and the vagabonds to have been as singular as Villon's *œuvre*, the expression of a single biography or vocation, or both. Perhaps it was no more than a fortuitous occurrence, which brought one artificial language into proximity, if not in unity, with another. One may, however, also reason otherwise, if at the risk of seeking a truth where there is only chance. Could there be some hidden link between the two hermetic forms of speech, which makes of verse a kind of idlers' talk, or jargon some variety of poetry? It is difficult to elude this question, even if Schwob, for his part, seems to have done exactly that. Because of his scholarly method, his writer's craft, or because few more years would be left to him, Schwob did not draw out the consequences of the discovery he made. Today, over a century later, they remain, therefore, still to be unfolded.

THE
CANTING
Academy;
OR
VILLANIES DISCOVERED.

WHEREIN IS SHEWN

The Mysterious and Villanous Practices
Of that wicked Crew, commonly known by the
Names of Hectors, Trapanners, Gilts, &c.

With several New Catches
AND
SONGS:
ALSO

A Compleat Canting-Dictionary, both of
old Words, and such as are now most in use.

A Book very useful and necessary (to be
known but not practis'd) for all People.

The Second Edition.

London, Printed by *F. Leach* for *Mat. Drew*, and
are to be Sold by the Booksellers. 1674.

Richard Head, *The Canting Academy* (second edition, London, 1674).

CHAPTER THREE

Principles of Cant

Our language contains several words for lesser varieties of speech. "Slang" refers to words and phrases that, within a single tongue, belong to particular segments of society defined by place, class, and association. Such expressions tend to live short lives, their fates being tied to fashion. "Jargon," in its common English usage, alludes, by contrast, to the terms and formulae employed by people who share a certain practice, activity, or knowledge. Those in possession of crafts and skills—artisans and doctors, students and teachers—tend to use such a type of speech, either knowingly or unknowingly. Yet there is also a third variety of discourse, distinct from both slang and jargon. Since the Renaissance, it has been known in English as "cant," a term that seems to represent an Anglicized form of the Latin word for church song or chant, *cantus*.[1] This word refers to an obscure form of speech, which is employed above all for the commission of crime. "*Cant*," as an historian of the subject has recently written, "goes one step further than jargon. Its primary purpose is to deceive, to defraud, and to conceal. It is the language used by beggars and criminals to hide their dishonest and illegal activities from potential victims. It is sometimes used as a disparaging synonym for *jargon* and applied to other groups, particularly religious hypocrites, and occasionally real estate agents."[2]

Such summary considerations run the risk of suggesting that as a rule, within a single language, all three varieties of special speech are discernible. This seems, however, not to be the case. If one considers the ancient cultures of Greek and Rome, it is striking that instances of the first two types of lesser discourse can be found. Classical literature contains many slang expressions, in Greek and Latin, long known to readers of Aristophanes, Petronius, and Plautus. That the ancient branches of learning, from philosophy to mathematics and medicine, developed their own jargons, moreover, has never been in doubt. Many of their technical terms, from "energy" and "square root" to "interval" and "melancholia," remain in use to this day. As a rule, whenever a new field of knowledge arises, it quickly develops a distinct lexicon, which in turn provides the matter for an unfamiliar jargon. The classical examples, like all others, illustrate this principle. Yet the case of cant is different. Among the remnants of the ancient world, one looks in vain for signs of a speech crafted so as not to be commonly understood. No classical bandits seemed to have forged a secret tongue, no antique ruffians a hidden idiom. The Amazonians may have invented a language all their own, as Herodotus, for one, reports, but no ancient author maintains that they did so to conceal their ideas from those hostile to their company.[3] The least one may say is that if ever there did exist classical idioms similar in form to thieves' cant, their traces are lost today.

The first references to a secret tongue of malefactors date to the end of the twelfth century, when various authors begin to write of obscure "jargons." The Old Occitan grammatical treatise *Donats proensals*, thought to have been composed in the second half of the century, includes one passing, pregnant reference to *gergons*, which it glosses in Latin as *vulgare trutanorum*, "beggar's" or "thieves' talk."[4] Only a few years later, Jean Bodel's play *Le jeu de saint Nicolas*, from the beginning of the thirteenth century, sets on stage two robbers who, conversing in a tavern with a disreputable young man, exchange phrases that, while clearly French, have long defied interpretation. They may constitute the earliest attestations of criminal jargon in French, although historians of the language continue to disagree about their relationship to modern argot.[5] In the same years, the unknown author of the romance *Richard li biaus* recounts how its eponymous hero, stepping into a lair of thieves, sought the advice of a knowledgeable esquire who "knew all the *gargoun*" of

32

crooks and robbers.[6] These are the first signs of the emergence of the artificial idiom of malefactors. Philologists have noted others in the fourteenth century, for example in *fabliaux*.[7] Yet it is only in the fifteenth century that one encounters a more complete account of cant. The age of the Coquillars' trial was that in which the "exquisite languages" of cheats and scoundrels began, for the first time, to make their strange sounds heard in public.

Early modernity proved to be an epoch favorable to rogue tongues. A few decades after the Burgundian bandits were condemned for their nefarious acts, plotted in "a jargon that no man understands," one Teseo Pini of Urbino wrote his *Speculum cerratanorum*, a treatise exposing the ways of beggars who defraud and prey on those so credulous as to believe in their apparent misery.[8] Pini identifies thirty-nine distinct classes of false mendicants and, in the conclusion to his book, offers a glossary of the many obscure terms that they employ, pairing each curious Italian word or phrase with a standard Latin expression.[9] Only a few years later, there appears the most famous of all early modern accounts of the ruses of mendacious idlers: *The Book of Vagabonds and Beggars* (*Liber vagatorum*, also known as *Der Betler Ordern*), thought to have been composed sometime after 1509 by an author who, withholding his full name, signed simply as one "expert in roguery": "Expertis in Truffis."[10] His treatise contains both a typology of cheats and a lengthy dictionary of their expressions. Its anonymity was no hindrance to its circulation, for it was soon reproduced in verse as well as in prose, and in 1527–1528, it appeared in print, with a preface by no less an authority than Martin Luther.

"I have thought it a good thing that such a book should not only be printed, but that it should become known everywhere, in order that men may see and understand how mightily the devil rules in this world," Luther explains in his introduction. He then advances a hypothesis concerning the lexicon of malefactors: "Truly, such Beggars' Cant has come from the Jews, for many Hebrew words occur in the Vocabulary, as any one who understands that language may perceive."[11] While conceding that there do exist genuine paupers whom towns and villages should help, Luther declares that "outlandish and strange beggars" employing unknown words ought not, under any circumstances, to be tolerated. By way of conclusion, he reveals that he himself has had bitter experience of their ways: "Of late years," he writes, "I have myself been cheated and befooled by such tramps and liars more than I should like to confess. Therefore, whosoever hear these words, let him be warned, and do good to his neighbor in all Christian charity, according to the teaching of the commandment. So help us God!"[12]

In the following centuries, the interest in rogue tongues continued to grow. In England, the literature on the subject begins in 1557, when Thomas Harman publishes his *Caveat or Warening for Common Cursetors*.[13] Here Harman dates the appearance of the secret language of criminals—which he calls "cant" or "peddler's French"—to thirty years before the time when he composed his book. He claims that cant was the invention of an individual, although he also suggests that the impenetrable tongue might be attributable to the Gypsies, those "wretched, wily, wandering vagabonds calling and naming themselves Egyptians, deeply dissembling and long hiding and covering their deep deceitful practices."[14]

Thomas Dekker continued Harman's research in a series of publications beginning with *The Bellman of London*, which dates from 1608. Dekker distinguishes between "Cursitors, alias Vagabonds," "Faytors," "Robardsmen," "Draw-latches" and "Sturdy Beggars," yet he argues that they all share a single language, cultivated for the commission of their crimes. This, he writes, is a matter of material necessity:

It was necessary that a people (so fast increasing, and so daily practicing new and strange *villainies*) should borrow to themselves a speech, which (so near as they could) none but themselves should understand. And for that cause was this language (which some call Peddlers' French) invented, to the intent that (albeit any spies should secretly steal into their companies to discover them) they might freely utter their minds to one another, yet avoid that danger. The language therefore of *canting*, they study even from their infancy; that is to say, from the very first hour, that they take upon themselves the names of *knichin coes*, till they are grown *rufflers*, or *uprightmen*, which are the highest in degree among them.[15]

In English, Dekker's work on the rufflers' "new speech or language" was hardly to be the last. From Richard Head's *The English Rogue* of 1665 and *Canting Academy* of 1673 to the books on cant published in the last years of the seventeenth century by one "B. E. Gen.," from Francis Grose's *Classical Dictionary of the Vulgar Tongue* of 1731 to the essays on "cant and flash language" published in Britain and America in the late eighteenth and early nineteenth centuries by such authors as Humphrey Tristram Potter, James Hardy Vaux, Peirce Egan, and John Bee, an entire literature on the special speech of criminals arose and came to maturity.[16]

The other cultures of Europe witnessed similar developments in these centuries. In France, Henri Etienne marvels in 1566 at the refinement of the new "jargon"; he speaks of the perfection of a language long rudimentary and suggests that Villon himself would have had much to learn from his criminal contemporaries. He declares himself "certain" that the language in which thieves converse in his day "was never yet of such perfection.... Without having taken any great pains, these men have so enriched their jargonlike language, and so well studied it, that without any fear of being uncovered by those not of their profession, they can negotiate calmly among themselves."[17] The first extended study of the subject in French dates to 1596.[18] It was followed, a few decades later, by an influential work, *Jargon, or The Language of Reformed Argot, as it is Now in Use among the Good Poor* and by a host of diverse discussions of the cryptic language of various tricksters (not least fishermen and prisoners) that continued to appear throughout the seventeenth, eighteenth, and nineteenth centuries. In 1837, E. F. Vidocq, once an infamous criminal and later the famous chief of police in Paris, set a new scholarly standard in the field. He published a philological monument to the world of thieves, *Les Voleurs*, which soon proved an indispensable source to both Balzac and Victor Hugo.

The interest in thieves' cant in these centuries traversed Western Europe. In Iberia, the hidden language of wrongdoers acquired the special name of *germanía*. It resounded, in different ways, in fictional as well as scholarly works, marking the literature of the picaresque with particular force. Hence the special terms employed and interpreted in the narrative of Quevédo's hapless *Swindler*; hence, too, the secret expressions learned by Rinconete and Cortadillo in Cervantes's exemplary tale of initiation to the world of roving thieves. In Portugal, the term of choice was *calão*, which evoked the special tongue of the Gypsies of Alentejo.[19] In German, one would speak of "red Welsh," *Rotwelsch*, or, alternately, to employ a word of different origins, "thieves' language," *Gaunersprache*.[20] The great monument to the study of this obscure idiom dates to 1858. This was the year when Friedrich Christian Benedict Avé-Lallement, scientist, explorer, and chief of police in the city of Lübeck, adduced new philological evidence in favor of Luther's old claim, aiming to demonstrate that the German language of criminals was, in fact, simply Yiddish.[21] Italian authors write of an idiom "wily" by nature, *furbesco* being the long-standing name of the special tongue in which cheats plot their illicit acts. The literature on the subject stretches from the Renaissance to the twentieth century, when Alfredo Niceforo published a series of influential works, in French as well as Italian, on the language of the pernicious fringes of society. They are well represented by his comprehensive treatise of 1897, *Jargon among the Normal, the Degenerate, and the Criminal*, whose well-ordered chapters consider the types of argot in use in "normal associations," "the amorous couple," "the lesbian, onanist, and pederast couple," "lower social stratifications," "feminine milieus," and "between the prostitute and her *souteneur*."[22]

From early to later modernity, one basic structure in the study of cant has remained in place. Publications on secret tongues can only be at odds with them. Since the jargons of cheats demands secrecy, any attempt to illuminate their elements, rules, and mechanisms undermines their force and validity. Despite the curiosity of the case in question, a fundamental characteristic of all linguistic study can here clearly be discerned. It has been observed that scholars of language tend to approach their objects as if they were immutable, even when they are in fact in variation; linguists thus treat living languages as if they were dead, grasping their rules in the artificial fixity of a single moment, if only to write their grammars. When it so happens that scholars do speak the languages that they study, they regularly approach them, for reasons of scientific method, as if they were foreign to them. In each case, the procedure remains the same: knowing subjects must exclude themselves from the realm of what they wish to know, precisely to bring it into focus in the light of scientific objectivity. This systematic self-exception of the linguist is perhaps nowhere as apparent as in the study of cants, which has the peculiar consequence that each increase in the scholar's knowledge brings about a corresponding decrease in the effectiveness of the hidden tongue. Hence the peculiar animus that writers on jargon tend to express, which insistently, if awkwardly, accompanies the scholarly tone in the analysis of thieves' speech. From Jean Rabustel to Martin Luther, Avé-Lallement, and Vidocq, the interest in the idiom of cheats is in turn denunciatory and scientific, aggressive and neutral, for reasons involving the epistemology of the knowledge of secret languages.

Several centuries of research have made it possible to grasp the fundamental characteristics of such forms of speech. They are less languages in the full sense of the word than "special languages," that is, forms of discourse that result from the modification of given tongues according to rules known only to a select few. It suffices to apply certain special principles to the vocabulary and grammar of a language to obtain such idioms, which, while altogether dependent on existing linguistic systems, may be effectively impenetrable to the untrained ear. Strictly speaking, they constitute not so much secret languages, therefore, as secret uses of languages. At times, they have been called "anti-languages," for they serve the interests of "anti-societies" that strive to protect themselves from threatening majorities.[23] From a linguistic point of view, they may be dubbed "parasitic languages," as Marcel Cohen long ago maintained. "Given any linguistic unit (ordinary French, the dialect of an Alpine

37

valley)," Cohen reasoned, one may conceive the existence of idioms that will borrow "their phonetics, their morphology, and their syntax from it," using them in their own way and for their own ends, at times submitting them to an "abnormal transformation."[24] Such idioms may be "incomprehensible to the noninitiate," being conceived as the instruments of defense or attack.[25] Yet it is certain that such linguistic parasites, like all others, possess their own means of subsistence. These involve both the sense and the sounds of the languages by which they live.

The simplest and most obvious modification from which a "special language" may be born is that by which a given lexicon comes to be increased, diminished, or deformed. Cryptic jargons, like all others, are made of new words and phrases, and the first step in their study consists in the enumeration and examination of formulae. At times, the usual vocabularies of languages will be reduced, such that a single expression comes to convey more meanings than it would in its ordinary usage; at other times, by contrast, vocabularies will be augmented by new expressions. Words and phrases may be forged by the most varied of rhetorical means: metaphor, metonymy, antithesis, and epithets, most obviously, can all have roles to play.

Among such lexical elements, moreover, one may discern a relation found in such special tongues alone. Marcel Schwob and Georges Guieyesse were perhaps the first to identify it when, in their 1889 "Study of French Argot," they maintained that slang admits of a curious mode of signification that they baptized "derivation by synonymy" (*dérivation synonymique*). To grasp the full force of their argument, one must recall that implicitly, if not explicitly, scholars of language often assume that no two words in a language possess exactly the same signification. Admittedly, the dictionary and the thesaurus indicate that within a single tongue, one may define the sense of a given word by means of other expressions. Yet the synonymy that such procedures establish is only ever relative. If the lexicographic analysis of a certain term succeeds, it reveals the traits by which that term may be distinguished from those of an apparently similar semantic value. In his analysis of the principles of linguistics, Jean-Claude Milner, for these reasons, has gone so far as to make of this an axiom in the science of language: absolute synonyms do not exist; or, positively stated, whenever two terms are in use, their lexical meanings must be distinct.[26]

Slang, jargon, and cant would all seem to revoke that principle of speech. Pointing to sets of terms signifying the same acts, objects, affects, and states, Schwob and Guieyesse argue that in special languages, every word can produce "an artificial double" that may, in fact, become interchangeable with it. It suffices to deform an ordinary expression by the rules of the parasitic idiom and, in a second step, to insert it into a hitherto unknown "synonymous series." An example may be of help. In nineteenth-century argot, the French word *bonneteau*, the name of the "three-card trick" or "monte" played by cheats, came to be reduced, by apocopation, to *bonnet*, a noun already in use in the language in the sense it also possesses in English: "hat, cap, usually soft and without a brim." Henceforth, the speakers of jargon could take this word and forge from it a set of doubles that, while produced on the basis of a metonymic association with the French word *bonnet*, would all share the lexical sense of the word *bonneteau*. Schwob and Guieyesse report, for example, that *bonneterie* ("hosiery") and *lingerie* could function as semantically equivalent to *bonnet* in its secret sense, meaning "three-card trick"; moreover, *bonneterie* and *lingerie* would, in this hidden usage, also function as semantically equivalent among themselves.[27] The two terms were no more and no less than artificial doubles of the phonetically altered term from which the "synonymous series" had begun: *bonnet*, as abbreviated form of *bonneteau*. Moreover, the doubles, in turn, could lead to other synonyms and so to other series of artificial, yet equally regular forms of designation. At any point along the chain of interchangeable terms, a new series might begin. "A metaphor can cause a cloud of synonyms to fall about it, like the mushrooms that, exploding, produce a haze of spores, destined to perpetuate their own kind."[28]

The principles of cant extend, however, beyond the level of vocabulary. The secret use of a language may also involve the alteration of its sound shape. It suffices to think of operations of syllabic scrambling, suffixation, infixation, prefixation, apocopation, and truncation, all of which may be conjoined in different ways and in accordance with rules too numerous to anticipate.

Restricting oneself to the special varieties of the French language, one might recall the idiom called *verlan*, which rests upon the inversion, according to fixed patterns, of the phonological and syllabic structures defining common words. *Envers* ("backwards") becomes *verlan*; *feuille* ("leaf"), *yeuffe*; *arabe*, *beur*, and, by virtue of a further inversion, which does not return the transformed term to its initial form, *reube*.[29] One may also cite the example of *javanais*, the cryptic special tongue of nineteenth-century French prostitutes, invented, if one believes the historians, for protection from male clients. This idiom arises from the insertion, after each syllable of a common French word, of an infix that begins with the consonant *v* and that usually assonates with the preceding vowel. Under these artificial constraints, entire sentences, with all their elements, may be transformed.[30] Hence Queneau's "Javanese" exercise in style: "Un jour, vers midi-vingt, sur un autobus de la ligne S, j'aperçus un jeune homme avec un long coup et un chapeau entouré par une ficelle au lieu du ruban" becomes "Unvin jovur vevers mividin suvur unvin vautobovus deveu lava livignévé essévé, jeveu vaperverçuvus unvin jeveunovomme vavec unvin lonvong couvu evet unvin chavapoveau envantouvouréré pavar uvune fivicévelle oveau lieuveu deveu ruvubanvan."[31] Or, in the "back slang translation" proposed by Barbara Wright: "Unway ayday aboutayay iddaymay onyay anyay essyay usbay Iyay oticednay ayay oungyay anmay ithway ayay onglay ecknay andyay ayay athay enyayircledcay ybay ayay ortsay ofyay ingstray inyayeadstay ofyay ayay ibbonray."[32] Then there is *largonji de loucherbème*, the secret jargon of nineteenth-century Parisian butchers, the rules of which are more complex. Here, in all words beginning with consonants, the first phoneme is erased, replaced by *l*, and moved to the end of the phonological sequence; then, to that new element, a new and meaningless morpheme is appended. Thus *jargon* becomes *largonji*, and *boucher*, *loucherbème*.[33] Countless other "special languages," built from different grammars, follow similar principles.[34] Each time, such forms of speech can prove impenetrable to the unadvised speakers of the idioms of which they nonetheless constitute regular, if subtle, deformations.

Yet the special alterations of given languages can be more complex. Hidden plays of meaning and sound may also be conjoined. Pierre Guiraud has called attention to the practice of what he calls "homonymous substitution" in twentieth-century French argot, whereby one expression comes to be replaced by another of a similar or identical phonological form.[35] It is this operation that allows one to apply the French word *blanchisseuse* ("female launderer") to those clients who, leaving a shop without making a purchase, promise the seller that they will return. A fact of pure homophony justifies this semantically unmotivated usage, for in French, the statement "I will return" (*je repasserai*) is phonologically identical to the sentence, "I will iron" (*je repasserai*), and this assertion, in turn, may be taken as synonymous to the declaration, "I will launder" (*je blanchirai*). On account of an identity of sound, two units of differing sense thus come to be substitutable: "returning" may be expressed as "laundering" and, by extension, as "ironing." The artifice at work in the special tongue in this case is that of the pun, which sets phonological equivalence against unexpected semantic divergence.[36]

One may also think of the related English-language procedure commonly referred to as "rhyming slang," which has variously been attributed to East London Cockneys and Australian and United States prisoners, among others. This curious operation consists in two basic steps. First, one replaces a word by an entire phrase whose ending rhymes with the word in question; then, an element of the rhyming phrase may be omitted. The remnant of the rhyming sequence will be grasped as synonymous with the substituted term. In a first step, for instance, the word "stairs" may be replaced by the phrase "apples and pears," on the basis of the rhyme between "stairs" and "pears." In a second step, "and pears" may be dropped. Through a procedure of suggested rhyme and partial deletion, a new synonym will be forged: "going up the apples" will signify "going up the stairs."[37] So, too, given the rhyme between "money" and "bees and honey," one may say simply "bees," for in its truncation, the part will summon the whole from which it was drawn.[38] Imperceptibly, the rhyme between "honey" and "money" still sounds. As a fact of phonological identity enables a lexical substitution that is partially elided, in turn, by a principle of syntactic truncation, the procedure quickly gives rise to the most enigmatic of equivalences.[39]

Like all arts, such procedures lend themselves to more than a single use. Techniques of appropriating languages are appropriable in many ways. One may imagine why historians have wished, at different times, to attribute such forms of cryptic speech to as diverse a cast of socially marginal characters as beggars, butchers, fishermen, prostitutes, and prisoners. Yet the principles of cant, no matter how varied, subtle, and complex their historical instantiation, are united in the minimalism of their material. Secret languages do nothing but recapitulate the various units that are operative in a grammar, from the phoneme to the syllable, the word to the phrase and the complete sentence. As arts of speaking that order and reorder the parts of language to willful ends, the procedures of such hermetic idioms may call to mind the techniques of rhetoric. Yet the uses of special languages far exceed the aims of "speaking well" (*bene loquendi*) that rhetoric, in its classical definition, strives to serve. With greater justice, one might view the opaque expressions of "anti-societies" as close, in kind, to literary discourse in the sense given to it by Viktor Shklovsky. Like the writer's speech, the tongue of cheats and scoundrels troubles the patterns that define known expressions. It is speech become unfamiliar.[40]

Yet one may also take a further step. To the degree to which thieves' cants join and disjoin the phonological and semantic levels in their procedures, they come close, in structure, to the variety of literary discourse that Valéry once defined as a "prolonged hesitation between sound and sense."[41] That variety is poetry. This proximity points to an aspect of criminal jargons that may not have received the attention it deserves. As arms or shields employed by the dangerous classes of modernity, grammatically regular cryptic idioms may be datable, in Europe, to the mid-fifteenth century. Yet as appropriations of language that set sound and sense against each other, simultaneously revealing and concealing what they suggest, they are far more ancient. Before the rise of late medieval rogues, before the emergence of Renaissance outcasts and more modern outliers, secret languages played a crucial role in the work of a different company of speaking subjects. Their old and foreign names today are largely forgotten: *aeidioi*, *brahmaṇa*, *vates*, troubadours and trobairitz, skalds, riddlers, and scribes. Their titles varied from epoch to epoch, culture to culture, vocabulary to vocabulary. Yet in each case, if in different ways, these versifiers and scriveners were perhaps the first to seek to make one speech divide in two, and to summon, within the limits of a shared language, an insistent and startling opacity.

CHAPTER FOUR

Signs

The vernacular literatures of medieval Europe are in several respects perplexing objects of critical study. They are written in idioms commonly taken to constitute the first attestations of the Romance, Germanic, and Slavic languages that are still in use today. In their forms, they are generally believed to represent early examples of what later became modern literary genres. One might, therefore, infer that medieval literary texts possess a clarity of language and form that renders them more immediately intelligible than the works of Graeco-Roman antiquity. Yet the literature composed during the medieval periods of modern languages remains, in several respects, impenetrable to the contemporary eye. This curious fact has been noted several times. It has led some scholars to write of the simultaneous "alterity and modernity" of medieval writing; it has prompted others to go so far as to assert that the vernacular works of the Middle Ages, despite their relatively recent date, are obscurer than those of antiquity.[1] "Medieval poetry!" Paul Zumthor exclaimed in 1963. "Let us admit it: in its most perfect forms, the civilization of the tenth, eleventh, and twelfth centuries is more foreign to ours than that of classical Rome."[2] Buried in the tongues of the first poets of the modern world lie signs that resist even the most erudite of interpretations.

One may take, as a first example, the oldest Romance literature in verse. This is the corpus of largely lyric works attributed to poets of the eleventh, twelfth, thirteenth, and fourteenth centuries who, in a geographical range stretching from northern Iberia to southern

France and northern Italy, called themselves "troubadours": according to the most accepted etymology, "finders" or "inventors," named after the Old Occitan verb *trobar*, "to find." Their works have often been considered to define, with the simplicity proper to beginnings, features that would soon become the hallmarks of the modern lyric: verse structure, measured by a regular number of syllables, with rhymes; grammar, characterized by a discourse in the voice of a first person singular; and topics, involving a being who speaks and sings to evoke the joy and pain of his amorous passion. Yet as Alfred Pillet observed long ago, "the troubadour texts, in themselves, present...more difficulties than any poetic texts of the old Romance languages."[3]

This fact is all the more striking if one considers that it cannot be explained by reference to problems of an exclusively textual or linguistic kind. The manuscripts containing the troubadour songs, which date mainly to the late thirteenth and early fourteenth centuries, are relatively few in number and have been edited, sometimes repeatedly, with great care and exactitude. Scholars possess a reliable critical repertory of the entire corpus, estimated to consist of 2,542 lyric works.[4] Their language, once called Old Provençal and now known as Old Occitan, has been subjected to thorough philological and linguistic analysis, as a whole and in its details. Verse forms have been identified and catalogued.[5] Yet despite the scholarly grasp of the troubadour lyric, there are elements in the medieval craft that remain to us opaque. To invoke a rhetorical and stylistic term used by the troubadours for some of their compositions, one may say that in certain respects, the entire corpus seems sealed, as if in accordance with an art of *trobar clus*, or "closed finding."[6]

If anything in this literature is certain, it is that at its center lies the figure of the poet's beloved. She is the "point," as one literary historian has written, "toward which the troubadour constantly turns his eyes."[7] For her, the troubadours generally employ the Old Occitan word *domna*: a term derived from the Latin *domina*, which, in feudal parlance, denotes a married lady.[8] Yet it is striking that although the troubadour always evokes such a beloved, on account of whom he has begun to sing and the poem, therefore, has begun to be, he refrains from offering of her anything resembling a description. From the earliest attestations of the troubadour tradition to its conclusion, from poet to poet, style to style, and school to school, this fact remains constant. Despite the variety of terms and tones with which they conjure their love in words and music, the medieval "finders" deny their public any representation of the physical, social, historical, or biographical characteristics of their ladies. From a modern perspective, it has been observed that the medieval treatments, for this reason, exhibit a somewhat dissatisfying uniformity. "One might think," André Moret commented of the troubadours' Middle High German followers, the *Minnesänger*, "that they all wrote in praise of the same woman."[9]

Similar claims could be made about the being who speaks in these poems. Although the troubadours sometimes evoke the conditions in which they have come to meet their ladies or learn of their renown, and although they depict the pleasure and sorrow that their love has brought upon them, they systematically avoid naming themselves in the principal portions of their poems. Many troubadours, indeed, never introduce themselves by name at all.[10] Those who do so restrict their self-identifications to the abbreviated stanzas with which they conclude their works. Here, in the lesser units of poetry that the medieval theorists of Occitan poetry call *tornadas*, some authors, such as Bernart de Ventadorn, reveal their names occasionally. Other troubadours, such as Marcabru and Cercamon, identify themselves more often. There are a small number of poets, finally, who name themselves in these stanzas almost regularly. Sometimes they join their names to carefully crafted epithets. The exemplary case is that of Arnaut Daniel, whom Dante's Guinizelli calls "the better craftsman of the mother tongue" (*miglior fabbro del parlar materno*).[11] This twelfth-century troubadour concludes a song by naming himself in three famously enigmatic lines: "I am Arnaut, who hoards the wind / And chases the hare with the ox / And swims against the swelling tide" (*Eu sui Arnautz q'amas l'aura / e catz la lebre ab lo bou / e nadi contra suberna*).[12]

As a rule, it is in these concluding portions of the poem that the Occitan poets also refer, in a single, elusive invocation, to their beloved ladies.[13] Yet it is striking that even when the concluding units of the poem seem to constitute "stanzas of address" (*Addressentornaden*), the medieval authors refrain from naming their *domnas*, at least by any ordinary nominal means.[14] The troubadours avail themselves, instead, of openly cryptic turns of phrase. The first modern scholars of the literature immediately observed this fact. They commented that the Occitan poets systematically substitute for the name of their beloved "an allegorical name of the lady" (*nomen allegoricum dominae*), as Alfred Kalischer observed in 1866, introducing, in place of an existing designation, a "pseudonym" or "disguise name" (*Versteckname*).[15] Guilhem de Peitieus, the earliest recorded troubadour, also known as William of Aquitaine, thus evokes his lady twice. Once he calls her *Mon Esteve,* "My Stephen"; once he names her *Mon Bel Vezi,* "My Fair Neighbor."[16] Admittedly, not all the troubadours choose to designate their loves in such a form. The twelfth-century poet Cercamon, for example, appears to avoid the practice altogether; none of his poems offers any name for the lady around which, nonetheless, they turn. Yet the Occitan minstrels who designate their *domnas* follow Guilhem. In the final lines of their work, they offer a noun, title, or phrase as a cipher of the name that they withhold.

In its form, the procedure obeys certain grammatical constraints. Edoardo Vallet has shown that as a rule, the designations adhere to one of four linguistic forms. They may consist of a single noun, such as *Dezirat,* "Desired One," or a proper name drawn from myth or literary history, such as *Tristan*; a nominal phrase, consisting of a noun and qualifying adjective, such as *Bel Cavalier,* "Fair Knight," or *Fin Joi,* "Pure Joy"; a comparative prepositional phrase, such as *Mielhs-de-Domna,* "Better-than-Woman"; or, finally, a verbal phrase (usually based on a present-tense verb, conjugated in the second person, singular or plural), treated as a single name, such as *Dreit n'avez,* "You Are Right."[17] It is remarkable that such appellations, as a rule, are masculine in gender, even when they appear to denote a female being. Within these limits, the troubadours form a vast array of elliptical titles and abbreviated descriptions. The poet may name the addressee of his poem by a formula of admiration, such as *Bel Esgar,* "Fair Look," *Bel Rai,* "Fair Ray," *Bel Vezer,* "Fair Sight," or *Plus Avinen,* "More Charming." He may, instead, build a name from the expression of an affective state, evoking *Mon Desir,* "My Desire," *Fin Joy,* "Pure Joy," *Mais d'Amic,* "More than Friend," *Mielhs de Be,* "Better than Good," *Gai d'Amors,* "Drunk with Love." He may allude to his own wishes and expectations, calling out to *Bel Esper,* "Fair Hope," *Bel Respeit,* "Fair Waiting," and *Conort,* "Comfort." He can also craft a name from the designation of his pleasure, addressing *Bel Gazanh,* "Fair Gain," *Mon Plazer,* "My Pleasure," and *Gen conquis,* "Nobly Conquered." More rarely, he will summon a figure named through bitterness or reproach, alluding, for example, to a lady named *Tort n'avez,* "You Are Wrong."[18]

In the fourteenth century, the principles of the troubadour poetic craft came to be recorded by a company of poets and grammarians from Toulouse. In a monumental treatise of Occitan poetics titled *The Laws of Love* (*Las leys d'amors*), or *The Gay Science* (*El gay saber*), these medieval scholars gave a name to the troubadour procedure of substituting one name for another. Forging a technical term from the common vocabulary of the Old Occitan language, the members of the *Gay Science* called the "allegorical names of the lady" *senhals.* That term may be translated in several ways, not least by the words "insignia," "sign," "mark," "seal," "proof," "signal," and "portent."[19] In the section of their treatise devoted to the formal structure of troubadour verse, the fourteenth-century writers explain that poems may be divided into stanzas (or *coblas*) of equal numbers of lines that end, for the most part, with a shorter strophic unit that is called *tornada.* "Let it be known," they declare, "that one can place and apply a *senhal* in the *tornada* and that everyone must choose one for himself, without doing any wrong to another, that is, that he must not put into his work or appropriate from another any *senhal* of which he knows someone else has made use" (*devetz saber . . . pauzar et aplicar a so senhal. lo qual senhal cascus deu elegir per si. ses far tort*

49

a autre. so es que no vuelha en sos dictatz metre et apropriar aquel senhal que saubra que us autres fa).[20]

One learns more about these "signs" from the anonymous works in prose that often accompany the troubadour poems in medieval manuscripts. These texts date from the thirteenth and fourteenth centuries and are known to the literary tradition as *vidas* and *razos*, "Lives" and "Reasons." They comment, in different ways, on the origins and sense of the Occitan poems. Often they furnish the modern reader with precious information about *senhals*. In the one-page "Life" of the twelfth-century poet Raimbaut de Vacquerias, for instance, we learn that this troubadour "fell in love with the sister of the marquis, who had the lady's name of Biatritz, and who was the wife of Enric del Caret. And in his songs, he called her 'Fair Knight' [*et appelava la en sas cansos Bel Cavaliers*]."[21] In a *razo* or "Reason" relating to Bernart de Ventadorn's famous song about a lark rising and falling in the air, we read that Bernart "called his lady *Lark*...and she called him *Ray*" (*apelava la B[ernart] Alauzeta...e ela apelet lui Rai*).[22] These expressions are often repeated in the medieval literature on the troubadours, which evokes practices of "naming," "calling," and "appellation" (*appelar*) that seem technical in kind. At the court of the count of Provence, the thirteenth-century poet Sordello "loved a beautiful and noble lady of Provence, and in his songs, which he made for her, he called her *Sweet Enemy* [*et apellava la en sieus chantars, que el fazia per liei, Doussa Enemia*]."[23] Richart de Berbezill, poet of the late twelfth century, "fell in love with a lady, wife of Master Jaufre de Taona...and the lady was noble and beautiful.... And when he began making songs of her, he called her *Better-than-Woman* in his songs [*apellava la Meillz-de-Domna en sus cantars*]."[24] Raimbaut d'Aurenga, twelfth-century lord of Orange and Aumelas "and great king of many castles," "for a long season loved a lady of Provence, who was called lady Maria de Vertfuoil; and he called her *His Playing* in his songs [*appellava (la) 'son Joglar' en sas chiansos*]."[25]

Yet the medieval "Lives" and "Reasons," while crucial, do not allow the critic to decipher all the medieval signs. Many of the *senhals* invoked in the Old Occitan songs remain opaque. The *vidas* and *razos* suggest, moreover, that the medieval designations should not be understood as referring solely to the poets' beloved ladies, for at least some appellations are of another kind. The "Life" of the twelfth-century troubadour Bertran de Born, for example, explains that this poet devised a set of titles to designate some of his noble contemporaries. "He called the count of Brittany *Rassa*, the king of England *Yes-and-No* [*Oc e no*] and the young king, his son, *Seaman* [*Marinier*]."[26] Building on such suggestions, critics have hypothesized that it is likely that other *senhals* in the corpus are of this nature. In an important essay on Peire Vidal, Ernest Hoepffner thus raised the question of the meaning of the name "Castiat," "Punished," which one finds often in the work of this troubadour from Toulouse. Through a careful reading of the poet's work and the extant sources relating to his life, the philologist argued that the Castiat against whom the troubadour rails in verse was, in truth, the count of Toulouse, the poet's own lord, whose wrath he had provoked.[27]

Certain passages in the medieval corpus suggest, moreover, that a *senhal* could also be employed by one troubadour poet to designate another. Such an act of allusion might be direct or indirect. There is no doubt that a minstrel could, for instance, cite a *senhal* invented by another, thereby evoking its referent, for "once one troubadour had imagined a title for a baron or a lady, others could adopt the same designation for the same character."[28] Yet there is evidence that the troubadours also invented titles for each other. A *razo* to Guilhem de Baus thus explains that the mysterious name "Engles" is the sign by which the poet chose to evoke Raimbaut de Vaqueiras.[29] An anonymous note inserted in the troubadour songbook H explains that "Desirat," in a lyric by Arnaut Daniel, refers to the troubadour Bertran de Born.[30] Modern interpretations of such appellations must be more conjectural, although critics have not hesitated to formulate their readings in terms of apparent certainty. According to Isabel de Riquier, the cryptic name "Linhaure" in the poems of Guiraut de Bornelh, which has been interpreted in more than a single sense, "is, or was, or could be, Raimbaut d'Aurenga, thus designated by his colleagues and friends, who gave each other names by *senhals*, signs of intimate recognition, which are often enigmatic for us."[31]

Scholars have proposed several accounts of the origin of the *senhals*. In his classic study of the troubadours, Alfred Jeanroy maintained that the Old Occitan pseudonyms constitute an utter novelty in the history of literature. "This usage," he commented, "has, as far as I know, not been observed in any literature. Under Charlemagne, the members of the Palatine school gave each other the names of great characters of antiquity. In a more recent period, John of Salisbury and Gautier Map designated their contemporaries by the names *Cornificius* and *Porphyrius*; but the *senhals* invented by the troubadours are ... of a completely different nature."[32] This was a polemical claim, for at least some of Jeanroy's colleagues had argued the opposite. Several years before Jeanroy, V. de Bartholomaeis suggested that "the use of the *senhal* is not ... a novelty, since the poets of the Palatine school had precisely the habit of designating each other by means of pseudonyms."[33]

One may recall that the classical Latin love poets, too, employed pseudonyms to designate their ladies. Catullus called his Clodia "Lesbia"; Propertius named his Hostia "Cynthia"; Tibullus evoked his Plania as "Delia."[34] The Arabic poets of medieval Iberia also cultivated an art of naming by dissimulation, availing themselves of poetic titles that could be elaborate. Long ago, A. R. Nykl argued that the troubadour procedure might well derive from that of the Arabic authors, who regularly gave their loved ones masculine "fictitious names," or poetic *kināya*: *amalī, munyatī, buǧyatī, ǧārī, sayyidī*.[35] Attending to the more immediate historical and social surroundings of the troubadours, Martín de Riquer has advanced a simpler historical explanation. The troubadour practice of poetic naming could also be derived from that of the feudal courts at which the poets presented their works. For there, the nobles themselves often bore surnames. It suffices to think of Richard "Lionheart" or John "Lackland." "Authentic pseudonymous" were also in use. Hence "the viscountess of Châtellerault, friend of Guilhem de Petieu, called *Dangerosa* and *La Maubergeonne*, after the castle in which she lived."[36]

Whatever their origins, there can be no doubt that the *senhals* play a crucial role in a fundamental aspect of the Old Occitan craft: what Bernart de Ventadorn, one of the greatest troubadours, calls *bel celar*, "fair concealing."[37] Yet critics have differed vastly in the readings they have given of this practice. At one extreme, one may interpret the troubadour names and phrases as willfully opaque: titles intelligible solely to the poet and his addressees or, perhaps, to them and to those few who remained in their immediate vicinity. If one grants, however, that the Old Occitan names were formed and used in accordance with the rules of an art, one may infer that they were also comprehensible to a public familiar with the conventions of the medieval craft. That a single *senhal* can be found in texts by several authors seems telling. The "allegorical name" may have been less than obscure to the medievals. Yet one can go further. If one grasps *senhals* as appellations of a public kind, titles such as "Lackland," "the Handsome," or *Court-Martel*, one may also draw a possibly discomforting conclusion: they may hardly have been secrets at all. At most, they could have been "open secrets," as Gérard Gourian maintained, or "functional elements" in a system requiring the pretense of obscurity.[38] The Old Occitan name for the poetic name is, in any case, richly ambiguous. "Cipher" or "insignia," "mark" or "proof," the word *senhal—signans* and *signatum—*remains decidedly equivocal.

This much, however, is certain: the Occitan "sign" possesses a role shared by none of the other constitutive elements of the troubadour song. Whether openly or enigmatically, exoterically or esoterically, the "allegorical name" points, by its nature, beyond the world conjured up by the poetic text. There is a simple reason for this fact, from which several consequences follow. The "signal" marks the bare condition of the poem's existence. One may give several names to this condition. More exactly, one may give exactly as many names to it as there are accounts of the sense of the *senhal*. The elliptical title or phrase may indicate the lady who allows the poem to be made, the noble patron at whose court it can be recited, or, finally, the troubadour who will enable to it to be received and integrated

53

into a tradition. The "sign" is in this sense ambiguous. Yet its function remains constant. From the eleventh century to the fourteenth, the *senhal* continues to point, within the poetic work, to a reality that precedes the poem and that enables it to be. The naming, for this reason, shelters a hidden reference to the "finding" at the origin and the center of troubadour song. Whatever else it may designate, a troubadour "insignia" always also alludes to the language in which the poets craft their work, being an index to the prime matter from which they draw the elements of their song. Among the troubadours, that allusion remains, for the most part, only implicit. At least once, however, a poet chose to identify that which these medieval signs obliquely, if obstinately, evoke. In the early thirteenth century, a *trobairitz,* Na Castelloza, noblewoman of Auvergne, left her readership a telling indication. The sole woman troubadour ever to employ a *senhal,* she called her beloved, in bright opacity, Bels Noms, "Fair Name."[39]

CHAPTER FIVE

Knowings

It can happen that words and phrases that are unknown to the
majority of those who speak a language sound not only in certain
portions of poems but throughout them, becoming, in their darkness, the signs of literary speech. Old Norse literature, in this
regard, contains perhaps the most brilliant of examples. They are to
be found only in part in the great prose works, the sagas, composed
in the twelfth, thirteenth and fourteenth centuries, which contain
occasional citations in verse. Perhaps the most striking witness to
the secret idiom of writers in the Middle Ages derives from a period
in Old Norse literature several centuries before the emergence of
poetry in the Romance languages.

Like that of all ancient literatures, the dating of the earliest
Old Norse verse is uncertain. This poetry was doubtless transmitted orally before being committed to writing, and today, scholars
maintain that it most likely came to maturity before the tenth
century. Its corpus is diverse. Some of the oldest poems in the
language record cosmology in narrative form, being traditionally
considered to be "the original storehouse of Germanic mythology."[1] These are the works of varying length contained in the thirteenth-century *Codex regius* discovered in Iceland in 1643, which
have been referred to since as the *Elder Edda* or *Poetic Edda*.[2] Other
Old Norse poems are of a fundamentally different form and matter. They arose between the ninth and eleventh centuries at courts
in Sweden, Denmark, and Norway, where authors wrote brief
poems, chiefly in praise of their noble lords and kings. These are

the works of the "skalds," the Scandinavian poets who crafted, as
E. V. Gordon wrote long ago, "a poetry more melodious, more
ornate, and more artificial than any other type that grew from
Germanic tradition."[3]

In its rhymes and in its rhythms, skaldic poetry is exceptionally
complex. The dominant verse form, the *dróttkvætt* stanza, obeys
redoubtable formal demands. Each strophe is composed of eight
six-syllable lines that bear three stresses and that fall into two lesser
units of four lines each. In the stanza, one observes a rigorous distinction between the lines that fall in odd-numbered positions (1,
3, 5, 7) and those that fall in even-numbered ones (2, 4, 6, 8), for
there is alliteration between two words in the odd-numbered lines,
tied to one alliterating word in the even-numbered ones. There are
two internal rhymes or assonances within every line, varying also
in nature on account of their position within the stanza: in the odd-
numbered lines, one may detect a partial internal rhyme, while in
the even-numbered lines, by contrast, there sounds a full internal
rhyme or assonance. Within these constraints of lengths and tim-
bres, quantity and quality, the skaldic poet composed sentences that
fully exploited the syntactic capacities of Old Norse. Relying on the
inflected grammar of the language, the court poet could subject the
order of words to considerable variation, intertwining and embedding entire sentences within each other.[4]

Yet the work of the skalds is no less carefully wrought in its diction and, for this reason, their poems tend to evoke the world in
ways difficult to decipher. That the *dróttkvætt* stanza poses a special
challenge to its listeners and readers has been noted often since the
waning of the Middle Ages. But this fact was already observed and
discussed in the monument of medieval poetics that is the *Younger
Edda* or *Prose Edda* of the Old Icelandic writer Snorri Sturluson. This
thirteenth-century work contains at its center an extended account
of literary discourse: a treatise titled "The Language of Poetry"
(*Skáldskaparmál*).[5] This work reveals, by way of introduction, that
the evident obscurity of poetic speech is nothing less than the consequence of a divine decision.

Toward the beginning of this book, the god of poetry, Bragi, instructs "a certain man named Ægir, or Hlér," on the fundamentals of literary craft. Bragi explains that "there are two categories into which all poetry is divided."[6] These are "language and verse forms" (*Mál ok hættir*).[7] Of the second, metrics, he says no more at this point. Here the medieval author concentrates, instead, on the special variety of "language" that is circumlocution, "the paraphrasing of one word by several."[8] "There are," we learn, "three categories [*grein*] in the language of poetry." Each consists of a type of naming. The first is "to call everything by its name; the second is the one called substitution [*fornofn*]; and the third category of language is what is called *kenning*."[9] The first "category" appears to pose no interpretative difficulties, for it consists in designation by customary names and nouns. The second "category" seems to involve the operation by which the proper name of an individual comes to be replaced by a nominal circumlocution, as in the classical figures of *pronominatio* and *antonomasia*.[10] It is the third category of poetry that interests the divine authority most, and in what follows, Bragi relates a host of periphrastic formulae to exemplify the technique to which the Old Norse poets and theorists of poetry gave the name "kenning" (or, as the figure is known in its original plural form, *kenningar*).

The Old Norse term *kenning* "is probably derived from the expression *kenna vid* (to express or describe something)."[11] It is constructed on the basis of the verb *kenna*, "to ken," "know," "perceive," "recognize."[12] Stretching a translation, one might conclude that the kenning implies a "knowing" of a kind. Yet one would need to add that the knowledge sealed in the kenning relates first and foremost to the structure of a language and, more precisely, to the distinct levels that, within it, tie one expression to another. If the kenning opens onto the world beyond the literary work, it does so by substituting for one ordinary element of speech another that is more complex than it is.

Snorri's god announces that he will hold forth on kennings with didactic precision, thus assuring the future of an art that might otherwise be lost. "These things," Bragi explains, "have now to be told to young poets who desire to learn the language of poetry and to furnish themselves with a wide vocabulary using traditional terms; or else they desire to be able to understand what is expressed obscurely."[13] He continues: "We speak of Odin or Thor or Tyr or one of the Æsir or elves, in such a way that with each of those that I mention, I add a term for the attribute of another or make mention of one or other of his deeds. Then the latter becomes the one referred to, and not the one that was named."[14] One may thus call the god Odin the "All-Father," "the hanged God," the "Strangely wise Raven-tester," "Vilir's brother," or "Mim's friend," just as one may refer to his wife, Freyja, as "daughter of Niord, sister of Freyr, wife of Od, mother of Hnoss, possessor of the fallen slain and of Sessrumnir and tom-cats, of Brisingamen, Van-deity, Van-lady, fair-tear deity."[15] So, too, by the art of kennings, things may be named and renamed in seemingly unlimited sequences of synonymous substitutions: "On a man there is what is called a 'head.' This shall be referred to by calling it toil or burden of the neck, land of helmet and hat and brains, of hair and eyebrows, scalp, ears, eyes, mouth."[16]

> How shall the sea be referred to? By calling it Ymir's blood, visitor to the gods, husband of Ran, father of Ægir's daughters, whose names are Himinglæva, Dufa, Blodughadda, Herfring, Unn, Hronn, Bylgia, Bara, Kolga; land of Ran and of Ægir's daughters and of ships and of terms for sea-ship, of keel, stem, planks, strake, of fish, ice; sea-kings' way and roads, no less ring of the islands, house of the sands and seaweed and skerries, land of fishing tackle and of sea-birds, of sailing wind.[17]

Modern scholars, following in Bragi's footsteps, have sought to refine the formal definition of the kenning. They have suggested that the Old Norse theorists of the thirteenth century, such as Snorri, no longer distinguished between two varieties of periphrasis whose difference one may still detect among the earlier court poets. One is the figure of the "qualified name" or *kend heiti*, which consists of "any circumlocution in which the base word literally refers to the concept designated by the whole."[18] Examples include constructions that refer directly to relations of kinship, such as "Vilir's brother," "husband of

Ran," and "daughter of Niord," or to a single or characteristic deed, such as "Strangely wise Raven-tester," or "Hanged God." By contrast, in its narrower definition, the kenning proper involves a "periphrasis, consisting of two or more substantive members, which takes the place of a noun."[19] Examples of kennings in this narrower sense include such phrases as "land of helmet," or "burden of the neck," for "head."

The skalds carried the art of naming by periphrasis to an extreme point. In her classic study of Old Norse strophic court poetry, Roberta Frank cites as an exemplary text a passage from the late eleventh-century Icelandic author Markús Skeggjason, which she renders, for the purposes of poetic and grammatical analysis, word for word into a "virtually uninflected English":

> Fjarðlinna óð fannir
> fast vetrliði rastar;
> hljóp of húna gnípur
> hvalranns íugtanni;
> bjǫrn gekk framm á fornar
> flóðs hafskíða slóðir;
> skúrǫrðigr braut skorðu
> skers glymfjǫtur bersi.

> Of the fjord snake waded through the snowdrifts
> Firmly the bear of the current;
> Jumped over the peaks of the mastheads
> Of the whale house the bear;
> The bear went forward on the old
> Of the flood sea ski's tracks;
> The storm-breasting broke through of the prop
> The skerry's clashing fetter the bear.[20]

Frank comments that "at first hearing, the stanza appears to be about an acrobatic, if damp, bear."[21] The lines evoke, no fewer than four times, a single motion that sets on stage a subject, a verb, and its objective complement. Each time, the poet names the elements of that motion by the art of kennings. Thus, the subject is alternately "the bear of the current," "the bear of the mastheads," "the bear of the flood," and "the storm-breasting bear of the prop." All are periphrases for "ship." The four verbs in the stanza (óð, hljóp, gekk, braut), while lexically distinct, designate, by a rule of synonymy, a single activity: despite their differences, they all signify a spatial displacement. Finally, the objects—"snowdrifts of the fjord snake," "peaks of the whale house," "old tracks of sea skis," "clashing fetter of the skerry"—are circumlocutions for "sea." In short, "the poem says—four times—'the ship sailed over the sea.'"[22] Yet it does so not by sequential repetition, but by the superposition and coordination of sets of formulae, from which an attentive reader can also glean the season and the direction of the poet's voyage.

The structure of such Norse periphrases has been studied several times. In what remains the single most comprehensive treatment of the literary device, Rudolf Meissner, in 1921, defined the kenning in its fundamental form as a "two-part substitute for a substantive of common speech."[23] He added that in this "two-part substitute," a formal distinction must be made between the "base word" (Grundwort) and the definer, which is the agent of its "determination" (Bestimmung). When the tenth-century Norwegian skald Eyvindr Finnsson Skáldaspillir speaks, for example, of "slim arrows of the sea" (mævǫrum sævar), meaning "herring," "slim arrows" is the base word, "of the sea" the determinant.[24] Likewise, in the thirteenth-century Icelandic writer Sturla Þórðarson's kenning for the sea, "eel ground" (álfoldur), "ground" is the base word, while "eel" is the determinant.[25] Such an analysis of the kenning has the merits of clarity as well as simplicity. Since the time of its formulation, it has allowed literary historians to identify a number of formulae in Old English poetic diction that seem to mirror the form of the Old Norse kenningar. Examples include Anglo-Saxon "sea stallion" (sæhengest) for ship, "whale road" (hron-rād) for sea, and "giver of rings" (beaga gifa) for king or chieftain.[26]

Meissner's account of the kenning, however, has not gone unquestioned. In an early review of his monumental book, Andreas Heusler argued that more is required for the Old Norse periphrasis than Meissner's theory suggests. Norse *kenningar*, Heusler maintained, are not merely condensed descriptions in several terms. These may be found in all traditions: it suffices to think of such circumlocutions as the "Protector of the Land" (*Schützer des Landes*) for "ruler," "which," Heusler remarked, "one can find everywhere."[27] One might add such expressions for divinity as the Hebrew "lord of hosts" (*adonai tzevaot*), the Latin "maker of the world" (*creator mundi*), and the Arabic "master of worlds" (*rabb' ul-'ālamīn*).

Heusler's criterion for the Old Norse kenning was more exacting. He characterized the medieval circumlocution as "a playful type of metaphor," being "in spirit, the relative of the riddle and the joke, since it demands a solution and glimpses the similarity of the dissimilar." In its simplest form, it rests on one structure: "metaphor with derivation" (*Metapher mit Ablenkung*).[28] The phrase can be simply explained. Metaphor operates by a rule of substitution, by which a stated term takes the place of another that remains unmentioned. In the kenning, Heusler suggests, one can identify such a substitution, yet one also finds something more: the index, namely, of its formulation, which functions as its "derivation." In the kenning "arrows of the sea," for instance, a metaphoric equivalence is established between the base word, "arrows," and the substituted term, "herrings," yet this periphrasis also contains a sign of the ground of its making in the definer "of the sea." One term is equivalent to another, in other words, because of the determinant: A ("slim arrows") may be taken in place of C ("herrings"), since A is said to be *of* B ("the sea"). As John Lindow, building on Heusler's argument, suggests, the kenning may therefore also be understood as an abbreviated riddle. One may always expand Old Norse periphrasis into a question, followed by an answer: When are slim arrows like herrings? When they are slim arrows in the sea. When is a road like the sea? When it is the road of whales. When is a bear a ship? When it is of the current.[29]

If one accepts Heusler's thesis, one will exclude from the field of kennings all circumlocutions that do not function according to the rule of "metaphors with derivation." It has been observed that this choice will significantly restrict the catalog of such periphrases in the literary corpus. Kennings will be distinct not only from "qualified names," such as "daughter of Niord, sister of Freyr"; these periphrases will also be irreducible to such formulae as "giver of rings" and "protector of the land," which imply shortened descriptions. In the West Germanic languages, such as Old English, kennings in the strict sense, then, must be considered to be relatively rare.[30] Yet they continue to proliferate in skaldic verse, despite the fact that the Norse court poets used kennings to name only some one hundred things.[31] There is a simple explanation for this fact, and it involves a basic feature of the medieval figure: the two-termed kenning is but the simplest of its kind. When an Old Norse poet chose to replace a substantive by a circumlocution, he need not stop when he had found two terms for one, or a single compound expression to substitute for a simpler noun or name. "Any member of a circumlocution might be expanded by further kennings."[32] In a passage of his *Prose Edda*, Snorri distinguished, for this reason, between varieties of periphrases, graded in terms of their rising complexity: "First there are simple kennings [*kenningar*]; second, double [*tvíkent*]; third, extended [*rekit*]."[33] At a first degree of periphrasis, one may, for instance, designate the sea by the kenning "earth of the fish"; at a second degree, one may expand "fish" by means of the circumlocution "snake of the fjord"; then, at a third degree, one may substitute for "fjord" the phrase "bench of the ship." In three steps, one thus reaches a single synonym for "sea" that is as prolix as it is enigmatic: "earth of the snake of the bench of the ship."[34] There is, moreover, no rule or reason why such circumlocutions must not be carried beyond the third degree. The Old Norse kenning is, at least in theory, indefinitely expansible.

That such a procedure could lead to poetry lacking in beauteous proportions has been stated more than once. Among twentieth-century critics, evocations of the "Baroque" dimensions of the Old Norse kennings are legion. Discussing the skaldic penchant for periphrasis, E. V. Gordon, for one, declared in 1927: "modern taste is offended by their wholesale use of this figure, which is usually regarded as mere frippery obscuring the more essential meaning of the verse."[35] Borges, who dedicated an essay to the *kenningar* in 1933, was considerably more equivocal. Admitting that he had amassed memorable examples of the Old Norse circumlocutions "with an almost philatelic pleasure," he nevertheless called the kennings, in his opening judgment, "one of the most frigid aberrations recorded in the history of literature." Yet he ended his considerations by stating that no aesthetic evaluation of the periphrasis could truly be conclusive. "We no longer know its laws," he wrote.

> The words left to us are so few. . . . It is impossible to know with what intonation of the voice they were pronounced, with what expressions. . . . What is certain is that they once fulfilled their function to astonish. Their gigantic impropriety enchanted the red-haired poets of the volcanic deserts and fjords no less than did their strong ale and their duels of raging stallions.[36]

More recent readers of the kennings have not resolved the question. It cannot be denied that, while unmistakably obscure, the kennings remained a basic element of medieval Scandinavian poetry for more than four centuries. That fact raises a question. How to understand the persistence of this figure? Various accounts of its literary and historical functions have been proposed. Social conditions may have demanded that poetic diction remain unclear. "Some *dróttkvaett* stanzas might be deliberately cryptic," Frank comments. "The syntactic ambiguity in stanza 25 allows the commemorated loyal retainer to share in his lord's glory; that in stanza 46 seems designed to protect its author from prosecution in a paternity suit."[37] Other critics have evoked tendencies proper to the grammar of the Old Germanic tongue that may, in some way, have suggested the art of periphrasis to the Scandinavian poets. Borges, for one, concludes that "the style codified by Snorri is the exasperation and, as it were, the *reductio ad absurdum* of a preference common to all Germanic literature: the preference, namely, for compound words."[38] Linguists have pointed out that from a syntactic point of view, the

circumlocutions, despite appearances, are a means to achieve concision, kennings possessing, as Gordon noted, "the meaning of a subordinate clause in briefer space and with less emphasis."[39] Rhetoric
and stylistics have also furnished explanations. It has been argued
that the periphrases are best grasped as Norse varieties of metaphor
or, alternatively, as the elements of a poetic system articulated in
several levels and governed by rules comparable to those of a single
language.[40]

The debates about the functions of kennings will doubtless continue. Yet it is certain that for them, a stratum of crafted impenetrability was crucial. It can be no accident that in his account of the
Old Norse poetic art, Snorri attributes to a god the insistence on
the hermetic quality of poetic naming. Divine authority establishes
that literary periphrases are to be opaque. Bragi recounts to Ægir
that when the giant Olvaldi died, his sons divided their inheritance,
measuring out their father's gold and "in turn taking a mouthful,
each of the same number." Hence the rise of a curious, yet divine
appellation. "Now," Bragi explains, "we have this expression among
us, to call gold the mouth-tale of these giants, and we conceal it in
secret language or in poetry, by calling it speech or words or talk
of these giants."[41] That gloss is well worth pondering. Bragi's kenning, "speech of giants," names a precious good hidden in "secret
language, or poetry" (í rúnum eða í skáldskap).[42] In those few words,
which interpret one circumlocution, another knowing lies safely
sealed. Implicitly, yet surely, the god establishes a second substitution: what is to be consigned to "secret language" (felum í rúnum)
reveals itself to be, whether by expansion or by reduction, synonymous with "poetry" (skáldskap). This is a language within language
in which one can rename anything in skilled obscurity. One must
only leave some trace or trail for the reader—god, giant, dwarf or
human being—who may come, at a future time, to recover its riddle.

CHAPTER SIX

Riddles

Every secret institutes a division. Its effects can be detected in the individual who, knowingly or unknowingly, conceals something from another. But they also extend to larger numbers of speaking beings. Friends, families, associations, and communities can set themselves against themselves by the silences they keep concerning certain matters. Two steps alone suffice for the production of such dissension in dissimulation. Something, first, must be distinguished, for whatever reason, as worthy of concealment; it must, second, be withdrawn from the usual field of perception. The etymology of the word "secret" suggests both acts. In English, the noun derives, by means of the French cognate *secret*, from the Latin *secretum*, past participle of *se-cernene*, meaning "to discern" and also "to separate."[1] One might deduce from this fact that for secrets to be held, two elements alone are therefore required: the thing set aside and the means of its concealment. Yet if the secret is not only to be made and kept but also transmitted as such, a third element will be demanded. There must be some mechanism capable of establishing and maintaining the division that results from the existence of a secret: a test of sorts, which will determine where certain individuals stand with respect to what has been "discerned" and "separated." The border between those who know and those who do not may, then, be both preserved and reproduced.

Defined in such terms, the mechanism of secrecy may seem abstract. Yet it is illustrated in a single linguistic and literary shape known to all. Riddles not only constitute examples of a minor type of folklore and literature that, like the proverb, exhibits a conventional and often formulaic structure. They also exhibit the form that secret knowledge takes in the moment that it passes from the field of the statement to that of the puzzle and the question. Any concealed matter can be safely conserved and transmitted in the perplexing shapes of enigmas, which only a few will know how to resolve. Hence the "virtual universality" that riddles would seem to possess.[2] They may be oral, being composed and transmitted between generations without writing. Folklorists have studied such riddles across the world, from the Americas to Europe, Asia, and Africa. They may also be written, either secondarily, in the sense that they are transcribed after being composed, or originally, as in the works traditionally designated as "literary riddles." Certain traits, in any case, mark the structure, function, and conditions of recitation of all these cryptic forms.

It is characteristic of riddles to express only established knowledge. They may test the ingenuity of those who hear them, but their primary aim seems less to prompt new responses than to determine the competencies of speakers with respect to a traditional corpus of special names and formulae. In a study of the practices of the Anang in southeastern Nigeria, John Messenger comments, in this sense, that "riddles are not told with the end in view of baffling the audience and stimulating its members to provide correct answers."[3] John Blacking, an ethnographer who has investigated the value of riddles among the Venda in the Northern Transvaal, advances a similar claim. "I never encountered anyone who thought about the meaning of an unknown riddle and tried to reason out the answer. Whenever someone knew a riddle well he answered it pat, as if the answer was an integral part of the question. Riddle and answer, therefore, are learnt as one unit, and it is knowledge of the riddle that is more important than the ability to work it out."[4]

Such terminology is traditional in form but may be questioned. That a single riddle falls naturally into two units—one obscure, one clarifying—is commonly accepted. The first portion has gone by many names, such as "riddle," "question," "query," "proposition," and "enigma." The second portion, which Blacking here calls "answer," has been variously named "solution," "reply," and "key." Some scholars have wished to avoid the confusion that results from so many terms of differing implications. In his work on African riddles, Lyndon Harries, for one, proposes a more formal distinction: that between "Precedent" and "Sequent," "both of which are neutral terms indicating only that one expression precedes the other."[5]

From Plato to Aristotle, from the Latin orators to Augustine and the medieval theorists of rhetoric, riddles have been defined in many ways.[6] Modern scholars of folklore have sought to offer a firm foundation for earlier accounts by proposing a systematic and comprehensive analysis of the form. In an important early contribution, Archer Taylor suggested that the riddle is essentially a device of comparison. "The true riddle, or the riddle in the strict sense," he wrote, "compares an object to another entirely different object."[7] The link between the "Precedent" and the "Sequent" would then have its basis in a principle of similarity. Some elements in the comparison, Taylor specified, will be positive, while others will be negative. As a rule, each type of characterization will possess a specific rhetorical valence. Positive descriptive traits, for instance, tend to be metaphorical, while negative ones are in general to be understood literally. One may take, as an example, the Irish riddled phrase for "potato": "What has eyes, but cannot see." The quality of "having eyes" must be understood figuratively, while that of "being unable to see" is literally true.[8] In "Towards a Structural Definition of the Riddle," Robert A. Georges and Alan Dundes, taking a further step, argued that a riddle may be more fully defined as "a traditional verbal expression which contains one or more descriptive elements, a pair of which may be in opposition: the referent of the elements is to be guessed."[9] That thesis has been criticized for several reasons.[10] Yet the characterization is helpful in its emphasis on the fixed form of the riddle, the contrast of its descriptive elements, and the challenge that it provokes.

That challenge, as Georges and Dundes indicated, is one of reference. The riddling phrase and its solution, "Precedent" and

"Sequent," point to one reality, whether it be natural, cultural, mythological, or linguistic. Its two parts indicate a single object, though by two distinct means: indirectly, then directly. From a logical point of view, one may note, moreover, that the riddle tends to recall and invert an old epistemological form: that of the predicative definition. For example, when Aristotle asserts that among animals, man is "the only one that has language," he names a predicate—possessing language—that defines a single species: humanity. When, by contrast, the Sphinx confronts the inhabitants of Thebes with her riddle, she proceeds along another path, albeit by denoting the same subject. She offers one complex predicative phrase composed of three seemingly incompatible elements: "Being a creature that moves on four legs in the morning, two legs in the daytime, and three legs in the evening." Despite its apparent contradictions, this "Precedent" alludes to a single being, which the "Sequent" must name. Oedipus, to his misfortune, knew its nature, for it was his own: "man." While the definition, in its classical form, passes from the given thing to its constituent traits, the riddle, in this sense, moves from a collection of distinct and apparently contradictory characteristics toward a single subject. Definition, in short, leads from a name to its multiple, consistent predicates; riddling, by contrast, winds a way from a set of seemingly incompatible attributes to the common term that can be substituted for them all.

One may go further still in the analysis of the structure of the riddle. Since the "Precedent" and the "Sequent," by definition, possess a single referent, one semantic relation obtains between them. It is that of synonymy. This term, to be sure, has several significations, and one may understand it in at least the two meanings famously distinguished by Frege: in terms of "sense" (*Sinn*) and, therefore, the semantic conditions under which an expression can name a certain thing, or in terms of "reference" (*Bedeutung*), that is, the act of indicating, denoting, or "picking out" one portion of reality.[11] If one defines the word "synonymy" in this second of these two meanings, it fits the riddle's two parts well. The "Precedent" and the "Sequent" point to the same part of reality, though the "Precedent" does so only obscurely. Successful riddlers are the ones who know the "Sequent" that will satisfy all the conditions of reference stipulated by the contradictory predicates named in the "Precedent." When faced with a seemingly impossible set of descriptions, they can find the one term to which they all can be attributed. Riddlers know, in other words, how to find a synonym for the oddest of long phrases. To resolve the enigmas put to them, they must call upon a special knowledge of names and predicates, terms and their descriptions.

Riddles, in this sense, test a kind of linguistic learning close, in nature, to that possessed by the scholars who write dictionaries and thesauruses. The crucial difference between the two sets of knowledgeable speakers is that lexicographers concern themselves with the vocabulary of a language that is (or that at least in principle may be) generally known to those who speak it. Those who solve riddles possess a different cunning. It bears on a language shared by many but employed, in technical ways, by few. The corpus of riddles, in short, composes less a language in any ordinary sense of the term than a special language, which arises in the process by which speakers make of their language a jargon incomprehensible to the uninitiated.

The oldest recorded Indo-European riddles confirm this hypothesis. The *Rig Veda*, whose most ancient stratum dates to the second millennium B.C., contains a host of formulae suggestive of "Precedents" disjoined from their "Sequents," and among the ancient hymns, one finds a poem composed almost wholly of such expressions, known in Sanskrit as the "Asya Vāmasya," "Riddle Hymn," or "Riddle of the Sacrifice."[12] In an influential study of these riddles published in 1925, Walter Porzig argued that they "clearly display a special terminology" with a tendency to denote certain objects according to fixed patterns of description. "Thus," he explains,

> mobile things (sun, moon, year, foot) are said to be wheel or wagon;
> equally ordered things (days, months) are said to be brothers; things
> that appear in the air (sun, sparks, lightning) are birds; things from

which other things come (clouds, dawn, fire) are said to be a cow; things that unite are called hub, navel, encompassing womb; that which is underneath is a foot; that which is above is a head.[13]

These facts are rich in implications. "In the language of riddles," Porzig writes, "we stand before a language that, once known, grants belonging to a certain circle. The coherence of this circle can be seen in this language and in the worldview it expresses. The language of riddles is a special language [*Rätselsprache ist Sondersrpache*]. The group to whom this special language belongs is, for the Veda, easy to grasp: it is the Brahmans, the priests separated off by their caste."[14] In an enigmatic passage, the ancient "Riddle Hymn" itself seems to suggest no less:

catvári vák párimitā padáni
táni vidur brāhmaṇá yé manīṣíṇaḥ
gúhā trīṇi níhitā néṅgayanti
turíyaṃ vācó manuṣíā vadanti

Speech was measured out into four tracks.
Brahmins with insight know these. People
Do not set in motion the three that are hidden:
They speak (only) the fourth track of Speech.[15]

Porzig maintains that the function of the Vedic riddles is in substance specific to classical India; in form, however, it is representative of a more general fact. "A glance at the riddles of other peoples shows that these, too, rest on special languages and even that the essence of riddles is everywhere special language."[16]

Such "special languages," as Porzig comments, appear to rest on certain fundamental rhetorical operations, such as metaphor and metonymy. "When we speak of the foot of the mountain, or the foot of a lamp," he writes, "then the word 'foot' has a meaning of the same kind as in the Rig-Vedic riddle of the dawn, which bears the sun 'by foot,' or the clouds, which drink water 'by foot.' These are processes of semantic modification that one tends to call 'metaphor' or 'figurative expression.'"[17] One may find echoes of such claims in scholarship on traditions as distant from Sanskrit as Old Norse. As early as 1923, Heusler called the kenning a "playful type of metaphor [...,] related to the riddle and the joke, since it demands a solution and glimpses the similarity of the dissimilar.[18] Lindow later observed that the affinities between the riddle and the Old Norse periphrasis are threefold. "1) Both expressions are composed of two or more components. 2) The 'meaning' or referent of each expression may be (usually is) different from each of the components. 3) The referent is found by identifying the nature of the relationship between the expression's components."[19] Riddles, like kennings, make of the words of one language the elements of a new lexicon that doubles, surely if impenetrably, the one commonly in use.

It would be a simplification, of course, to assume that any language contains solely two such registers: one general and known, the other special and opaque. Multiple secret idioms may all be lodged within a single tongue. One of the Elder Eddas, "The Lay of Alvís" or *Alvíssmál*, sets on stage a learned dwarf who, to win Thor's daughter for himself, must first meet the challenge of an extended examination in not one but five riddled languages, all somehow composed from the standard linguistic material of Old Norse. The work opens as Alvís arrives in the dwelling of the gods, eager to claim for himself the divine bride whom he believes has been promised him. Thor, reluctant to remit his daughter to the knowledgeable dwarf, demands that Alvís first prove to all that he is, in truth, as "all wise" as his name suggests. To this end, the god submits him to an examination in five varieties of synonyms. For thirteen Old Norse words uttered by Thor, Alvís must give equivalent expressions in the languages of Æsir divinities, the Vanir divinities, the giants, the dwarves, and the elves. The examination fills the entire Edda, constituting, in Hugo Gering words, "a versified chapter from the skaldic Poetics."[20] The god's question about "earth" is exemplary:

(Þórr kvað:)

Seg mér þat, Alvíss,

ǫll of rǫk fira
vvrumk dvergr, at vitir,
hvé sú jǫrð hęitir,
er liggr fyr alda sonum
hęimi hvęrjum í?

(Alvíss kvað:)

"Jǫrð hęitir með mǫnnum,
ęn með ǫlfum fold,
kalla vega vanir,
ígrœn jǫtnar,
alfar gróandi,
kalla aur uppręgin."[21]

"Tell me this, All-wise, since, dwarf, I suspect
  you know every creature's whole history:
  what the earth's called, spread out before the songs of men,
  in every world there is."

"'Earth' it's called by men, by Æsir 'ground,'
  the Vanir call it 'ways';
  'evergreen' giants, 'growing' elves,
  the lofty powers call it 'mud.'"[22]

Alvís succeeds in proving his mastery of the five secret languages. Yet in the end, he fails. As he lays bare his knowledge of names by night, day begins to dawn. The first rays of light strike his body and for reasons that remain obscure, the dwarf turns, as the god had foreseen he would, to stone.[23]

The "Lay of Alvís" is exceptional in the minimalism of its synonyms. The Old Norse work tends toward establishing a term-for-term identity of reference between words in the common language and in the cryptic tongues of the gods, giants, elves, and dwarves.[24] Formulaic riddles, by contrast, usually consist not of two expressions but of two asymmetrical linguistic parts. To a single word in the common language, there tends to correspond a synonymous phrase built from a chain of several disparate descriptions. Other Old Norse works offer clear examples of this pattern. In the "Lay of Vafthruthnir," or *Vafþrúdnismál*, it is a god, Odin, who must answer questions. He has disguised himself as one "Gagnrath" and resolved to seek out the giant Vafthruthnir, so as to test his renowned knowledge against his own. Accepting the challenge, the giant proposes description after description. In each case, the god must provide a proper name that will satisfy the conditions of reference stipulated by the giant's representation:

(Vafþrúdnir kvad:)

Sęg mér, Gangrádr,
Alls á golfi vill
þíns fręista frama,
hvé hęstre hęitir

Sás hvęrjan dręegr
Dag of dróttmǫgu.

(Odinn kvad:)

Skinfaxi hęitir,
es hinn skíra dręgr
dag of dróttmǫgu;
hęsta baztr
þykkir með Hręiðgotum;
ęy lýsir mǫn af mari.[25]

(Vafthrúthnir said:)

"Tell me, Gagnrád, since you wish from the floor
   to make a test of your talents,
what's the name of the horse who always drags
   the day over troops of men?"

(Odin said:)

"He's called Shining-Mane who always drags
   the day over troops of men.

73

The glorious Goths think him the best horse:
His mane shines always aflame."[26]

A chapter of the medieval prose *Hervarar saga* contains a contest of riddles in a stricter form. A man named Gestumblindi must settle a dispute with his famously learned king by an act of verbal battle. The man, fearing for his fate, makes a sacrifice to Odin, who in recompense offers to disguise himself in mortal shape and to go "bring up riddles" (*béra upp gátur*) to the king. Repeatedly, Odin, dressed as Gestumblindi, advances expressions in dark terms, which King Heidrik must reformulate and explain in clear speech. "Precedents" are here in verse, "Sequents" in prose:

Hverr er sá inn mikli,
er líðr mold yfir,
svelgr hann vǫtn ok við;
glygg hann óast,
en gumna eigi
ok yrkir á sól til saka?
Heiðrekr konungr,
hyggðu at gátu!

'Góð er gáta þín, Gestumblindi, getit er þessar; þat er myrkvi; hann líðr yfir jǫrðina, svá at ekki sér fyrir honum ok eigi sól, en hann er af, þegar vind gerir á.'

"Who is that great one
Over ground passing,
Swallowing water and wood;
The wind fearing,
But fleeing no man,
And waging war on the sun?
This riddle ponder,
O prince Heidrek!"

"Your riddle is good, Gestumblindi," said the king; "I have guessed it.

74

That is fog; it passes over the earth, so that one cannot see because of it, not even the sun; but it is gone, so soon as the wind gets up."[27]

Similar contests can be found in many Indo-European traditions. Medieval European literature, for instance, contains parallels in the Anglo-Saxon *Solomon and Saturn* dialogue and the Old Irish *Colloquy of the Two Sages*.[28] Old and Middle Iranian literary texts have been said to contain traces of similar confrontations, in which learned minds evoke obscure and formulaic phrases, demanding that their interlocutors interpret and explain them.[29] Ancient Sanskrit literature abounds in such examinations, which are known by the name of *brahmodya*.[30] Ernest Renou was the first to offer a sustained analysis of these simultaneously poetic and liturgical tests of riddled speech. One of the oldest Vedas, the *Shukla Yajurveda*, represented by the *Vajasaneyi Samhita*, dictates that the sacrifice of a horse be followed by a contest in which the two officiating agents, a presiding priest, or *brahmán*, and a reciter of invocations, or *hotṛ*, sit on either side of the sacrificial stick. From there, they are to engage in a ritual dialogue of question and answer. First the *brahmán* asks and the *hotṛ* answers; next the *hotṛ* poses queries to which the *brahmán* responds. Such exchanges, measured out in verse, obey a regular form:

kā́ḥ svid ekākī́ carati
ká u svij jāyate púnaḥ
kím svid dhimásya bheṣajám
kím u āvápanaṃ mahát

sū́rya ekākī́ carati
candrámā jāyate púnaḥ
agnír himásya bheṣajám
bhū́mir āvápanam mahát

Who is he who moves alone?
And who that is born again?
Who is the remedy for cold?
And who is the great sowing?

75

Sun is he who moves alone.
Moon is who is born again.
Fire is the remedy for cold.
Earth is the great sowing.[31]

Longer *brahmodya* may display more "formulaic, repetitive and catechistic" traits, which may function also in the absence of an interrogative syntax:[32]

pṛchámi tvā páram ántaṃ pṛthivyáḥ
pṛchámi yátra bhúvanasya nábhiḥ
pṛchámi tvā vŕṣṇo áśvasya rétaḥ
pṛchámi vācáḥ paramáṃ víoma

iyáṃ védiḥ páro ántaḥ pṛthivyá
ayáṃ yajñó bhúvanasya nábhiḥ
ayáṃ sómo vṛṣṇo áśvasya réto
brahmáyáṃ vācáḥ paramáṃ víoma

I ask you of the far end of the earth.
I ask where the world's navel is.
I ask of the seed of the stallion.
I ask of the highest heaven of speech.

This altar is the far end of the earth.
This sacrifice is the world's navel.
This Soma is the seed of the stallion.
This Brahmin is the highest heaven of speech.[33]

However obscure they may at first glance appear, "Precedent" and "Sequent" here refer to one event: the taking place of the riddle as a performance. The formulaic construction "I ask" (*pṛchāmi*), like the response beginning with the demonstrative pronoun "this" (*iyáṃ* or *ayáṃ*), alludes to the liturgical occurrence itself: the conditions of questioning, as well as the occasion for correct response. The enigma can be solved only when the one who hears it knows that it turns, allusively, yet systematically, back upon itself.

Such riddles, like all others, function within certain unstated constraints. Formulaic expressions may demand corresponding synonyms only if they exhibit two features: opacity and the hidden principle of their interpretation. That summary may appear willfully paradoxical, yet enigmas verify its truth. Were a riddle immediately intelligible, it would be none at all. Comprehensible in itself, it would neither call out to a synonym in ordinary parlance nor allow the mind to linger on the passage from "Precedent" to "Sequent." Yet there is another possibility that would be no less threatening to the form of riddles. Were an enigma solely solvable by means of knowledge extrinsic to its construction, it, too, could hardly be called an "enigma."

Mythology, folklore, and literature abound in examples of "false riddles," which violate the conventions of contests of wisdom by presenting apparent "Precedents" from which even the cleverest and most learned of hearers cannot deduce the correct "Sequents." Fearing that there is no enigma that King Heidrik cannot solve, Odin, in the *Hervarar saga*, for example, poses an unanswerable query to foil him. It appears, deceptively, in the same metrical form as his preceding questions: "What said Odin / in the ear of Baldr, / before he was borne to the fire" (*Hvat mælti Óðinn / í eyra Baldri, / áðr hann væri á bál hafiðr*)?[34] The clever king, however, will not be fooled. Heidrik immediately sees that his interlocutor is Gestumblindi only in appearance, for if he knows the answer to such a question, he can be none but the god Odin himself, who accompanied Baldr to his death. Striking his interlocutor with a magic sword, Heidrik thus exclaims: "Only you know that, wicked creature" (*þat veiztu einn, rǫg vættr*)![35]

The angrily impious king is not unjustified in his act. In such contests, linguistic knowledge that is accessible to a single speaker alone is inadmissible. A secret tongue can never be strictly private. To function within the conditions of conversation, even in the most restricted form, it must, in principle, be decipherable, however indirectly, by the one who is to hear it. "Special languages" must, in short, be regular in structure, like the grammatical tongues from which they are forged. The rules in question, of course, may be difficult to discern; they may be complex and ideally so. Yet every enigma, no matter how hermetic, must contain within its form the key to its unlocking. Only then may it become productive of expressions made in its mold. Those who know its hidden sense must be able also to grasp the principles of its construction, such that they can appropriate them, in turn, to devise new riddles similar in their patterns to the old.

The true secret of the riddle, therefore, lies less in the "Sequent" that is synonymous with the "Precedent" than in the structural bond that unites them. This bond may take a number of shapes. Yet research on riddling suggests that there are two fundamental means of tying "Precedents" to "Sequents," of which all others are, in essence, variations.[36] The first is rhetorical and relies on the arsenal of tropes and figures familiar to orators. The Sphinx's riddle is of this kind. To pass from its "Precedent" to its "Sequent," Oedipus must distinguish between the literal and the figural: "creature" is to be taken in its usual meaning, while the distinctions between "morning," "daytime," and "evening" are all metaphors for three stages in life. Similarly, if one believes Porzig, the enigmas of the *Rig Veda* display regular rhetorical substitutions, such that one can establish correspondences between certain types of objects and certain figured shapes that signify them according to regular patterns. Riddles that rest on metonymy, rather than on metaphor, are also of this kind. The Old Norse periphrasis for "sea" as "eel ground," for example, functions by such means: it replaces one term by another, linking two expressions that are already united by association. Traditional enigmas built from implicit comparisons also belong to this set. Consider the English lines:

In spring I am gay,
In handsome array;
In summer more clothing I wear;
When colder it grows
I fling off my clothes;
And in winter I quite naked appear.

78

Only if one considers the terms of this "Precedent" as essentially the elements of a simile may one pass to the "Sequent": *A Tree.*[37]

The second variety of riddle may be dubbed "grammatical," if one takes the term "grammar" as the designation of the linguistic system as a whole. Such enigmas play one element or domain of a single tongue against another. Individual words, for example, may be simultaneously yoked in multiple meanings; simple facts of lexical ambiguity will work to cloud comprehension. Thus a host of familiar forms of English riddle questions and answers: "What turns but does not move? *Milk.*" "What has a mouth but does not eat? *A river.*" "What has an eye but cannot see? *Needle.*"[38] Yet the ambiguities exploited by enigmas may also affect other domains of language. Word structure may play a crucial role. Take the question and answer: "Why is coffee like the soil? *It is ground.*"[39] The ambiguity is in this case morphological, rather than lexical. As W. J. Pepicello and Thomas A. Green observe, "the lexical item / *grawnd* /, a noun, is homophonous with the past participle of the verb / *graynd* /."[40] Phonology may play a similar role. The link between "Precedent" and "Sequent" can be a matter of as minimal a distinction as that between one vowel and another. "What is the difference between a baby and a coat? *One you wear, the other you were.*"[41] Confusion may also be sowed at the level of the entire sentence: "Why is a goose like an icicle? *Both grow down.*" Here the two elements of the riddle may be understood to form a whole only if one succeeds in detecting, in a single "Sequent," two fundamentally distinct syntactic structures. In the first, "down" functions as a direct object and thus as a noun phrase; in the second, it is, instead, an adverb.[42] Often these domains, however, can be compressed and superimposed. Phonology and syntax can collide. "When is it hard to get your watch out of your pocket?" finds a resolution in a single phonological chain, which is susceptible, by a fact of homophony, to two different chains of words: "*When it keeps sticking there*" or "*When it keeps ticking there.*"[43]

Rhetorical and grammatical conceits, of course, can also meet. Principles of carefully crafted speech may dictate that in the language

of the "Precedent," the "Sequent" be concealed, albeit in ways difficult to discern. Literary riddles often follow such a rule. A poem
by Cervantes, for instance, ends with a challenge to the reader: "Tell
me what is one thing and another!" (*Decidme qué es cosa y cosa*).⁴⁴ The
answer lies inscribed in the question: "one thing and another" (*cosa y
cosa*) is a common expression for "riddle." The seventeenth-century
Hebrew poet Moshe Zacuto devised a like enigma: "If a man is bewildered by a secret sealed, / He should learn the concealed from the
concealed."⁴⁵ The key to these lines is buried in one of their words.
As Dan Pagis has observed, "the reader assumes the word 'secret'
refers to the riddle as a genre, but here the word also implies that
the solution of this riddle is the 'secret.'. . . If you are bewildered by
a sealed secret, by the solution, deduce what is concealed (i.e., the
encoded solution, here: secret) from the concealed, from the lines
of the poem itself, which mention the 'secret' explicitly."⁴⁶ Writers
have carried such operations to an extreme point. Riddles in one
tongue have been written so as to sound aloud, in another, the solutions for which they call. The early modern Jewish poets, who wrote
in the language of the Bible while speaking European vernaculars,
practiced arts of this kind. They would embed, within their Hebrew
verse, words homophonous with others in Italian, Spanish, or Portu-
guese.⁴⁷ "In the riddle *Miyom nivra 'olam* by Jacob Vita Israel (Amsterdam, mid-eighteenth century)," Pagis relates,

> the hidden speaker says, "My friend in the hills, I say to you, / If you
> ask Shlomo he will reveal it to your ears / Ask Esther as well, go then
> to / Seek, and find me among her perfumes." Shlomo and Esther are
> the couple in whose honor the riddle was composed. "In the hills"
> alludes to Mt. Morah (*har hamor*); "among her perfumes" (*tamruqeha*)
> is *hamor*, myrrh; thus, in accordance with their pronunciation, we are
> led to *Amor*, love. The word *omar* (I say) suggests the solution as well,
> inverting its vowels.⁴⁸

Spoken riddles are rarely so sophisticated. Yet within the con-
fines of one language, they also exploit patterns of sound, word,
and sentence in ways no less surprising. In them, too, a "Sequent"

can lie hidden in a "Precedent." Italian affords an example: "I will say to you, I repeat to you, and if you do not know what it is, you will truly be donkeys" (*Velo dico, velo ripeto, se ancor non lo sapete, dei ben asini sarete*). Within the repeated expression "to you" (*velo*) one finds the homophonous noun "veil" (*velo*), which points to the enigma itself.[49] Linguists who have studied folk riddles have found that such procedures are more common and more deeply rooted than one might think. Developing research begun by Osip Brik and Roman Jakobson, the philologist and chess composer Alexander Gerbstman has shown that one type of Russian folk riddle demands, as a formal feature, phonological affinity between "Sequent" and "Precedent."[50] The sounds of the solution, in other words, must in principle be scattered throughout those of the enigma. Consider the example "*Net ni okon ni dverej. Posredine—arkhierej.—Orekh.*" "It has neither windows nor doors. In the middle there is a bishop. *A nut.*" A phonological analysis of this riddle reveals that the sounds of the solution are distributed across it, not once, but almost three times. Hence the choice of the "bishop," as Tzvetan Todorov, commenting on Gerbstman's work, has remarked: "Among all the possible inhabitants of this strange house, this one clearly follows from the phonic relation of *orekh* to *arkhierej.*"[51] Vladimir Toporov and Tatyana Elizarenkova have argued convincingly for the presence of such "anagrammatic" procedures in Vedic enigmas, and Vladimir Milicic has shown that certain Macedonian and Bulgarian riddles follow similar patterns.[52] Milicic has suggested that such procedures can also be found in English-language riddles, although the speakers who transmit them may be unaware of this fact. A few examples suffice to illustrate the principle of such "subliminal structures in folklore." "It goes upstairs and all downstairs and never makes a track. *Air.*" "Two lookabouts, two hookabouts, and four big standers. *A cow.*" "Which is the biggest saw you ever saw? *Arkansas.*"[53]

Riddling here reaches a point of maximal abstraction and simplicity. The secret is hidden, with the greatest surety, precisely in being exposed. Two synonymous expressions are at once disjoined, conjoined, and superimposed upon each other: one, in being uttered, beckons to another, whose sounds lie quietly in it. To find the way from "Precedent" to "Sequent," it suffices, then, to listen closely. The syllables, sounds, and letters that compose an enigma simultaneously, if inaudibly, spell out its certain solution. Those in possession of the rules of the special language will know to grasp it. To the question of the identity of these masters of speech, several ancient and medieval traditions suggest an answer. From Vedic India to archaic Greece and the medieval North comes the same startling suggestion: those who long ago appropriated a shared means of communication, making of a common idiom an opaque jargon, were those who claimed to act with the knowledge of the gods. Before the emergence of modern crime and its calculatedly cryptic cants, divinities demanded that a secret be kept and spoken, concealed from some and transmitted, at the same time, among the members of a single company. Piety sowed the first seeds of dissension, for it exacted what must not be said. Tradition followed. Priests and their helpers—poets and scribes—obliged.

CHAPTER SEVEN

Nomina Divina

To know a language is to be in a position of mastery and uncertainty for reasons that follow from the nature of the faculty of speech. It is a widely known fact that before beginning to form utterances in any given tongue, speaking beings possess an intuitive, yet complete grasp of its grammar. They are somehow aware of the rules that define the set of signifying sounds from which words can be composed, as well as the principles that determine the ways in which words can follow each other in correct sentences. Yet it is also common knowledge that even the most learned of speaking subjects can always, unexpectedly, come face to face with a linguistic barrier. It suffices for them to run up against one or more impenetrable expressions. These may consist of words or phrases that are new in their basic shapes, yet they may also consist of ordinary locutions employed in an unfamiliar manner. One might be tempted to attribute their possibility to ignorance of a subjective kind; individuals, after all, tend to move in circles in which the same special vocabularies are in use, a fact that doubtless limits their knowledge of the lexicon. Yet there is an objective reason for which speaking subjects can always find themselves at a loss in the languages that they would seem to master. It involves the special uses that individuals and groups can make of a tongue. From their unconscious knowledge of a single grammar, speakers can draw the form and matter of unattested expressions. To the degree to which they respect the phonology, morphology, and syntax of a given grammar, such utterances may be considered to be limited in scope. They will not, for example, involve sounds that cannot be pronounced by speakers of the language, or that cannot possibly be recognized by them. In this sense, such formulae will be consonant with the languages in which they appear. Yet they may be utterly incomprehensible nonetheless. The threat would be minimal were the set of such possible terms restricted. The truth, however, is that within the terrain circumscribed by a grammar, obscure expressions can always be invented. They can, moreover, proliferate without end, for the parts of speech can be recomposed in infinitely new ways.

The oldest literatures of the Indo-European traditions suggest, in striking unison, that the true masters of such obscure expressions are divine. A corpus of ancient sources leads one to believe that the gods of the ancient Greeks, Celts, Norsemen, Indians, and Anatolians, in particular, employed a set of special terms and phrases that were at once similar in form to those commonly recorded in human tongues and noticeably distinct from them. Such expressions appear to have been largely nouns and nominal phrases, like the elements of the argots that developed across Europe centuries later. In the Greek tradition, the examples begin with Homer. His two epics contain six references to a special lexicon: a jargon of sorts, that, to use an irreverent yet entirely appropriate term, one might name "godly cant." After Homer, Greek literature contains over a dozen more allusions to such a form of hidden discourse that offer, in each case, a term and its translation. From Hesiod and Pindar to more minor authors, such as Pherecrates and Maximus of Tyre, no fewer than twenty precious lexical items have be found.[1] In the fullest treatment of the Indo-European language of the gods, Françoise Bader has shown that these mentions generally display two characteristics:

> From a formulaic point of view, the names of the language of gods and men form two couples (or give rise to more distinctions in more recent texts), and they are accompanied by the author's reference to the giving of the name: "among the gods (or men), X is called..." or, in an active form, "the men (or gods) give the name X...." Another characteristic

involves the referent: it is one and the same, and the divine name grants it a cosmic dimension that the human name does not possess.[2]

The *Iliad* contains the most important Greek examples of these names. Four times, the Homeric narrator interrupts his discourse to introduce an expression in need of special commentary. The term, in each case, appears to be an unusual Greek word for which the poet hastens to offer a synonym in the vocabulary that would have been immediately intelligible to his audience. Book 1 contains the first evocation of such a term in the scene in which Achilles converses with his divine mother, Thetis. Speaking of Zeus, "the son of Chronos," the Achaean hero recalls: "You came, goddess, and freed him from his bonds, when you had quickly called to high Olympus him of the hundred hands, whom the gods call *Briareus*, but all men *Aegaeon;* for he is mightier than his father [*hon Briareōn kaleousi theoi, andres de te pantes / Aigaiōn, ho gar aute biēi hou patros ameinōn*]."[3] The other three examples in the epic set godly terms against human ones in like fashion. "Now," we learn in book 2, "there is before the city a steep mound afar out in the plain, with a clear space about it on this side and on that; this do men truly call *Batieia*, but the immortals call it *the barrow of Myrine*, light of step [*tēn ētoi andres Batieian kiklēskousin, / athanatoi de te sēma poluskarthmoio Murinēs*]."[4] Elsewhere, Homer evokes the "clear-voiced mountain bird, that the gods call *Chalcis*, and men *Cymindis* [*khalkida kiklēskousi theoi, andres de kumindin*]"[5] and "the great, deep-eddying river, which gods called *Xanthus*, and men *Scamander* [*hon Xanthon kaleousi theoi, andres de Skamandron*]."[6]

The *Odyssey* contains only two terms belonging to the divine jargon. Once, the poet explains of a special herb: "*Moly* the gods call it, and it is hard for mortal men to dig; but with the gods all things are possible" (*mōlu de min kaleousi theoi: khalepon de t'orussein / andrasi ge thnētoisi, theoi de te panta dunantai*).[7] Later, Circe, revealing wonders to her parting guest, explains that Odysseus, when at sea again, will reach straits where "on the one hand are beetling crags, and against them roars the great wave of dark-eyed Amphitrite; *the Planktai* do the blessed gods call these [*Planktas dē toi tas ge theoi mak-ares kaleousi*]."[8] It is striking that both these terms remain without apparent synonyms in the language of the Homeric epics. Homer's twelfth-century commentator Eustathius of Thessaloniki explained the good reasons for this fact. *Moly* and *Planktai* remain nameless in the discourse of men, he commented, for they are unknown among mortals.[9] While the double terms of the *Iliad* "may suggest the relative superiority of divine to human knowledge," Jenny Clay notes, "the *Planktai* and *moly* belong to a kind of knowledge available to the gods alone."[10]

Less evident is the nature of the words that belong to the godly argot. Plato already raises the question in the *Cratylus*. Socrates enjoins Hermogenes to learn from "Homer and the poets" about the "correctness" (*orthotēs*) of expressions by attending to the passages in which he indicates the ways in which "gods and men designate the same things."[11] In jest or in earnest, the philosopher suggests that the unfamiliar names of divine origin must be taken to be correct, the human to be false.[12] There remains the problem, however, of the features that define divine words. Philologists and linguists have sought to resolve it in several ways. In one of the first studies of Homer's references to a godly speech, J. van Leewen suggested in 1892 that the immortals' words could be distinguished from the mortals' in being Hellenic in origin, rather than non-Hellenic.[13] In 1910, H. Jacobsohn pursued the argument, holding that one can find in the differences between the two types of designations the signs of a partition of an ethnic and therefore interlinguistic kind. While the divine terms are Greek, he reasoned, the human terms recall various tongues of Asia Minor.[14] In a similar vein, Paul Kretschmer suggested, a decade later, that one can recover in the two sets of words a distinction between "the national [or 'popular'] speech of the poet" (*Volkssprache des Dichters*) and expressions deriving from a "foreign dialect."[15]

Such claims have proven difficult, if not impossible, to demonstrate. More recent scholars have held that human and divine words are equally Greek and foreign in origin and that the difference between them is more exactly intralinguistic, involving two levels of a single language. Hermann Güntert thus maintained in 1921 that the divine words constitute archaic expressions deriving from the field of religious terminology, while the human words, by contrast, were in Homer's time all terms of common use. Antoine Meillet, in response, appealed to the possibility of a linguistic prohibition that could have caused certain terms to become unspeakable. Homer's divine names could then be explained as "circumlocutions of the kind that are used to avoid words that have been forbidden by taboo."[16] Romano Lazzeroni later developed Meillet's argument in greater detail. In an incisive essay, he recalled that the Homeric gods do not, as a rule, use a special language, either among themselves or in conversation with men. Homer's allusions to a divine idiom, therefore, are in need of explanation. This Lazzeroni offered by maintaining that whenever a specifically divine lexical item appears, it functions to denote "a natural object that, in a specific context, has taken on a sacred character," withdrawing it from the reach of mortals. "'Divine terms,'" he concluded, "have the structure, the sense, and the value of tabooed expressions." Yet he also conceded, following Gunther Ipsen, that the literary practice nonetheless remains something of a mystery: "It is difficult to understand what stylistic effect Homer was aiming for in giving a 'divine' denomination for an object."[17]

Early in the development of modern philology, scholars noted that Homer's allusions to divine speech, however curious, are not entirely unique. In his *Germanic Mythology*, first published in 1835, Jakob Grimm remarked on this unexpected and suggestive fact: "concordant information reaches us from our own antiquity, as well as the Greek, regarding the *language* of gods."[18] The classic Germanic example, of course, was the Eddic "Lay of Alvís," which evokes not only the tongues of gods and men, but also those of dwarves, giants, and elves.[19] Grimm's remarks were to be the starting point for the first major study of the subject: Herman Güntert's 1921 book, *On the Language of the Gods and the Language of Spirits: Historical-Semantic Investigations into the Homeric and Eddic Divine*

Language.[20] Conducting an extensive examination of the Old Norse and ancient Greek literary works, Güntert reached the conclusion that what appears in both texts as an opposition between languages reflects, in truth, two types of designations in one tongue. In the Homeric epics, as in the Edda, godly terms are not foreign words, or *voces mysticae*, or even, as some had held, artificial lexical constructions. They are, instead, "poetic circumlocutions of a general kind" (*poetische Umschreibungen allgemeiner Art*), being distinct in structure from the standard nonpoetic designations of things in Homeric Greek and Old Norse.[21] In the closing pages of his book, Güntert enjoined his readers to see in the language of the gods one variety of artistic creation, a variety whose origins might well lie in acts of inspired utterance, such as those of speaking in tongues, that, when transcribed and studied at a later date, had engendered new expressions. Yet he also argued that such designations are close in nature to those employed by the modern poets who have invented new "spiritual languages." "Such poetic testimonies," he wrote, "bring us news of the most beautiful and the deepest spiritual language, which is close in its effects and its mode of expression to music, and to which the poet's word alone, among all the arts, gives speech."[22]

As research in the fields of ancient literature and poetry continued, philologists became increasingly aware that languages of the gods are more extensively documented than Güntert had recognized. In an excursus, Güntert had alluded in his book to the existence of passages in Sanskrit literature that seemed to echo those in Homer and the *Elder Edda*. The classical commentators of the *Rig Veda*, he recalled, maintain that there are discernable differences between words in the tongues of gods and men:

> Thus, for example, Mahidāsa, the compiler of the first six books of the *Aitareya-Brāhmaṇa*, often says, *yad vai devānāṃneti tad eṣām o3m iti,* "what is 'no' to the gods, is 'yes' to human beings," which, according to B. Liebich, *Introduction to Native Indian Linguistics* (1919, II, 6), means that *na*, the particle that later was to mean "not," clearly also appears

in the *Rig Veda* in affirmative sentences, where it has the meaning of "how," "just as if."[23]

"Somadeva 1.59.64 contains a discussion of four languages: Sanskrit, Prakrit, popular dialect and the language of demons." There are even "individual 'divine words,'" Güntert added, "which confirm these findings; I not only mean such *nomina sacra* as *svāha, hiṇ, om, vauṣat* and so forth, but also individual expressions, which in their form recall the Homeric divine words."[24]

More recent scholars, following in Günter's steps, have studied these terms in detail. They have thus been led to propose a new interpretation of the lines of the Vedic "Riddle Hymn" that state that speech has been divided into "four tracks," of which only one is known among mortals.[25] The three hidden tracks, it has been said, are idioms known solely to the *Rishi*, the poets who composed the ancient hymns, and to the priests who, officiating at Vedic sacrifices, employ a secret terminology. "This esoteric knowledge," M. L. West has commented, in reference to the three secret tracks of speech, "must have included the 'hidden names of the gods' (RV 5.5.10, *devānām guhyā nāmāni*), needed for the successful ritual; the expression implies that the gods had names for themselves that differed from those in common use," yet that were known to the learned Vedic poets.[26] "In 4.58.1 'the secret name of the ghee,' understood to be the holy Soma, is called 'the tongue of the gods,' apparently because it causes the sacral vocabulary to be uttered at the sacrifice."[27] There are several other examples. One Sanskrit prose text "describes a ritual in which the priest takes a black antelope skin (*carman-*) with the words 'You are a defence (*śarman-*),' and it is explained that while *carman-* is its human name, 'it is *śarman* among the gods.'"[28] Strikingly, the ritual of the horse sacrifice, or Aśvamedha, "the principal Indo-European kingship ritual,"[29] names the horse four times, according to a pattern reminiscent of the Old Norse "Lay of Alvís":

háyo bhutvá deván avahad vājī́ gandharvā̀n
árvā ásurān áśvo manuṣyā̀n

as *háya* he bore the gods, as *vājín* the gandharvas,
as *árvan* the Asuras, as *áśva* human beings.[30]

The Vedic text offers three synonyms for the "mortal" word
for "horse," *áśva*: in M. L. West's transposition, "as it were, steed,
courser, racer."[31] The suggestion is clear. To each type of being—gods,
Gandharvas, Asuras—there corresponds a different cryptic tongue
with its own vocabulary.[32]

Signs of godly cants have also been found in several other archaic
Indo-European traditions, which do not appear to have influenced
each other. The earliest records are those contained in the oldest
known Indo-European tongue of all: the ancient Anatolian language,
Hittite, generally believed to have been in use between the sixteenth
and the thirteenth centuries B.C. Bilingual tablets inscribed both
in Hittite and in Hattic establish a series of parallelisms between
two sets of names for gods: the human and the divine. "For mankind, thou (art) Taḫattanuit, but among the gods, the Mother of the
Spring, a queen [(art) thou].... For mankind, Wašizzil, but [among]
gods a Lion-King (art) thou, and [thou holdest] Heaven and Earth....
For mankind, Tašimmit, but among gods Ishtar the Queen (art)
thou."[33] A formal "schema," as Johannes Friedrich has observed,
is evident even in such a translation: "first we are told what the
divinity is called among human beings (*ḫa-pipunan*), which is its
everyday name; then follows the divinity's name among the gods
(*ḫa-yašḫaḫipi*), accompanied by an attribute."[34] The first designation
situates the divinities in the mortal realm, the second in the world
of the immortals. Literature in Avestan, the Iranian language of
the second millennium B.C., may furnish related cases in texts that
offer, for a single object, two sets of strictly synonymous names, one
of which is lowly, the other of which is elevated.[35] Finally, Calvert
Watkins has maintained that Old Celtic literature transmits a distinction that mirrors that of the archaic Greek, Indian, and Hittite
traditions. His source is "one of the most curious of all Irish texts,"
the *Auraicept na n-Éces*, known in English translation as *The Scholar's
Primer* or *The Handbook of the Learned*.[36] This work survives solely in

a manuscript dating from the twelfth century. Yet there are reasons to believe it contains material that may bear witness to "a doctrine of poetic learning" developed in an earlier epoch. In one precious, albeit obscure passage, the treatise justifies certain grammatical features of the Irish language by appealing to the three successive "'legendary races' of men and gods which occupied Ireland: the Milesians (Sons of Mil), ancestors of the Gaels; the Fir Bolg invaders; and the ancient Celtic pagan gods, the Túatha Dé Danann."[37]

Such accounts can be interpreted in several ways. For some comparative philologists, they offer compelling evidence of a single Indo-European poetic technique transmitted in different languages for millennia: in Watkins' words, "a conscious tradition of obscurantism, of secrecy, which serves like a cipher to protect the poetic message."[38] Yet one may also question the unity of this "conscious tradition." Whether by chance or by necessity, the documents suggest less a single inheritance than a corpus in bits and pieces, not all of which are incontestably Indo-European. That the twenty Greek works in the language of the gods and the terms of "Lay of Alvís" are straightforward Indo-European witnesses can be granted. Yet the Hittite texts are also transcribed in Hattic, a non–Indo-European language; they have often been considered to bespeak Hattic religious rites.[39] The classical Sanskrit testimonies of the jargon of the gods, while numerous, fail to conform, as a whole, to the models presented in the other examples; even as convinced a proponent of the idea of an Indo-European hermetic tradition in poetry as Françoise Bader admits, in this regard, that "it is perhaps for India that the language of the gods leaves the most to be desired."[40] The Avestan sources are few in number, and while evoking a partition of tongues similar to the others, lack any explicit reference to the language of the gods. There is the Middle Irish allusion to the form of speech of the "ancient pagan gods," to which Watkins accords considerable importance, yet it consists of one sentence, copied in a medieval Christian intellectual milieu that can hardly be considered to have been exclusively Celtic. Moreover, even if one accepts that these various sources all bear witness to a "conscious tradition of obscurantism" in poetry, one may still wonder about the degree to which the "tradition" in question is Indo-European in character. It could be so on account of its remotest historical and linguistic origins, which still survive in fragments in later form. It could also be so on account of accidental borrowings made after the period in which the Indo-European languages would have diverged. Finally, it could be so on account of the nature of sacred speech, which may, in the most disparate of linguistic cases, demand linguistic obscurity.[41]

Certain common traits among these various forms of poetic "obscurantism" in any case merits close study, for they cast a bright light on the structure of jargons and cryptic tongues in general. In a penetrating paper, Calvert Watkins has identified a feature that marks all the examples of Indo-European lexical doubling. He notes that in each case of opposition between an expression in the language of the gods and an expression in the language of men, one may observe the same "metalinguistic poetic figure." This figure functions to exhibit a semantic hierarchy that is already present in the lexicon: that, namely, between terms of different levels that refer to a single object. "The lower level," Watkins writes, "that of ordinary language, is figured as 'the language of men,' the higher and more restricted level of formal, poetic or otherwise exotic language is figured in this ancient metaphor as the 'language of the gods.' This metaphor represents a conscious signalization of an opposition existing in the lexicon, between the common, *semantically unmarked term*, and a rarer, more 'charged,' *semantically marked term*."[42]

Watkins's thesis, in short, is that seemingly theological distinctions between two expressions are linguistic and, more precisely, lexical in nature. Gods and men are the elements of a single figure for the division of one vocabulary into several sets of hierarchically distinct, yet synonymous terms, among which a fundamental distinctive opposition can always be discerned: that between the "common" and the "rare," or, in the Jakobsonian terminology evoked by Watkins, between the structurally "unmarked" and the "marked."[43] As Watkins writes elsewhere, "it is the semantic hierarchy that is basic, and the metaphor of 'language of men' and 'language of gods' is derived from it."[44] One might add that the fact of synonymy is also basic, for only where several terms share a single referent can they be distinguished solely by virtue of "markedness" or "unmarkedness," lexical rarity or commonality. Watkins's principle nonetheless remains valid, as well as impressively supple. "From these examples," he writes, having surveyed the Indo-European instances of divine naming, "it should be clear that the social groups can be multiplied to fit the number of synonyms or quasi-synonyms in the lexicon to be contrasted. "[45] Poetic theology, in any case, will recapitulate facts of grammar: the opposition of the speech of gods and men will mirror the distinctions implicit in the lexicon, and the poet's "obscurantism" will draw its crucial matter from the relative darkness of certain appellations in the language.

This hypothesis is seductive, but one may object that it is one-sided. For it rests on the crucial presupposition that the grammar of a language precedes and determines the special idioms evoked in its poetry. Only if one grants that the lexicon of a language essentially preexists the literary act can one reason that given certain synonyms, a poet may conceive certain expressions, multiplying "social groups" in numbers mirroring those of words. One might also entertain the possibility that makers of poetry, in crucial ways, always also invent aspects of their languages, not least their vocabularies. Their discourse is not only given in advance; it is also forged, each time anew. Into a set of existing synonyms, a poet can always introduce a hitherto unknown distinction of markedness and unmarkedess, not least by assigning one expression to the idiom of the immortals and another to that of mortals. Poetic theology, then, would determine a feature of the common language, for composers of epics, hymns, and narratives would alter the sense of some names in distributing them to the different beings who inhabit their worlds. Jargons can also bring about changes in the tongues of which they are a part, and the cant of gods, no less than that of criminals, can exert an influence on the common idiom in which it is evoked. The possibilities are doubtless many. It would perhaps be misguided to linger on questions of precedence and consequence, for on this level, they can hardly be resolved. As Walter Porzig observed in his study of Vedic enigmas, "one should not ask which of the two is older: common language or special language."[46] The truth is that they are strictly simultaneous. The philology of Indo-European languages has demonstrated that even the most ancient of idioms had its jargons; already in the second millennium B.C., tongues were seized and altered in secret by "canting crews" no less hermetic for being priestly. Speech, one might conclude, is always imparted in parts waiting to be taken. It is in the nature of the rules of grammar, however bounded they may be, to leave a space for speakers to craft new expressions from them and for writers, with or without written signs, to make the idioms they inherit their own.

CHAPTER EIGHT

Nomina Sacra

To devise an impenetrable expression, one need not compose an entirely new word. It can suffice to alter those already present in the language. The simplest level on which to intervene is that of the smallest units of meaningful sound, which coincide, in certain writing systems, with the letter. Speaking beings possess a consciousness, or credulity, so acute that they can be led astray by the alteration of even one of the phonological atoms that, when ordered and combined with others, make up known words. Of course, if the need to conceal a certain term or phrase is great, it may be wiser to effect a systematic set of changes to the chain of signifying sounds. Suetonius reports that Julius Caesar, for one, did so with some frequency. Whenever he had something of a private nature to divulge in a letter to a friend, he would "write it out in signs [*per notas scripsit*], that is, by so changing the order of the letters, such that not a word could be made out." The key to his alphabetic procedure, nonetheless, was rudimentary. "If anyone wishes to investigate these letters and peer into their meaning," Suetonius explains, "he must substitute the fourth letter of the alphabet, namely D, for A, and so for with the others."[1] Augustus, after him, employed a simpler system. "When he had occasion to write in signs [*per notas*]," his biographer recounts, "he put *B* for *A*, and so forth, and instead of *Z, AA*."[2] The Biblical practice known as *atbash*, recorded in the Book of Jeremiah, rests on a similar conceit. *Tav*, the last letter of the Hebrew alphabet, takes the place of *aleph*, the first, even as *shin*, the penultimate, takes the place of *bet*, the second. The Hebrew name of Babylon, *Bavel* (בבל),

thus becomes *Sheshakh* (ששך), according to a secret system whose exact function is no longer clear today.[3]

Such procedures long outlived classical and Biblical antiquity. The curious seventh-century Latin grammarian Virgilius Maro, once believed to have been a Spanish Jew, later thought to be an Irish monk, included in his *Epitomae* a lengthy treatment, "On the Art of Scrambling Words" ("De scinderatio fonorum"), in which he distinguished several ways to disorder the letters of known expressions. From classical Roman literary texts he made new and unintelligible series of signs, grouped together as words. Virgilius listed, in didactic terms, at least three reasons for such practices: "First, so that we may test the ingenuity of our students in searching out and identifying obscure points; second, for the ornamentation and reinforcement of eloquence; third, lest mystical matters, which should be revealed solely to the initiated, be discovered easily by base and stupid people."[4] In hindsight, one may say that such "scramblings" were to be, in a sense, only beginnings. Starting with the Renaissance, ever more complex forms of artificial encipherment and decipherment came to be devised. The modern cryptographers might begin, as did the ancients and medievals, with the signs and expressions of natural languages, but they quickly made of them new "secrecy systems," often unspeakable as well as unrecognizable in form.

Arts of dissimulation of this kind may be effective in concealing speech. Yet they possess a weakness, and that is that they are manifestly occult. Confronted with sentences reordered by the Caesars' cipher or the prophet's *atbash*, speakers of Latin and Hebrew could hardly fail to observe that into their customary speech, an unheard expression had suddenly been inserted. The craft is too apparent. Subtler techniques of hiding efface their traces, becoming almost undetectable to the ear and to the eye. The gods of ancient India, according to the classical Vedic sources, cultivated such procedures. Tradition teaches that on earth, the bodies of these deities can cast no shadows, being absolutely clear.[5] They themselves speak the truth, for it is their nature. Their language is the "refined speech" known as Sanskrit (*saṃskṛtā*): an idiom in which words are the fitting names of the things they designate and are, in structure, susceptible to a grammatical analysis so thorough as to leave no remainder, thereby justifying each of the linguistic traits perceptible in words. Yet it is also repeatedly reported that the gods, by nature, "delight in what is concealed" (*paro'kṣakāmā hi devāḥ*) and "detest what shows itself in plain view" (*pratyakṣadviṣaḥ*).[6] "This statement," Jan Gonda has commented, "implies that gods like to use, among themselves, a vocabulary which is not intelligible to (most) men. They like to keep the names of important beings and objects secret."[7] The ancient Sanskrit prose works known as *Brāhmaṇa*s amply confirm his interpretation. They furnish precious accounts concerning how the gods, in a time almost before all human reckoning, secretly altered the form of words in ways that might easily have escaped all mortal perception.

Charles Malamoud has dedicated an exemplary study to these changes made to the language shared by mortals and immortals. That such alterations confound grammatical analysis can hardly be doubted; the divine changes work both to disguise etymology and to cloud morphology. "A great many passages tell us that the original form of this or that word has been slightly modified, becoming a hidden form."[8] Human beings, for example, believe themselves to be familiar with a god named Indra. But they reason with a term artificially made by the gods on the basis of a related word. The god's true name, we learn, is "Indha, that is, 'what lights,' a name derived from the verbal root *INDH*, 'to light, burn,' and justified by a fire function attributed to this divinity."[9] Elsewhere, however, another origin and another disguise are suggested: "Indra," we are told, derives in truth from *idaṃdra*, "he who has seen this," "since as soon as he was born, Indra looked about him and saw a man who was none other than the *Brahman* (that is, the Absolute), in all its extension, and he said, 'I have seen this.'" The explanation could hardly be clearer: "That is his name. We call the one who is *Idaṃdra* Indra, in a hidden fashion, for the gods delight in what is hidden."[10] So, too, the name of the god commonly called Agni is, in truth, "Agri"; it derives from the adverbial forms *agram*, "in front," or *agre*, "in the first place," though few mortals know it.[11]

Common nouns have also undergone such processes of phono-logical deformation. Thus, the Sanskrit word for sweat, *sveda*, can be etymologically tied, by means of an explanatory myth, to a word apparently unrelated to it, *suveda*, "happily found." "What is *suveda* is called, in secret, *sveda*, for the gods delight in what is concealed and detest what lies in plain view."[12] The sources suggest that even one of the oldest Indo-European designations for humanity has also been altered in such a way. When pierced by a three-pronged arrow, the creator god Prajāpati was wounded, and his sperm descended to earth and formed a lake. "The other divinities exclaimed: 'May this sperm of Prajāpati not be spoiled (*mā duṣāt*)!' Because the gods said *mā duṣāt*, the lake of sperm came to be called *mādusa*." But, once again, "the gods like to express themselves in terms unknown to men": *mādusa* thus "changes to *manuṣa*, 'human,' 'man.'"[13]

To a certain degree, the alterations recounted in these Vedic sources can be seen to involve a cryptic tongue invented within an existing grammar. Yet this divine jargon works in ways unlike those of other special languages. The gods, the texts relate, willingly divulge their artificial vocabulary to mortals; what they conceal is the common lexicon from which they departed. The "secrecy" of this godly cant is therefore in some senses unique. Malamoud observes: "The word that results from the alteration inspired by the desire for esotericism is not occult in the sense that it belongs to a language of a closed group. On the contrary, it is the falsified word that belongs to ordinary language; everyone says Indra, and not Indha, Agni, and not Agri." By an unexpected artifice, jargon, the special tongue, thus becomes "the common language," while "inno-cent and intact words" are veiled in secrecy.[14] If human language appears obscure in its origins and form, one can then infer that it may be the work of divine minds, who distorted grammar accord-ing to rules that they alone—with certain rare exceptions—master. What they guard to themselves is not a lexicon but a systematic mechanism: "The secret of the gods is the secret of a fabrication and deformation of a product that is everywhere in use."[15] It is a "fab-rication and deformation" that proceeds, at each step, by the most minute of changes to given words. Letters may be either added or subtracted to the items in the vocabulary. Most often, however, they are merely substituted for each other, one by one, in elementary phonetic forms. That is enough to confuse our mortal minds.

One might imagine that for such operations, writing would be crucial. How could one change *Indha* to *Indra*, *Agri* to *Agni* without decomposing these names into the minimal units now represented as letters? It is remarkable, however, that while according such importance to details of a grammatical variety, the Vedic corpus refuses to admit the role of *grammata*, "letters," scripts, and books, in the transmission of revealed tradition. In classical India, Malamoud writes, "knowledge is above all sonorous speech, *vāc*, and writing grants access to knowledge only if it leads to familiarity with sounds."[16] Not by accident does the Sanskrit term for "revelation," *śruti*, mean "hearing." Although the Vedic poet is considered a "seer" (*ṛṣi*), he is not thought to read or write. Nor are the guardians of Vedic tradition to frequent books. Commandments, both positive and negative, are explicit on this matter. "Vedas are to be learned orally," declares the *Gopatha-Brāhmaṇa*.[17] "It is held that no knowledge of *dharma* can result from a Veda known improperly, either from a written text or studied by a servant [*śūdra*]."[18] "Innumerable signs indicate that in any milieu dominated by Vedic religion or by the Hindu religion that derives from it, writing is held to be vile and suspect. At best, it is useful as a last-resort technique. But it is inadequate to the task of preserving the most prestigious bodies of works, which, though they can be very voluminous, must be committed to memory."[19]

More than once, the foreign visitors to ancient India expressed some surprise about this fact. Megasthenes, Greek ambassador to King Kandragupta in the fourth century B.C., reported, for example, that the Indians of his day "have no knowledge of letters and regulate every single thing from memory" (*oude gar grammata eidenai autous all'apo mnēmēs hekasta diokeisthai*).[20] The soundness of that general pronouncement has been questioned, for in India writing was used from an early date, and books were neither rare nor strange.[21] As an observation about the Vedic tradition, however, it is not implausible. The eleventh-century Persian geographer al-Bīrūnī visited India at a time when sovereign administrative practices, in particular, relied crucially on letters, books, and note keeping. Yet the classical Arabic author reports that the Brahmans would not allow the Vedas to be transmitted by any means other than oral recitation. "They do not allow the Veda to be committed to writing, because it is recited according to certain modulations, and they therefore avoid the use of the pen, since it is liable to cause some error, and may occasion an omission or defect in the written text."[22]

This exclusion of writing from the domain of priestly and poetic practice, while striking, is not entirely without parallels among ancient cultures. In a famous passage of his *Gallic Wars*, Julius Caesar leads one to believe that the company of Druids played a role similar to that of the Indian priests. Druids, the Roman author explains, "are engaged in things sacred, conduct the public and the private sacrifices, and interpret all matters of religion," being "supreme authorities" among the Celtic people of Gaul.[23] Yet Druids "do not go to war, nor pay tribute together with the rest; they have an exemption from military service and a dispensation in all matters." They are, moreover, entrusted with a large body of poetry, which they must memorize: "They are said to learn by heart a great number of verses; accordingly, some remain in training for twenty years." Graphic arts, we learn, are expressly forbidden to the Druids, though the ancient Celts otherwise do avail themselves of writing: "Druids do not regard it as lawful [*fas*] to commit [their great number of verses] to writing, though in almost all other matters, in their public and private transactions, they use Greek letters."[24] Caesar advanced two explanations for this habit, which clearly struck him as in need of commentary. The first is that the Druids do not "desire their doctrines to be divulged among the mass of the people." Their teachings are instead to remain esoteric. The second is that the Celts do not wish to weaken the powers of their recollection, "since it generally occurs to most men, that, in their dependence on writing, they relax their diligence in learning thoroughly, and their employment of the memory."[25] Modern scholars have offered their own interpretations of the druidic ban.[26] Yet they have largely agreed with Caesar in holding that if the Celtic priests refused to commit their ancient poetry to writing, it must have been to preserve some knowledge of a hermetic kind that letters, being public, would destroy.

Such an opposition between writing and secrecy is all too apparent. One might choose to doubt accounts of civilizations that, while conceding the existence of writing, insist that it was unknown or forbidden to priestly classes. Yet there is a more compelling reason to question the familiar dichotomy of common techniques of writing and secret practices of oral wisdom. It is that writing, no matter how formal, may also be a means of concealment. Under certain conditions, it may even itself become a matter of some secrecy. The ancient world was also familiar with peoples who, while apparently without writing, nonetheless employed arts of marking signs in special circumstances. Tacitus reports in the *Germania* that the Germanic tribes, while illiterate, practiced an art of divination that relied on inscribing "marks" on bits of wood:

> A little bough is lopped off a fruit-bearing tree, and cut into small pieces. These are distinguished by certain marks [*notis*], and thrown carelessly and at random over a white garment. In public questions the priest of the particular state, in private the father of the family, invokes the gods, and, with his eyes towards heaven, takes up each piece three times, and finds in them a meaning according to the mark previously impressed on them.[27]

The nature of these "marks" is to us, as perhaps it was to Tacitus, obscure. Yet it is difficult not to interpret them as the elements of some variety of writing.

There are also examples in literary history of graphic arts of linguistic representation that are thought to have once served hidden and magic ends. A famous example is that of the Northern European letters called "runes," whose related names in Old English, Old High German, Old Norse, and Old Irish evoke not only written signs but also "mysteries," "whispers," and "secrets."[28] They have

been identified with the very Germanic "marks" evoked by Tacitus, although one cannot establish the link with certainty.[29] There
is, however, evidence that those who copied runes in the Middle
Ages believed themselves, at times, to be transmitting knowledge
of secret things. A ninth-century scribe in England who annotated
rune lists in Latin, for instance, explains to his readers in a note that
"these forms of letters are said to have been invented among the
people of the *Northmanni* [or *Nordmann*]," adding that "they still use
them to commit their songs and incantations to memory. They give
the name 'rune-staves' [*runstabas*] to these letters, I believe, because
by writing them they used to bring to light secret things."[30] The
copyist, of course, may well have been mistaken. Yet where runes
appear in Anglo-Saxon literature, they bring to it a palpable layer
of opacity.

This is due in part to the fact that in the Old English tradition,
each rune bears a special name that, in addition to designating
the written sign, also has a function in the language as a common
noun denoting a worldly object. In the eighth- or ninth-century
Rune Poem, which has parallels in the so-called *Icelandic Rune Poem*
and *Norwegian Rune Poem*, every stanza turns around a single rune,
whose various associations it explores in Latin letters. "Rather than
using runes," Robert DiNapoli has commented, "the poem is gener-
ated by them, or more precisely by their names, which introduce a
note of ambiguity from the outset, since each is the name of both a
runic character on the page and an object, being, or concept in the
world."[31] Several of the riddles in the tenth-century Anglo-Saxon
Exeter Book exploit such ambiguities to an extreme degree. Here,
runes can be the keys to encryption and decryption, even where,
strictly speaking, they do not appear in the text. Riddle 58, for
example, ends with the following pronouncement, uttered in the
first-person singular of the riddle: "There are three right runes in
my name, the first of which is *Rad*" (*Þry sind in naman / ryhte runsta-
fas, þara is Rad forma*).[32] To solve the riddle, one must first recover
the "three runes" concealed in these lines of poetry in Roman
letters. The reader must decide whether *Rad* is to be taken as the

name of physical being, such as a "rod," or as the rune commonly called *Rad* (ᚱ), or, by extension, as the sign of the phoneme /r/ it represents, which is commonly written in Latin letters by "r." Only by conducting these various procedures can one reach the riddle's most probable, if uncertain solution.[33] Even more hermetic are the conceits of Riddle 19, in which a dozen runes appear in nine lines of Anglo-Saxon poetry. The two types of writing oblige the eye to read in two directions at once, for to spell intelligible words in the language, the runes must be sounded out from right to left, while the Roman letters continue to move from left to right. The solution, *snac*, "a light, swift ship," is inscribed in the riddle itself, but as an acronym. Its four letters are distributed across those of four common nouns. "The words are spelled backward, so that one takes the 's' from *hors* 'horse,' 'n' from *mon* 'man,' 'a' from *wega* 'warrior,' and 'c' from *haofoc* 'hawk,' to find the answer."[34]

Such texts may well be exceptional in the arts of their obscurity. Yet there are practices of writing that, while far more common, rest on techniques of ellipsis and dissimulation that are not dissimilar in structure. One may take, as an exemplary case, the standard methods of transcribing holy names in the Christian manuscripts of antiquity and the Middle Ages, which Ludwig Traube analyzed in his path-breaking 1907 book, *Nomina sacra*.[35] Traube borrowed the expression in his title from his older British colleague, Sir Edward Maunde Thompson, who had employed it to refer, as he wrote, to "sacred and liturgical contractions" found in Greek and Latin manuscripts. Such "contractions" or abbreviations are ubiquitous in the tradition and can render works obscure even to those who have mastered both languages.

Traube began by showing that such abbreviations are fundamentally of two kinds. There are those, first, in which a word, title, or name is shortened by the removal of its final letters: such is the case, for example, of *Imperator*, contracted as "IMP.," *Consul*, abbreviated as "C.," and *Dominus*, "Lord," shortened as "DOM.," "DO." or simply "D." In such cases, a dot is placed after the last remaining letter to indicate that an omission has been made. The second variety of shortening results from the decision to remove middle letters from a word while retaining, in each case, the last. Then the final letter or letters will be written next to the first. *Dominus*, in this form, can appear as "$\overline{\text{DS}}$." In such cases, no dot will be employed; instead, a superscript stroke will hover over the entire shortened form. Traube called the first variety of abbreviation "suspension," reserving the old name, "contraction," for this second. While the first consists in a "setting aside" (*Weglassen*) of parts of a word, the second, as he put it, brings about an "omission" or "leaving out" (*Auslassen*) of letters. Traube showed that while examples of "suspension" can be found in pagan as well as Christian manuscripts, the first instances of "contradiction" are no older than the third century A.D. and can be found solely in Christian texts. With considerable clarity and precision, Traube posed, then, two basic questions: that of the origin of the nonclassical form of abbreviation and that of the reason for its general adoption by Christian copyists.

Traube argued that the curious technique of shortening by contraction could be explained only with reference to a culture distinct from those of both Greece and Rome. One must, he wagered, recall a basic belief of ancient Judaism: "the four-letter name is taken to be holy, rife with magic, and unspeakable."[36] For this reason, biblical Hebrew scribes avoided transcribing it in its entirety. That medieval Latin manuscript practices should derive from an ancient Jewish faith in the magical properties of Hebrew letters, to be sure, was in 1907 anything but self-evident. In an early appraisal, W. M. Lindsay noted that Christian paleographers and classicists were bound to greet Traube's thesis with a "first attitude of startled incredulity."[37] Yet Traube marshaled compelling philological evidence in favor of his thesis. He showed that only words related to the Christian deity and holy things were ever subject to contraction. Some such words, moreover, were at times also abbreviated by suspension; but in all such cases, a theological difference explained the two techniques. Thus *Deo*, "God," might appear as "DO.," but only where it signified a pagan god, such as in Latin transcriptions of Virgil's *Aeneid*; wherever the manuscripts employed the word to signify the Christian deity, they had "$\overline{DO}$" instead. Similarly, "$\overline{SPU}$," for *spiritu*, always represented the Holy Spirit, although the Latin word *spiritu* might equally have signified profane "breath." Suddenly, it became clear why an anonymous seventh-century corrector of an Oxford manuscript had emended every complete mention of *deus* and *dominus*, such that both these sacred names appeared solely in contraction.[38] It was hardly to save space on the page, for the words were already in place, and nothing new would be written over the areas from which letters were deleted. Omission, in this case, expressed an act of pious reverence. The art of transcription reached a high point when the holy name came to be rewritten, its letters blotted out in such a way to give rise to a new and obscure sign. In time, however, the principles of the scribal technique were forgotten. Abbreviation by contraction, once a basic feature of manuscripts in Latin, Coptic, Gothic, and Armenian manuscripts, was by the ninth century a practice whose principles European scribes could no longer decipher.[39]

According to Traube, the reasons for this art of writing lay in a specifically Jewish relation to the holy name. Yet the Christian *nomina sacra* also illustrate a linguistic phenomenon that is by all accounts more general. There are certain words and phrases that no one wishes openly to express, and in all human societies, there are linguistic prohibitions that characteristically affect those areas of life considered to be subject to taboo. In some cases, silence is formally imposed. Since, however, it cannot always be assured, a set of substitutions is also required. Antoine Meillet commented on this fact in a classic essay, first published in 1906. "In various of the most diverse parts of the world," he wrote, "one may observe vocabulary 'taboos.'"[40] By way of introduction, he mentioned South Africa, the Malayo-Polynesian languages, the Far East, Europe, and North America, where "certain words are forbidden by usage either to a whole group of people, or to certain particular individuals, or during certain periods and in certain settings." A taboo, he explained, may concern "the name of the deceased, or a leader, or those from whose family one takes a wife, etc." Yet prohibitions can also affect common nouns, "which may or may not be identical with those names, which sound in some way identical or analogous, or even only partially analogous, to them."[41]

Half a century later, Émile Benveniste pursued Meillet's reflections. Meillet had concentrated above all on individual terms that are subject to taboo in Indo-European languages. He had observed that certain common names of animals, such as "bear" and "snake," appear to have been avoided by the speakers of languages as diverse as Russian, English, French, and Greek; as a rule, they substituted for them words unrelated to them in their roots. Benveniste noted that taboos not only dictated forms of lexical substitution. Subtler modes of deformation could also respond to the risks of speech. One may, he observed, in technical terms, "mutilate the word 'God' through the aphaeresis of the final syllable" or by the substitution of an assonating term: in place of the exclamation "by God!"("par Dieu!"), for instance, one may say "pardi!" or "parbleu!" although neither phrase, strictly speaking, can be reduced to words present in the lexicon of the language.[42] To avoid the infraction of a prohibition, speakers may even go so far as to create an entire "form of non-sense" produced by the scrambling of the sounds that make up a single, blasphemous phrase. Thus, in place of "par le sang de Dieu!" ("by God's blood!"), Benveniste reports, one says "palsambleu!" and instead of "je renie Dieu!" ("I deny God!"), one will prudently, if somewhat meaninglessly, exclaim "jarnibleu!"[43] It is not difficult to find examples of analogous formulations in other tongues. In 1944, H. L. Mencken recorded no fewer than ten phonologically related English euphemistic substitutes for the single name "Jesus," all of which were in use in the language spoken by one inhabitant of Dalton, Pennsylvania: "gee," "jeez," "jiminy" (or "jeminy"), "Jemima," "Jerusalem," "Jehosaphat," "gee-whizz," "gee-whillikins," "gee-whittaker."[44]

Such distortions all involve the constituent elements of forbidden words, being examples of reorderings of letters. Yet they presuppose no craft of writing, at least in the usual sense of a conscious practice of transcription. The passage from "par Dieu!" to "pardi!" or from "Jesus" to "gee," "gee-whizz," "gee-whillikins," and "gee-whittaker" requires neither pen nor paper. Nor does it rely for its workings on any knowing representation of the units of sound. Sacred words can be modified—and deformed—without a moment's thought. It is often said that once it is invented and established, a system of writing transforms the sense that speaking beings possess of their language and its elements, from the sentence to the word, the morpheme, and the phoneme. Yet such modes of linguistic representation have their foundation in the sensitivity to oppositions that is the condition of the faculty of speech. Only beings to whom the distinction between "parbleu!" and "par Dieu!" is evident—and, one might add, of religious significance—will devise a means to represent it in the building blocks of signifying sounds. For the same reason, only they will act, whether in speaking or in writing, to alter the expressions of their languages—letter by letter, syllable by syllable, according to the occasion—at times to conceal them, at times to mutilate them. To this degree, at least, mortals act, by nature, like the gods of the Vedic tradition. By substitution, suppression, addition, and contraction, they work and play, modifying the constituents of speech to render the familiar unfamiliar. One might object that the changes wrought upon a language to avoid blasphemy or the infraction of a taboo proceed from a powerlessness that lies at the furthest extreme from the mastery with which immortal beings must act. The difference is certain, yet it may be of less consequence than it appears. One fact, in any case, cannot be doubted. Whether for piety or for pleasure, mortals, too, like to keep names of important persons and objects secret. All speaking beings, swearers and scribes no less than gods and priests, share an attraction to what is hidden and a discomfort before "what lies in plain view."

CHAPTER NINE

Anaphones

In the winter of 1905, Ferdinand de Saussure, professor of Indo-European languages at the University of Geneva, took a leave from teaching. He meant to make a "complete break" with his "customary occupations and preoccupations," as he recalled in a letter to his former student, Antoine Meillet.[1] In the company of his wife, Marie-Eugénie, he traveled to Italy. Saussure spent a month in Naples before moving on to Rome, where he lingered in the Forum, pondering the remains of its monumental inscriptions. "No need to tell you," he wrote to Meillet in a note from January 1906, "that here I am not doing much. The archaic inscription in the Forum is just the diversion I need to rack my brains. Nothing to be drawn from it, of course, but it is interesting to contemplate the enigmatic block and, by sight, to confirm the transcriptions."[2] Among the texts chiseled on stone were some of the oldest surviving examples of Latin poetry: epitaphs and triumphal commemorations dating from as early as the third and second centuries B.C. These brief and often fragmentary texts, the oldest in the Roman literary tradition, are composed in the Italic verse form commonly known as the "Saturnian," which the Roman authors employed before their successors adapted the meters of Greek literature to suit the Latin language. It would seem that in the Roman Forum, it was this archaic metrical form, more than the contents of any one inscription, that unexpectedly caught Saussure's attention.

The Saturnian was, and still remains today, in large part, a mystery.[3] The Romans of the classical age may themselves not have understood it. Often they claimed that the old Roman form of verse possessed no rhythm whatsoever. Grammarians decried its linguistic liberties and lack of order; poets described it as belonging to a crude and undisciplined epoch in history. Horace, for one, did not hesitate to call it "horrid" (*horridus*).[4] In Saussure's own lifetime, however, a new interpretation of the meter had been proposed. It was argued, particularly in Germany, that the Saturnian was not quantitative, like Greek and classical Latin poetry, but rather accentual in nature, like verse in German, Russian, and English.[5] Its lines, in other words, would have been organized not by the regular alternations of long and short vowels but by the ordering of sets of accented and unaccented syllables. Saussure does not appear to have commented extensively on this hypothesis, either to assert it or to deny it, although having studied in Germany and having continued to follow the research of his colleagues beyond the Rhine, he most likely knew it well. As he examined the archaic Roman inscriptions, his attention was drawn, instead, to what seemed to be an odd linguistic phenomenon: "something as bizarre," as he later wrote to Meillet, "as phonic imitation."[6] Elements in the sound structure of the archaic Italic poetry seemed to mirror each other, as if obeying some unknown law of "phonetic harmonies."[7]

Upon his return to Geneva, Saussure persevered in his Saturnian studies. He began to investigate the entire corpus, which has been transmitted in a small number of precious manuscripts as well as epitaphs. Soon he believed he had found the forgotten key to the Italic form of verse. "By dint of turning the Saturnian upside down in all directions," he wrote in a letter to his former pupil, Charles Bally, in July 1906, "I have reached a solution."[8] He added that it was only provisional, and he entreated his correspondent to keep it to himself. "The solution," he announced, "is so simple that it makes me laugh when I think of the detours I had to go through to get there. For me, the Saturnian is no longer anything but the pure and simple Greek hexameter, adapted in such a way so as to allow substitutions of spondees by anapests, <the tribrach>, and the amphibrach as well as the dactyl."[9] This adaptation of the "pure and simple Greek hexameter," Saussure added, merely requires certain "licenses," which he went on to enumerate in detail.

Soon that metrical explanation seemed to him inadequate. Later the same month, Saussure wrote again to Bally, correcting his account. "Without abandoning what seemed to me true in metrics," he wrote, "that is, that it is a question of a dactylic or rather *spondaic* meter of five or six feet, with an anapest or an amphibrach as an acceptable substitute of a spondee (since they too hold as – –), I see now that one must at all costs resolve the problem of Alliteration."[10] This "problem" was not strictly speaking metrical, since it affected neither vowels nor accents taken in quantitative proportions. "The problem of Alliteration" involved, instead, other relations of words: affinities and symmetries between the textures of vowels, consonants, and whole syllables of Saturnian poetry that seemed to Saussure to echo each other, both within individual lines and across them, in almost systematic form. The linguist was now convinced that these striking symmetries of letters played a crucial part in the art of Saturnian verse.

Saussure, however, also took a further step. He held that the traits he had noted in the Forum were not exclusive to archaic Latin literature in verse. Similar phonetic phenomena could also be found in later Roman poetry. Moreover, he now explained, even beyond the limits of the Latin literary domain, one can find examples of a systematic mirroring in the vowels, consonants, and syllables of the kind present in the Saturnian. In the hymns of ancient India, the songs of medieval Germany, and the epics of classical Greece, Saussure detected something that had gone unnoticed by scholars: a shared Indo-European poetic technique involving the sound shape of words. Comparative grammar had, by this point, established that many of the ancient languages of Latium, India, Germany, and Greece were structurally as well as genetically related. Now Saussure suggested that one might find analogous correspondences between the poetic practices attested in these various languages. "All this leads me to think," he wrote, summarizing the path his research had taken, "that if the Saturnian, with its considerable *metrical* affinities for other ancient Indo-European types of verse, concealed, moreover, an extraordinary system of combinations of syllables, consonants, and vowels, all regulated by an *unapparent* law, perhaps there was something similar in the poetry of India, and Greece itself?!"[11]

Saussure distinguished this *"unapparent* law" from the various rules of language that define individual grammars and that linguists aim to lay bare. Those rules, he maintained, obtain in the absence of any clear awareness on the part of speaking subjects, in the sense that those who speak a language need not possess any conscious knowledge of its grammatical system to produce utterances that will nonetheless conform to its many constraints. The "bizarre" principle of Indo-European poetry, he held, was of another kind. Saussure wagered that it was a conscious inheritance that rested on an art knowingly, if secretly, passed on from poet to poet, generation to generation. "The results are no less confounding for their Indo-European significance," he observed. "It is no longer a question of something unconsciously transmitted, such as a language, or, in poetry itself, rhythm and visible form; it is, rather, necessarily a secret of the poets, the *Kavayas*, the *vates*, which requires that a formula be learned and then transmitted from master to disciple over thousands of years."[12] An archaic convention would have demanded, in other words, that poets acquire not only "the traditional Indo-European versification" that was "immediately grasped by the ear," but also something else: "an obscure, almost secret thing, which is, for us, absolutely astonishing, a thing such as the counting of phonetic elements by 'regular' arithmetical addition and subtraction."[13]

In the years following his return from Italy, Saussure dedicated the greatest attention to the study of this "obscure, almost secret thing" in poetry. Suffering from what he once termed an "incurable *graphophobia*," he neither sought to publish his findings nor expressed any wish to see them in print.[14] Yet between 1906 and 1909, he devoted no fewer than ninety-nine notebooks to elucidating the principles of the Indo-European "phonetic harmonies" that he first perceived in fragments of old Italic verse. The existence of these notebooks was generally unknown at the time of the linguist's death in 1913, and it remained so for half a century after the posthumous appearance of the famous *Course in General Linguistics* in 1916, which Charles Bally and Albert Sechehaye prepared on the basis of notes taken from Saussure's lectures.[15] Only in the mid-1960s did Saussure's research into the "*unapparent* law" of Indo-European verse come to be known, thanks to the five articles on Saussure that Jean Starobinski collected in his 1971 book, *Words upon Words: Ferdinand Saussure's Anagrams.*[16]

In deference to Starobinski's subtitle and Saussure's own suggestions, the notebooks are today generally thought to contain a theory of anagrams. That term, however, is for several reasons imprecise. Strictly speaking, an anagram consists in the reordering of the letters in one name (or noun), such that they come to form another expression. William Camden, one of the first English writers to discuss the procedure, defined it in classic terms when, in his *Remains concerning Britaine* of 1605, he explained that "*Anagrammatisme*, or *Metagrammatisme*," is "a dissolution of a Name truely written into his Letters, as his Elements, and a new connexion of it by artificiall transposition, without addition, substraction, or change of any letter into different words, making some perfect sence applicable to the person named."[17] Examples of such transpositions can already be found in the literature of the ancient Greeks, who coined the noun "anagrammatism" (*anagrammatismos*) and the verb "to anagrammatize" (*anagrammatizein*) for such "artificial transpositions."[18] In the second century B.C., Lycophron, for example, made of the name Ptolemaios "Apo melistos," "From Honey," and turned Arsinoê into "Hera's violet," "Ion Hêras."[19] The "phonic imitations" that Saussure believed he had discovered in ancient Indo-European poetry are of a different nature. Their rules are more numerous, their elements are more complex, and their reality is less certain.

Between 1906 and 1909, Saussure's theory underwent several changes. One may nonetheless present its basic lineaments in a single form. First, Saussure established, through a close study of Saturnian poetry, that, within a single line of verse, individual sounds—vowels as well as consonants—appear in groups of two: phonological "couplings" are the rule. "A vowel has the right to appear in the Saturnian," he explained, "only if it has a *countervowel* in some place whatsoever in the line."[20] The only liberties that the ancient poets gave themselves for vowels were three "compromises" (*transactions*) bearing on timbre: "1st, between short ĕ—short ī, short ō—short ŭ; 2nd, sometimes ē : ei; 3rd, sometimes ō: ū."[21] Similar "couplings," Saussure argued, dictate the quantity of consonants. Where the number of vowels or consonants in a line is odd, rather than even, there will naturally be a "remainder" (*résidu*), an element without a corresponding partner in the line. Yet in such cases, Saussure remarks, "one sees it reappearing *in the next line* as a new remainder, corresponding to the overflow of the preceding line."[22]

Next, Saussure applied this principle to a higher level of verbal construction. As he explained to Meillet in a letter dated September 23, 1907, when one pushes one's analysis beyond the level of the single sound or "monophone," one observes a more complex phenomenon that is at once "more easily grasped, yet more difficult to reduce to a fixed formula."[23] Sets of two and three phonemes—"diphones" and "triphones"—will mirror each other in remarkable symmetry. "In fact," Saussure notes, "almost any Saturnian passage is no more than a swarming of syllables or phonic forms echoing each other." As an example, he cited two lines from Livius Andronicus:

{ Ibi manens sedeto donicum videbis
Me carpento vehente dōmum venisse.[24]

There followed the following "polyphonic" analysis:

DĒ: DĒ in *sedēto: vidēbis.*
BĬ: BĬ in *ibi: vidēbĭs.*
DŌ: DŎ in *dōnicum: dŏmum*
VĔ: VĒ in *vehente: vēnisse*
TŌ: TŌ in *sedētō: carpentō*
NĬ: NĬ in *donĭcum: vēnĭsse*
ĒN: ĒN in *man-ēn-s: v-ēn-isse*

$$\left\{ \begin{array}{l} \text{SĔ: SĔ} \\ \textit{or } \text{SSE: SSE} \\ \textit{or } \text{ĒNSSE: ĒNSSE} \end{array} \right\} \quad \begin{array}{l} \text{in } \textit{sĕdētō: vēnis-sĕ} \\ (\textit{manēnssĕ-: vēn(i)ssĕ} \end{array}$$

ĔNT: ĔNT: in *carp-ĕntō: veh-ĕnt-e*
ŬMV: ŬMV in donic*umv*id: dom*umv*ēn[25]

Such a reading reveals several of the fundamental principles that underlie Saussure's representation of the "counting of phonetic elements" in verse. The elements in question, first, are not letters but phonemes. They may therefore be spelled in different forms with varying diacritics, their letters halved or doubled and treated in isolation and in larger groups. Monophones, diphones, and polyphones, second, are dispersed across both the single line and beyond it; there can then be parallelisms between not only *sedēto* and *vidēbĭs* in the same line but also between *dōnicum* and *dōmum* between two. Third, single elements can be counted in different forms according to their position. In Saussure's representation, the single word *venisse*, for example, contains no fewer than six distinct units of phonic imitation: *vĕ*; *nĭ*; *ēn*; *sĕ*; *ssĕ*; and *ēnsse* (according to a spelling nowhere present in the transcription). One might well understand such sonic poetic material in terms of alliteration. Yet Saussure argues that such a traditional figure of sound play cannot do justice to the "*unapparent* law" that commands the construction of this form of verse. "The whole phenomenon of alliteration (and also rhyme) that one may observe in the Saturnian," he asserts in 1907, "is nothing but an insignificant part of a more general, or, rather, an *absolutely total* phenomenon."[26] Here one finds far more than the alliterative echoing of certain letters with each other, for each and every portion of the poem can play several parts in this "extraordinary system of combinations of syllables, consonants, and vowels."

The formulation of the system demands, however, a further principle. Not only do the vowels and consonants in individual and adjacent lines correspond to one another, and not only do whole groupings of syllables also echo each other in fixed form. These elements, when conjoined, also spell out special nouns and names. "As soon as the occasion is given," Saussure continues, "the polyphones visibly reproduce the syllables of a word or an important name for the text, then becoming *anagrammatic* polyphones."[27] It seems that Saussure was quick to reach this conclusion. In a letter to Bally from 1906 evoking his Homeric studies, Saussure reports having detected the presence of "theme words" (*mot-thèmes*) or "key words" (*Stichwörte*), whose constituent phonic and syllabic elements are scattered across the epic texts. "What is most absolutely certain for me," he declares,

> is that the entire text of the Homeric poems (or, if it is not entire, this will be one easy way to see which parts were added) rests on a secret law, <in which> the repetition of vowels and consonants of an absolutely fixed number, on the basis of a keyword [*Stichwort*], a THEME WORD, is observed, from line to line, with an admirable and total precision.... One can <already> say that the whole text of Homer is nothing but a vast and continuous anagram, running on the key word [*Stichwort*] or key words [*Stichwörte*] that are renewed every two, or two and a half, or three lines, without the least imprecision with respect to the number of consonants, vowels, and hiatuses demanded in this space by the key word.[28]

Audible phonetic play, therefore, points to an unspoken noun or name. Saussure did not hesitate to evoke an art of circumlocution. Vowels, consonants, and syllables might all compose a "phonic paraphrase" "according to regular forms."[29] As long as he pursued his studies of Indo-European poetry, Saussure sought the rules that would define these forms. He believed them to be independent of purely metrical considerations:

> If all syllables can lay claim to phonic symmetry, it follows that what dictates these combinations in no way depends on the line and its rhythmic scheme. A second principle, independent of verse itself, was joined to the first to constitute a specific poetic form. To satisfy the condition of the "poem" (*carmen*), which is completely independent of the feet or *ictus*, I state, in fact, (*and this is my thesis*) that the poet, in

his vocation, dedicated himself to the phonic analysis of words. It is most probably this science of the sonic forms of words that from the earliest Indo-European period lent superiority, a particular quality, to the Hindu *Kavis*, the Latin *Vates*, etc.[30]

Saussure's "thesis" is worth unfolding. It holds that despite their apparent diversity, the Indo-European poets all possessed a special knowledge of the properties of sound structure, which they jealously kept to themselves: hence their tacit "superiority" with respect to the other members of their societies. Their special "science" would have allowed the poets to order and reorder units of sounds, just as mathematical knowledge allows those who possess it to submit individual numbers to the operations of "'regular' arithmetical addition and subtraction." "Every Latin poet [*Vates*] was above all a specialist in facts of phonemes."[31] For this reason, Saussure saw no difficulty in holding that the Sanskrit *Kavis* and the Latin *Vates* also carried out complex procedures of phonological inversion and transposition. Metathesis, he suggested, was, to the archaic poets, a familiar transformation. In reading and in analysis, one must keep its incessant possibility in mind. *EM*, in an ancient text, can also be *ME*;[32] *RT* may be deciphered as *TR*;[33] *TAE* can become *TA—E*, or *TE—A*.[34]

If one approaches the Saturnian by means of "this science of the sonic forms of words," hidden "theme words" and "key words" suddenly appear. Saussure cites, as an example, a single line of a Roman epitaph that conceals the constituent elements the name *SCĪPĬO* in dislocated form:[35]

Taurasia Cisauna Samnio cepit

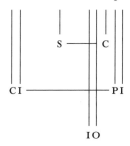

Yet this example runs the risk of simplifying the principle of phonic harmonies, for it suggests that the units of a "theme word" can be restricted to the space of a single line of poetry. This need not be the case. The elements of a certain "key word" can also be distributed over more than two lines. To be sure, Saussure began with the supposition that there would be, at most, one or two phonic "remainders" in each line; but he soon came to renounce that principle. He remained committed to the task of establishing some criterion that would allow for the identification of an "anagrammatized" term in a given work, yet the conditions that he demanded ran the risk of becoming ever less exacting. He diminished the number of the phonic imitations he required and extended the textual space over which they might be strewn. He began with the supposition that the correspondence would be distributed over a single line; failing that, he later added, one may study two, six, or even eight lines.[36]

There is no doubt that the "law" of sounds, then, grows increasingly lax. Some have wondered pointedly whether the entire theory of anaphones does not become "deeply questionable" as a result.[37] Saussure himself appears to have noted this danger. As if to ward it off, he developed a further rule that was to allow him to assert the existence of a technique of "phonic paraphrase" with greater certainty. He argued that at certain points in ancient literary works, one can detect a passage in which the trace of the entire anagrammatized word appears: "a closed and limitable sequence" in the lines of the poem that "one may designate as the place specially devoted to this name."[38] Saussure called this site the *locus princeps*. A "key word" can appear in several ways within its borders.[39] Its first and last letters may coincide with the first and last letters of this *locus*; in such cases, it may be called a "mannequin," which "encloses, within its own limits...the complete syllabogram."[40] At other points, Saussure granted that "theme words" can be present in works by more and less visible means. Sometimes *Stichwörter* may be explicitly stated, being the names of the fundamental figures of the literary works that contain their dismembered parts. In the *Rig Veda*, a collection of poetry "literally covered with anagrams," as Saussure wrote to

Meillet, entire hymns are made from the names of gods.[41] Evoking the first text in the collection, a poem in praise of the god Agni, Saussure comments that "this hymn positively *declines* the name of Agni, and it would be very difficult to think that the succession of lines—some of which begin with '*Agnim* îdê,' others with '*Agninâ* rayim açnavat,' others with '*Agnayê*,' '*Agní*,' etc., mean nothing for the divine name."[42] In other cases, however, Saussure suggested that the phonic shape of texts might be crucially determined by words that remain unsaid in them. In the opening of Lucretius's *De rerum natura*, Saussure thus found the many sonic elements of a Greek name nowhere mentioned by the Roman poet: "Aphroditê," whom Lucretius, for this part, names only "Venus."[43]

Over the course of the four years in which he sought to recover the secret art of the Indo-European poets, Saussure gave several names to the ancient practice of "phonic paraphrase" that he believed he had uncovered. "Anagram" did not fully suit him, for several reasons. In addition to evoking the procedure of reordering elements within the limits of individual words, that term refers, in its root, to the elements of writing: *grammata*, "letters." Saussure's archaic literary corpus was in large part transmitted orally, and he did not wish to suggest that the system of phonic paraphrase he had reconstructed rested essentially on a graphic practice. He sought, therefore, to dispel the misconception that might follow from his usage. "Employing the word *anagram*," he specified, "I certainly do not mean to appeal to the intervention of writing.... *Anaphony* would be better, in my mind, but this last word, if one creates it, seems suited to performing another duty, namely, that of designating an incomplete anagram."[44] Elsewhere, Saussure referred to "hypograms," evoking the Greek word for the inscriptions at the bottom of steles, or the pigment used for the makeup that lies under (*hypo*) the eyelid.[45] He also evoked the "paragram," a classical term for the rearrangement of letters in coded messages, and other neologisms and technical expressions: "paramorph," "homogram," "logogram," "antigram," as well as "homogram."[46] For cases in which "key words" remained unspoken in the works that systematically recombine their phonic elements, he wrote of "cryptographic" anagrams, for which, at times, he also used the simpler term, "cryptogram."[47] Yet if one recalls that the phenomena he conceived need not rest on techniques of writing, one may consider them all to be, more simply, varieties of "anaphones."

Saussure's theory of the secret science of sonic forms remained equivocal in several crucial respects. Beginning with his first investigations into "phonic imitation," he appears to have held that the regularities he detected were essentially lexical in structure and that the units of sound he tracked, although scattered across many lines, composed important words. For Saussure, this appears to have been a point of fundamental importance, which distinguished the poetic regularities he posited from traditional Indo-European features of versification, such as alliteration, assonance, and rhyme. Those were, to him, strictly metrical phenomena, transmitted from poet to poet and generation to generation, like all the properties of individual languages and language groups, in the absence of conscious decision and awareness. "Anagrammatic" or "anaphonic" regularities were, for him, of a different nature. They bore witness to a self-conscious knowing, a "science" possessed by poets that they could exploit as they saw fit, concealing precious terms. Yet precisely on this matter, Saussure seems to have left one question open. What are the precious words that poets wished to conceal: names or nouns? Does the difference matter? Names could be read as signs of individuals, nouns, by contrast, as allusions to concepts or the things that they subsume. But the possibilities are many. In the notebooks, scattered names outnumber dispersed nouns. Writing to Bally in 1906, Saussure goes so far as to assert that the "main word" (*mot principal*) is "always a name" (*un nom propre*).[48] Yet Saussure also uncovered nouns. Of the eighty-eight "cryptograms" the linguist identified in the *De rerum natura*, for example, only forty-three are names.[49] Sometimes he argued that both types of words function in the same work: in his Lucretius notebooks, for example, Saussure tracked the movements of both the name "Aphroditê" and the noun *postscēnia*, "backstage."[50]

The sign that the ancient poets systematically sought to dis-
simulate—be it name or noun, person or thing—remains, therefore,
obstinately opaque. Yet there is more. The reason for which the *vates*
developed and employed their "science" is also unclear. Saussure
suggests two possibilities: anaphones may have served a "religious"
or a "poetic" aim. This possibly exclusive alternative already appears
in the first of the linguist's notebooks: "From the moment in which
the poet was obligated, by religious or poetic law, to imitate a name
[or noun: *nom*], it is clear that having distinguished the syllables,
he was, without having willed it, forced to distinguish its forms."[51]
Elsewhere, writing of the Saturnian, Saussure explicitly confronts
the question of the purpose that Indo-European "phonic paraphrase"
was to serve. Underlining his uncertainties, he notes: "The reason
may have been the religious idea that an invocation, a prayer, a
hymn, is only effective on condition of mixing the syllables of a
divine name into the text.... The reason may have been nonreligious
and purely poetic, of the same kind that determines rhymes, assonances, etc."[52] He could also present this hesitation in positive form:
"The function of the anagram (as such) can be understood, without contradiction, in many ways, just like its relation to the more
general forms of phoneme play; thus, the question, in all respects,
admits of many solutions."[53]

Most important to Saussure, it seems, was the principle that
"phonic imitation," in any case, be an intentional procedure in the
making of the poem. Only an anagram consciously willed, for him,
counted as a "real anagram."[54] Yet the intention is susceptible to
several readings, which may be not only distinguished but opposed.
One can certainly imagine a case, such as that of the Vedic hymn, in
which the religious function includes the poetic; but one may also
conceive a case, such as that of Epicurean treatise *De rerum natura*,
in which the poetic function excludes any positive religious meaning. The reason for the secret art, in any case, remains structurally
indeterminate: a datum as impenetrable as the grammatical object
of the hermetic technique. Just as it is necessary that the "*unapparent
law*" of phonetic distribution conceal a word whose formal identity

need not be revealed, so the effects of phonic paraphrase result from
an intention whose identity cannot be unveiled.

Yet the most manifest mystery of the anagram notebooks involves
the place they occupy in Saussure's new conception of the science of
language. That Saussure's study of the Saturnian and other ancient
Indo-European poetic forms is linguistic in character may seem an
obvious fact today. Saussure, after all, shows little interest in the
interpretation of the works he reads; at each stage, he focuses instead
on the phonological composition of the poems, as well as on the
nouns and names that they suggest. Saussure was, moreover, active
in those years as a professor of linguistics. The period in which he
worked on the "obscure, almost secret thing" of the archaic poets
was also, in part, that in which he gave the lectures in Geneva from
which his students would later draw the *Course in General Linguistics*.
Saussure worked on cryptograms from 1906 to 1909, and he gave his
famous course on the science of language in 1906–1907, 1908–1909,
and 1910–1911. Yet the relation between Saussure's study of phonic
harmony and his general linguistics is anything but simple. On several counts, it even seems that the theory of anaphones is at odds
with the fundamental principles of the *Course*.

It is well known that in his systematic account of the science
of language, Saussure teaches that the object of linguistics is "language" (*langue*), grasped as a system of signs susceptible to synchronic and diachronic study. The investigation into anagrams
seems irreducible to both these forms of research. It is clearly not
synchronic, for it does not examine a single state of a language in
the "static perspective" in which it presents itself to its speakers.
Saussure showed little concern, for example, for the system of Latin
anagrams in the archaic period of the Saturnian, in distinction from
those that followed it. But the analysis of anaphones is obviously also
not diachronic in character.[55] Saussure seems to have no interest
in any "evolutional fact" (*fait évolutif*) in phonic mirroring, for the
notebooks contain no study of the process, whether "prospective" or
"retrospective," by which the "*unapparent* law" developed.[56] Just as
Saussure passes from one language (*langue*) to another, as if "phonic

harmony" remained essentially untouched by grammatical variation, so he moves, without methodological scruples, between the
most distant of epochs. There is evidence that Saussure believed the
technique that he had recovered was practiced in the Middle Ages,
the Renaissance, and even the recent past. "From the most ancient
Saturnian monuments up to the Latin poetry written in 1815 or
1820," we read in one note, "there has never been any other way of
writing Latin verse than by paraphrasing every proper name by the
regular forms of the hypogram."[57]

Even if one sets aside the question of the distinction between the
synchronic and the diachronic, however, the contrast between the
principles of the *Course* and the method of the notebooks is striking
and far-reaching. The lectures on general linguistics define the unit
of language as the sign. This fact entails, for Saussure, at least three
basic theoretical consequences. The two faces of the sign—signifier
and signified—are tied by a principle of association; their link is
"arbitrary" in nature and, as a two-faced whole, they form a being
defined in purely differential terms with respect to all others.[58]
Jean-Claude Milner has shown that the notion of the Indo-European
"anagram," as Saussure treats it, excludes each of these three principles.[59] Saussure considers the anagrammatized name or noun, first,
not as an element of a certain language, but as the name of a referent
or a part of the world: not, in short, as a "signified," but as a "sense,"
a linguistic expression that, for the purposes of analysis, has become
synonymous with a real thing. The anagrammatized term, second,
cannot be considered to be arbitrary; on the contrary, "its function consists in imposing a necessity on the phonemes in the poem,
withdrawing them from the contingency that affects lexical units."[60]
Finally, the "anagrammatic" word is fundamentally nondifferential,
for its identity can be established independently of its opposition to
any other words. The sign exists only in the system of differences
that links it to and distinguishes it from all other signs in a given
language; it has, that is, no positive self-identity. The *Stichwort*, by
contrast, requires no opposition to be recognizable as such. It is an
axiom of Saussure's method that wherever it appears in the literary

work, no matter the degree of phonic decomposition, the crucial term—whatever it may be—will continue to appear as itself.

Yet the notebooks belie another linguistic principle that is fundamental to the teachings of the *Course*. It is the principle of the "linearity" of speech.[61] In his general linguistics, Saussure accords great importance to this point: "The signifier, being by nature auditory, unfolds in time alone, and it has the characters that it borrows from time: a) it represents an extension, and b) this extension is measureable in one dimension alone: it is a line."[62] "In discourse," we read later in the *Course*, "words, by virtue of their sequence, maintain relations founded on the linear character of language, which excludes the possibility of pronouncing two elements at once.... They always come after each other in the speech sequence."[63] Saussure's anaphones openly flout both consequences of this principle. Several of their parts, in the unfolding of a poem, may well appear "at once." It suffices to consider a "polyphone" that can be counted simultaneously in several forms: once, for example, as *TAE*, once as *TA* and *E*, and once as *TE* and *A* or *TA* + *TE*. The idea of "phonic mirroring," moreover, suggests that "sonic forms" can appear not only at once and in succession, but also in transposition: backward and forward, in retrogression no less than in progression.

That Saussure was aware of the troubling implications of these facts can be gleaned from several passages in his notebooks, where he explicitly raises the question of forms intelligible "outside" the order of time. "Can one present TAE as TA + TE," he asks in one manuscript, "that is, invite the reader not to juxtaposition in consecutivity, but to a means of acoustical impressions outside time? Outside the order that elements have in time? Outside the linear order that is observed if I present TAE as TA-AE or TA-E, but not if I present it by TA + TE, amalgamated outside time, as I could do if they were two colors?"[64]

One may certainly wonder how Saussure would have reconciled the methods and findings of his notebooks with the science taught in his *Course*. It is worth recalling that he chose to publish neither. Yet it must also be said that in the four-year period in which he worked on anaphones, he appears to have passed from a state of conviction to one of skepticism, then grave doubt. In 1906, writing of the Saturnian, he had evoked the discovery of a "solution ... so simple that it makes me laugh when I think of the detours I had to go through to get there." He already had announced the possibility that the "phonic mirroring" he had observed might be common to other Indo-European poetic traditions, such as that of Sanskrit poetry. By 1907, he believed the Vedas to be "literally covered with anagrams" and Homer's epics to be "a vast and continuous anagram."[65] In January 1908, he wrote to Meillet: "I have attained a state of certainty that far exceeds, and that has no analogy with, the one I reached during these last months."[66] That, however, was the year that Saussure's anagrams began to "proliferate."[67] He now concluded that the "furor of phonic play" was more long-lived than he imagined.[68] Not only did the linguist now claim to find its signs in the classical Roman poets, such as Ovid; he also announced that he had found examples of the secret procedure in the neo-Latin writers of the Renaissance, such as Angelo Poliziano, and even in more recent Latin poets, such as the late seventeenth-century English Latin author Thomas Johnson.[69]

In an experimental science, confirmation by numbers is double-edged. Saussure responded with elation at the discovery of increasing examples of the "obscure, almost secret thing" he believed he had discovered. Yet it also occurred to him that should he be able to find no examples of speech from which the effects of phonic play were absent, their presence would mean little. The notebooks suggest that he sought a rigorous demonstration of his thesis. Strictly speaking, the proof of his theory of anagrams, as Milner has written, "would have to have the following form: establishing 1) that there are texts without anagrams; 2) that all the anagrams observed are the effects of a specific technique."[70] Saussure did not prove the first of these two propositions. One may, of course, interpret the widening of his corpus, from 1906 to 1909, from Saturnian poetry to Vedic hymns, Homeric epics, and modern Latin verse, as an indication that he was searching for some index of falsifiability: evidence of literature that, precisely in lacking "phonic mirroring," might confirm its certain presence elsewhere. Yet Saussure appears to have found no texts that did not obey the "*unapparent* law" he discerned in the Saturnian. Even classical prose proved no exception. In works by Pliny, Caesar, and Cicero, Saussure detected a "constant preoccupation" with the shapes of sounds that, when examined closely, pointed "hypogrammatically" to certain key words.[71]

Perhaps for this reason, Saussure finally chose to test the principle according to which anagrams, when present, are the signs of poetic intention. In 1909, he wrote to a living Latin poet, Giovanni Pascoli, to ask whether "certain technical details" in his verse resulted from a special system. Saussure promised that, if Pascoli obliged, he would send him a full exposition of the regularities he had observed in Latin poetry.[72] The Saussure archives do not contain the poet's response, but it appears that he did answer Saussure. The linguist's archives contain a copy of a second letter to Pascoli, in which Saussure permits himself to go into greater detail about the phonic procedure. This letter, however, seems to have met with no response. Saussure appears to have abandoned his studies of "phonic mirroring" soon thereafter. It is possible that, as Starobinski maintains, Pascoli's silence was the cause of the linguist's decision to "interrupt his inquiry into anagrams."[73] Yet by 1909, Saussure also had his own reasons to doubt the likelihood of the system he had reconstructed. He had repeatedly confronted a troubling question that he had no means to resolve: that of chance, or contingency. The "materiality" of phonic facts, as he admitted in one notebook, "might be due to chance." In another passage, an imaginary opponent to his theory similarly declares: "Chance can do anything in three lines."[74] Repeatedly, Saussure suggests that only a calculus of the probable distribution of sounds in a language would be capable of determining whether "anaphonic" effects are intentional or contingent.[75] In 1909, however, the tools needed compute such statistical facts of language were lacking.

When, over half a century later, Starobinski first began to publish portions of Saussure's notebooks, they provoked an immediate critical response. The interest in the founder of structural linguistics was at its apogee. Readers found in the notebooks the signs of a "second Saussure," a "dark double" of the thinker who had first defined language as a system of signs.[76] In *Words upon Words*, Starobinski presented a critical account of Saussure's research that determined much of its subsequent reception. Having retraced and commented upon the genesis of the theory of anaphones, Starobinski judged Saussure's findings to be questionable, and he concluded that in any case, the linguist's critical methods were unsound. He had mistaken unintentional literary effects for the signs of a willed system. To this degree, he argued, "Saussure's error" taught one "exemplary lesson":

> how difficult it is for the critic to avoid taking his own find for a rule followed by the poet. Having made a discovery, the critic has trouble accepting that the poet did not consciously or unconsciously *want* what analysis only *supposes*. The critic has trouble remaining alone with his discovery; he wants to share it with the poet. But the poet, having said what he has to say, remains silent.[77]

Those who followed Starobinski often echoed that judgment. The scholarly value of Saussure's findings was generally considered null. Critics had few hesitations about evoking a mental malady that would have besieged the linguist: "madness," "dementia," or even "schizophrenia," they variously argued, could be detected in the pages of the anagram notebooks.[78] Such wishfully medical judgments of the linguist were once commonplace.[79] The critics failed to note that in issuing such pronouncements, they merely echoed the linguist's own doubts, while adding to them a diagnosis of mental illness. One might also reason otherwise. The fact that Saussure chose to end his inquiries into anaphones could also be taken as a sign of his scientific rigor. John E. Joseph, the linguist's biographer, has advanced this argument. "Oddly enough," he writes, "the anagram research is one of the few projects Saussure pursued that did *not* fail," in the sense that having tested his hypothesis and observed that it did not lead to certain conclusions, he resolved to set it aside.[80]

Other views of Saussure's investigations, however, have also been expressed. Upon their first publication, Roman Jakobson hailed the

anagram notebooks as the beginning of a second Saussurian revolu-
tion, after that of the *Course*, opening "unseen perspectives for the
linguistic study of poetry." "If Saussure's manuscripts of this massive
work had not been spurned for many decades as supposedly 'futile
digressions,'" Jakobson later wrote, "the international struggle for
a science of poetics would have received beneficial incentives."[81]
That judgment was general in force; it bore on the conception of
poetry as involving a "furor of phonic play" and patterning in sound
structure. Yet it is worth noting that in the years that have passed
since the first appearance of Saussure's research into "anaphones,"
details of his analyses have found more support among scholars than
one might have first expected. In her important work on the poetic
structure of the *Rig Veda*, Tatyana Elizarenkova, for example, treats
Saussure's study of Sanskrit anagrams as a major contribution, which
casts significant light on the ancient literary corpus. In Vedic hymns,
she argues, the name of a lauded deity can be explicitly expressed,
yet it also "appears as a distinct pattern, embroidered on the can-
vas, as it were, of the metrical scheme. It can also be indicated by
sound-hints intertwined in the hymn's texture. That this is a fully
conscious effort, and not an accident, is suggested by those cases in
which instances of surface sound-play share a common etymological
basis."[82] In different settings and for different reasons, several comparative linguists have similarly argued that Saussure's notebooks,
however problematic in parts, constitute a basic element in the study
of Indo-European poetic techniques.[83]

Most remarkable is perhaps that some twenty years after publish-
ing his influential study of Saussure's "anagrams," Starobinski himself suggested, albeit only implicitly, that his early appraisal may have
been inadequate. Without formally retracting the judgment he made
two decades earlier, Starobinski admitted in 1995 that his treatment had perhaps been peremptory. In an article bearing the telling subtitle "Complement to a Reading of Ferdinand de Saussure's
Anagram *Notebooks*," he stated that it would be an error to exclude
from poetry the possibility of phonic play based on names. "Today,"
he granted, one may "admit that there was once a real procedure,

though it was neither general nor secret." That "procedure" was linked, he explained, to the genre of the encomium and, more precisely, to the poetic praise of a name. "In order to establish properly the glory of a name," he wrote, the elements of a certain special word can be "mobilized in an exalted fashion...as if the reordering of the letters and the phonemes in a name better twisted the branches of the crown belonging to the subject of praise." Within the limits of this "genre," he stated, "the use of anagrams is regularly present."[84] Without reasoning in terms of genre, Saussure, of course, had said no less.

In this article, Starobinski cited only early modern texts: Latin Renaissance inscriptions and Romance poetry, such as that of Petrarch and his followers, which extract and scatter the parts of important names across the lines of many lyric forms, such as the song, sonnet, sestina, and ballad. Starobinski avoided confronting the question from which Saussure had begun. Could the archaic Roman poets not also have practiced such a "procedure"? In the modern period, authors of treatises of poetics explicitly refer to figures such as the anagram, William Camden's "*Anagrammatisme*, or *Metagrammatisme*" being but one example. Saussure had sought indications of a similar kind among the authors who most interested him, but the ancient and even archaic sources were naturally more exiguous. He was the first to recognize, in any case, that he was no scholar of the history of poetic theory. "Without having made a special study of the writings of Latin prosodists," he wrote in one notebook, "it would be difficult for me personally [to say] if there is some allusion in their writings to the necessity of hypograms. Since such an allusion has never been pointed out, one must suppose that the ancient theorists of Latin versification constantly abstained from mentioning an elementary and primary condition of this versification."[85]

Here, however, Saussure encountered a literary fact as impenetrable as the triumphal lines of verse inscribed on the tablets of the Roman Forum. "Why they observed this silence," he commented briefly, referring to the ancient specialists of poetry, "is one problem to which I have no solution."[86] That the system of phonic doublings and scattered polyphones had been the content of "an occult tradition" was one axiom that Saussure did not question during the entire period of his research into the techniques of anaphones.[87] Yet how had the teaching passed from master to student for millennia? Transmission was perhaps the final mystery that the linguist must confront. "How Naevius, Ennius, Pacuvius, Attius still preserved a tradition that might have seemed inviolable in their imitative epoch," he wrote, "is something I can understand. But how could Virgil, who, after all, possessed the breath of original poetry, how could Lucretius, with his intense preoccupation for the idea, how could Horace, with his good common sense about everything, how could they all adopt this incredible relic of another age?" To these questions, Saussure offered no answer. "There is something there, I admit it, that escapes me altogether. I see no other thing to do than to present the riddle such as it presents itself."[88] Yet the riddle barely "presented itself" at all, for Saussure alone perceived it. The art of anaphones was so secret that it almost effaced itself. What they were to guard, the reason they were to guard it, and the form by which the method had persisted—all had vanished. Saussure retained only the uncertain signs of a nameless linguistic technique, and the one hypothesis to which they led him during his four years of study: that something, for some reason, had knowingly been scattered in speech, almost inaudibly, almost invisibly, and that its hidden places were in poetry.

CHAPTER TEN

Patterns

From 1909 till 1961, the existence of Saussure's notebooks on the sound system of Indo-European poetry remained almost entirely secret. Saussure did not mention them in his publications, nor does he appear to have discussed them in the courses he gave at the University of Geneva. He undertook his research in private and, with the notable exception of letters to certain friends and colleagues, he appears to have kept his findings to himself. When, after his death, his former students arranged to turn his teaching into a book, to be called the *Course in General Linguistics*, they limited their editorial activities to the materials pertaining to the lectures held between 1906 and 1910. The notebooks went unnoticed. Half a century later, in 1960, Robert Godel published a brief article, "Inventory of the Ferdinand de Saussure Manuscripts Held by the Public Library and University of Geneva" in which, after enumerating the unpublished papers on general and historical linguistics, he designated a last set of manuscripts, least, one might infer, in importance: "Ms. fr. 3963-3969, ANAGRAMS (or HYPOGRAMS)," consisting, as he wrote, of "ninety-nine notebooks" and a "dossier of tables written on large sheets."[1] Four years later, Jean Starobinski published an article on these documents.[2] He followed it in 1967 with a second essay bearing what was to become, in 1971, the title of his book on "the anagrams of Ferdinand de Saussure": *Words upon Words*. The essay appeared in a collective volume, *To Honor Roman Jakobson*.[3] Starobinski's choice of contribution was carefully weighed. When revealed, Saussure's inquiries into the law of poetic sounds met with almost unanimous skepticism from linguists and literary scholars. Among major figures in the fields of language and literature, only Jakobson dissented. His engagement with Saussure's research on poetry was to be unique, on account of both the aspects of the theory of "anaphones" that he retained and those that, by contrast, he set aside.

Jakobson was hardly known as a commentator on Saussure. Yet in 1971, he edited and published a document from the Genevan's archive: a letter addressed to Antoine Meillet from November 12, 1906, to which Jakobson gave the title "Ferdinand de Saussure's First Letter on Anagrams."[4] In the lengthy note that accompanied the text, Jakobson lamented the delay with which Saussure's research had been brought to light. "It is truly astonishing," Jakobson wrote, "that Saussure's ninety-nine manuscript notebooks on 'sounding poetics' [poétique phonétisante], and in particular on 'the principle of the anagram,' could have been hidden from readers for almost a half century."[5] He recalled that as early as 1966, when Starobinski published his first article on the "anagrams," Jakobson chose to express his admiration for Saussure's hitherto neglected research into phonic poetics. "The theory and analysis of the sound figures [jeux phoniques]," Jakobson had written, "particularly anagrams, and their role in the diverse poetic traditions as elaborated by him simultaneously with his renowned courses of general linguistics may certainly be counted among Saussure's most daring and lucid discoveries."[6] Jakobson dismissed the idea that Saussure's decision not to publish his research pointed to any particular dissatisfaction with its results. "Must one recall," he asked, "what Saussure himself says about his 'gift' of interrupting the publication of his linguistic articles when they were 'not only written, but also almost entirely composed'?"[7] Jakobson went so far as to suggest that in a certain sense, it was in the study of poetic textures, and not general linguistics, that Saussure had made his most original discoveries, "discoveries all the more striking," he added, "if one considers the fact that on this path, Saussure had no signposts to follow, whereas in the theses of his Course in General Linguistics, he was inspired by several precursors."[8]

Jakobson singled out only one element in the theory of ana-phones that was in need of correction, being, as he argued, both questionable in itself and a methodologically superfluous supposi-tion. Saussure, however, had held it to be a fundamental point in his investigations. It was the "the hypothesis," as Saussure had written, that the Indo-European procedure of sound mirroring in poetry was the object of "an *occult* tradition" that had remained, for the course of centuries, "a secret carefully concealed."[9] Jakobson was quick to point out that despite continuing to maintain this principle, Sau-ssure had alluded, albeit in passing, to the fact that one could also set the postulate of secrecy aside, considering phonic structure in itself. One could focus on the mere "materiality of the fact" of sonic symmetries, without advancing any theses about their subjective causes.[10] In a notebook on Homer, Saussure had even suggested—in terms Jakobson would cite repeatedly—that in certain conditions, one might concede that anagrammatic sound play can mark poetic language "whether the critic, on the one hand, and the versifier, on the other, wishes it or not."[11] This was the theoretical possibility that Jakobson deemed most worthy of exploration. Phonic mirroring, he argued, need not be considered the object of a conscious will, on the part of either those who compose poetry or those who transmit it. The intuition that poetry rests on a "furor of phonic play" can be freed of any thesis about poetic intention. The secret, in other words, may be eliminated. The many varieties of anaphones can then be considered for what they truly are: patterns of language percep-tible, to different degrees, in poetry.

By the time Jakobson advanced his reading of the theory of ana-grams, he himself had devoted half a century to the study of sound structure in verse. In his youth, he had participated in the first years of the Linguistic Circle of Moscow, formed in the winter of 1914–1915 to further, as its founding statement declared, the study of "problems of linguistics, metrics, and folklore poetics."[12] Implicit in that research program was the principle that forms of discourse as apparently diverse as literature and riddles exhibit certain common characteristics, which are susceptible to a single linguistic analysis.

In 1917, Jakobson became a founding member of the Society of the Study of Poetic Language (known by the acronym OPOJAZ), which also counted among its members Victor Shklovsky, Boris Eikhenbaum, and Yuri Tynyanov, as well Victor Mayakovsky, Osip Mandelshtam, and Boris Pasternak.[13] Jakobson would later recall how his involvement in these two associations led to his work on popular and literary verse forms. It also served to spur him on to what would become a lifelong search for a linguistic criterion for the distinction, in any given tongue, between poetic and nonpoetic sequences. By 1933, if not sooner, Jakobson had begun to envisage this search in terms that derived directly from the research program of the Moscow Circle. The crucial question, for him, was that of "poeticalness" or "poeticity," defined as the function by which literary language is distinct from other types of speech. Unlike poetry, "poeticity," Jakobson argued, remains constant across cultures, traditions, and languages. It may be recognized by certain signs. "Poeticity," he argued in a lecture given in Czech to an artistic society in Prague, "is present when the word is felt as a word, and not as mere representation of the object being named, or an outburst of emotion, when words and their composition, their meaning, their external and inner form acquire a weight and value of their own, instead of referring indifferently to reality."[14]

That statement offers a key to Jakobson's entire literary scholarship. From his 1919 essay, "The Newest Russian Poetry," which appeared as a preface to Velimir Klebnikov's collected works, to his 1921–1922 book on the comparative structure of Czech and Russian metrics, to his later studies of German, French, and English "verse and its masters," Jakobson sought to define the forms and rules by which, in the most diverse of languages, the "word" comes "to be felt as a word and not as a mere representation of the object." His theory of the poetic function was perhaps never more fully and precisely presented than in the famous lecture "Linguistics and Poetics," which he gave at the "Conference on Style" held at Indiana University in the spring of 1958.[15] Here he stated that his aim would be, as it had been decades earlier, to characterize literary discourse in relation to other forms of language. He aimed, in short, to situate the "poetic function" with respect to "the other functions of language."

To this end, Jakobson began by identifying "the constitutive factors in any speech event." He reduced them to six elements that may be related in a simple form. An "addresser" (1) sends a "message" (2) about a "context" (or referent) (3) to an "addressee" (4), a message that will be expressed in a certain "code" (5) and assured by a "contact" (6) (which Jakobson glosses as a "physical or psychological connection").[16] "Each of these six factors," he explained, "determines a different function of language." All six may be present, albeit in differing degrees, in a single utterance. The first five are most easily defined. The "referential" function, which focuses on extralinguistic reality, depends primarily on "context." The "emotive function," which involves the expression of affect, reflects above all the state of the "addresser." The "conative" function draws attention to the "addressee." The "phatic function" involves the "contact" by which communication occurs, being displayed, for example, "by a profuse exchange of ritualized formulas, by entire dialogues with the mere purport of prolonging communication."[17] The "metalingual function," finally, focuses speech "on the code," in science or everyday discourse, for the sake of clarifying terms that would otherwise remain ambiguous or unknown.

The "poetic function," as Jakobson defines it, approaches the "metalingual," in that it draws the attention of speakers toward language itself. The aims of metalanguage and poetry, however, are fundamentally distinct. Taking the term "message" to signify not a particular semantic or propositional content but the utterance as such, Jakobson asserts that "focus on the message for its own sake...is the POETIC function of language."[18] In content, if not in form, this was a claim shared by several of Jakobson's early colleagues, Viktor Shklovsky not least. Jakobson's original thesis is diffferent, consisting in a proposition all the more remarkable for its formal simplicity: that there exists "an empirical linguistic criterion of the poetic function."[19]

To define this "empirical linguistic criterion," Jakobson distinguishes "two basic modes of arrangement used in verbal behavior, *selection* and *combination*." Those "two basic modes" allude to an opposition set forth in Saussure's *Course in General Linguistics*: that, namely, between "associative" and "syntagmatic" relations.[20] According to the *Course*, any linguistic expression may enter into these two formally distinct types of arrangement. For example, the word "relation" may be related to others by association: terms related to it by its root, such as "relative," "relatively," or "relationship"; terms related to it by its form, such as "animation," "station" or "equation"; terms related to it by its meaning, such as "connection," "tie," "link," or "bond." The possibilities of association are many, if not infinite. "Syntagmatic" relations are of a different kind. They consist in the relations that words bear to those that precede and follow them in fully articulated speech. Morphological and syntactic rules bear on such relations to the degree that they define the sequence in which words may be placed in correct sentences. Saussure observed that syntagmatic and associative relations may be generally distinguished by their mode of appearance in language. The first sequence is actualized in discourse; the second is only ever potential. "The syntagmatic relation," we read, "is *in praesentia*; it rests on two terms that are equally present in an effective series. The associative relation, on the contrary, unifies two terms *in absentia*, in a virtual mnemonic series."[21]

In defining the empirical linguistic criterion of the poetic function, Jakobson treats Saussure's "associative" relation as an arrangement of "selection," which conditions and anticipates every particular choice of terms. If the "topic" of a certain message is to be a child, Jakobson explains, "the speaker selects one among the extant, more or less similar, nouns like child, kid, youngster, tot, all of them equivalent in a certain respect, and then, to comment on this topic, he may select one of the semantically cognate verbs—sleeps, dozes, nods, naps."[22] Selection is thus "produced on the basis of equivalence, similarity and dissimilarity, synonymy and antonymy," each of the terms that may be chosen being a member of a "virtual

mnemonic series." "Combination," instead, involves Saussure's syntagmatic type of arrangement. It is "based," in Jakobson's terms, on
not "equivalence" but "contiguity." Certain features involving the
lexicon, for example, may decide which terms in a given language
may be substituted for each other, while rules of syntax, among others, will determine which linguistic elements can follow or precede
each other in the articulation of grammatically correct phrases
or sentence.

Only if one grasps this distinction between "selection" and "combination" can one understand the "empirical linguistic criterion of
the poetic function" that Jakobson proposes as a major contribution
to the linguistic study of poetry. He explains the criterion in the
following terms:

> *The poetic function projects the principle of equivalence from the axis of
> selection into the axis of combination.* Equivalence is promoted to the
> constitutive device of the sequence. In poetry one syllable is equalized
> with any other syllable of the same sequence; word stress is assumed to
> equal word stress, as unstress equals unstress; prosodic long is matched
> with long, and short with short; word boundary equals word bound-
> ary, no boundary equals no boundary; syntactic pause equals syntactic
> pause, no pause equals no pause. Syllables are converted into units of
> measure, and so are morae or stresses.[23]

When the principle of equivalence passes from the "axis" of
selection to that of combination, from the associative order to the
syntagmatic, and when such equivalence in the "effective series" of
consecutive utterances dictates an entire sequence of speech, the
poetic function may be said to be operative. Hence the proximity
and distance, for Jakobson, of metalanguage and poetry. The "metalingual function" focuses language on "the code" in such a way as to
construct a single equation that clarifies the meaning of a particular
term: "$A=A$," Jakobson explains, giving, as a single example, "*Mare* is
the female of the horse."[24] By contrast, the "poetic function" concentrates attention on the "message for its own sake," such that syntagmatic equivalences come to form hierarchically stratified sequences

of measured units. In a strophic poem, for example, syllables, at a first level, will be treated as equal in their durations or stresses. In their concatenations, they will compose substitutable metric feet. Such feet, grouped together in fixed patterns, will constitute lines of verse, which may be exchanged according to certain prosodic rules. Lines, finally, in various commensurate relations, will form the strophes or stanzas that articulate the poem.

That equivalence is the fundamental formal principle of poetry was an idea Jakobson could find in several of the writers who mattered most to him. In "The Rationale of Verse," Edgar Allan Poe made this one of his central points, declaring: "*Verse* originates in the human enjoyment of equality, fitness. To this enjoyment, also, all the moods of verse—rhythm, metre, stanza, rhyme, alliteration, the *refrain*, and other analogous effects—are to be referred." In this sense, the idea of "equality," Poe explained, "embraces those of similarity, proportion, identity, repetition, and adaptation or fitness."[25] Perhaps most important, for Jakobson, was the recurrence of measured linguistic units in the simplest form of distinction, namely, opposition. The patterns of such recurrence constitute, he wrote, the "much more general, we may even say the fundamental, problem of poetry, namely, *parallelism*."[26] He repeatedly evoked Gerard Manley Hopkins's programmatic pronouncement, recorded in an entry of his *Journals and Papers* dating from 1865: "The artificial part of poetry, perhaps we shall be right to say all artifice, reduces itself to the principle of parallelism. The structure of poetry is that of continuous parallelism, ranging from the technical so-called Parallelism of Hebrew poetry and the antiphons of Church music up to the intricacy of Greek or Italian or English verse."[27]

Jakobson grasped immediately that Saussure's account of the Saturnian offered an exemplary illustration of such a "continuous parallelism." According to the Genevan linguist, in the archaic Roman form, Latin phonemes always appear in pairs, a vowel, for example, "having the right to appear in the Saturnian only if it has a *countervowel* in some place whatsoever in the line."[28] In one of his last books, *The Sound Shape of Language*, which he wrote with Linda

Waugh, Jakobson favorably evoked this aspect of the Saussurian theory of anaphones. The "constituents" of Latin verse are "exactly coupled, reiterated in even numbers." Hence the "slogan" that Saussure had transcribed in his notebooks in capital Latin letters and that Jakobson recalled: "NUMERO DEUS PARI GAUDET," "God delights in even numbers."[29] With his theory of the "projection of the principle of equivalence from the axis of selection to the axis of combination," Jakobson provided a linguistic foundation for such phenomena. It is not so much God, he might argue, as the poetic function that dictates that in utterances considered to be poetic, the many parts of speech tend toward equivalence, composing patterns that, however complex, may always be reduced, like the numbers of classical arithmetic, to commensurate collections of equal units.[30]

In his reconstruction of the "occult tradition" of phonic mirroring, Saussure had observed that anaphonic recurrences seem to be at odds with the consecutive character of linguistic relations. If the phonological elements that make up a single noun or name can appear out of their customary lexical order, their last letters, for example, preceding their first, while nonetheless evoking the word that they all compose, one may deduce that signifiers can function outside "juxtaposition in a sequence" and perhaps even, as Saussure had wondered, with some perplexity, "outside time."[31] To the theorist of the *Course*, who stipulated that the elements of language, being linear, "always follow each other in the speech sequence," such a possibility was troubling. In itself, it sufficed to cast doubt on the theory of anagrams. Jakobson, for his part, drew the opposite conclusion. He argued that the notebooks had intuited an aspect of language that the lectures had dogmatically excluded. Against one Saussure and for another, Jakobson concluded that where equivalence is "promoted to the constitutive device of the sequence," symmetry emerges beyond the apparent linearity of time.

As early as 1942, in the lectures that he gave at the École Libre des Hautes Études in New York and that appeared as *Six Lectures on Sound and Meaning*, Jakobson had judged the theory of the linearity of the signifier a "serious obstacle" to progress in phonology.[32]

Saussure's *Course* famously declared that "the linear character of language [*langue*] excludes the possibility of pronouncing two elements at the same time."[33] Jakobson objected, remarking that when referred to signifying sounds, such a claim is either tautological or incorrect. If one defines the "element" in question as the minimal unit of sound articulated in an instant, the statement, by definition, must be true; yet if one takes "element" to refer to a single phoneme, it is misleading at best. The reason involves the nature of the phoneme as Jakobson conceived it. Linguistics before him had commonly defined the phoneme as a minimal unit of signifying sound that exhibits a certain feature, such as being voiced or unvoiced or being occlusive or nonocclusive. Jakobson proposed a new conception. He argued that the phoneme be defined not as a minimal unit, but as the representative of distinctive features more minimal than the phoneme itself.[34] He argued, in other words, that the qualities of being voiced, occlusive, and alveolar, for example, do not define the English phoneme /d/ in the way that certain predicates, in a classical predicative definition, may be referred to a certain subject. Rather, the phoneme /d/ is no more than an abbreviated sign of these three "features" when clustered together. It is, in short, strictly equivalent to them.[35] The phoneme, in this sense, resembles less an individual musical note than a single "chord," being "unit and bundle at once."[36]

Such an argument could be seen as announcing the "nonlinear phonology" that, starting at the end of the 1970s, would show that speech patterns are not chains of individual elements but hierarchically stratified systems that may be studied on several levels.[37] Jakobson had, of course, drawn the elements of his phonology from research in general linguistics that suggested to him that the "linearity" of speech is far from absolute. He cited the phenomenon known to linguists as "regressive dissimilation," by which, as if in a curious chronological distortion, "in a sequence, a prior moment depends on a later one": "for instance, when Spanish and English changed the first /l/ of the world *colonel* into /r/ in anticipation of the final /l/."[38] Yet Jakobson's critique of the doctrine of the consecutive order of speech also drew on his study of poetic language, in which he had observed formal correspondences between lines and metrical positions separated in time. "Parallelism at a distance" may be found in many literary forms; it suffices to think of "compositions of the rondo type, which are based on a regular link between the end and the beginning of a piece."[39] Poe himself explained, in "The Philosophy of Composition," that he had begun "The Raven" with the word that constitutes its terminal refrain, "Nevermore."[40] Jakobson added that the words of the poem's title and refrain could be related as two lexical figures in retrogression, on condition of bracketing the order of temporal succession. "The never-ending stay of the grim guest is expressed by a chain of ingenious paranomasias, as we would expect from such a deliberate experimenter in anticipatory, regressive *modus operandi*, such a master in 'writing backwards,' as Edgar Allan Poe. In the introductory line of this concluding stanza, 'raven,' contiguous to the bleak refrain word 'never,' appears once more as an embodied mirror image of this 'never': /n.v.r./ $-$ /r.v.n./."[41]

This reading could be viewed as an ingenious application of the theory of "hypograms" to a literary corpus that Saussure did not take into account. The American poet would have scattered the phonic elements of the noun—or name—"Raven" in the bird's own insistent, exclamatory refrain: "Nevermore!" Yet one might also reason otherwise, for "Raven" could be read as a rewriting of "Never." Jakobson's comments suggest both possibilities. They thus also allude to a third literary and linguistic interpretation. "Raven" and "Never" may be grasped as two arrangements of a single sound sequence: "/n.v.r/" or "/r.v.n./." Such an interpretation may seem improbably abstract. Yet it is worth recalling that Poe, for his part, alleged that the poem had arisen from even simpler phonemic matter. He recalls that once he had decided that his composition would be organized by a refrain consisting of a single word, the question "arose as to the *character* of the word":

> Having made up my mind to a *refrain*, the division of the poem into stanzas was, of course, a corollary: the *refrain* forming the close to

each stanza. That such a close, to have force, must be sonorous and susceptible of protracted emphasis, admitted no doubt: and these considerations inevitably led me to the long *o* as the most sonorous vowel, in connection with *r* as the most producible consonant.[42]

"Raven" and "Never" would then be no more than the lexical progeny of the mournful, phonetically back diphthong, conjoined with the eminently "producible" liquid consonant. Jakobson could integrate this account, which he knew well, into his theory. Poe would have begun his composition with a linguistic relation of association: in this case, that of the vowel /o/ (or /oʊ/). He would then have projected the equivalence it suggested from the "axis of selection" to the "axis of combination," the metric recurrences of the vowel in the refrain word being the result.

The example illustrates the affinities and divergences between Saussure's theory of anagrams and Jakobson's idea of the poetic function. For Saussure, there exists a categorical distinction between forms of linguistic arrangement based on metrical principles, such as quantity, alliteration, and rhyme, and the art of "phonic mirroring" cultivated by the Indo-European poets. Metrical structures, for him, are essentially of a piece with a language. They are passed on unconsciously from generation to generation, like the many phonological, morphological, and syntactic rules of individual grammars. The principles of verse forms, in this sense, demand no special commentary. Anaphonic procedures are of another nature, for they bespeak a particular poetic technique that, to persist over time, must be consciously transmitted. They have as their basic objects not grammatical elements, such as syllables or accents, but rather certain nouns and names of particular importance. From Jakobson's perspective, this distinction is of no theoretical consequence. Poetic patterning can be of any element of speech. What matters, above all, is that in each case there be a projection of the principle of equivalence, such that the poetic sequence have as its basic principle a system of recurrences.

In his essays on poetry, Jakobson, for this reason, entertained many possibilities. At times, he detected measured recurrences of phonic elements that evoked particular nouns and names disseminated across lines of verse. In addition to finding the "Raven" in "Nevermore," he recalled how Velimir Khlebnikov, commenting on his own poem years after composing it, had been "charmed by the anagram" he discovered hidden in a gerund. "The word *uškúj* ('pirate ship,' metonymically 'pirate') sits in the poem 'as if in the Trojan horse': KRYLyšKÚJA 'winging' sKRÝL uŠKÚJA *derevjánnyj kón'* 'the wooden horse concealed the pirate.'"[43] In his "Microscopy of the Last 'Spleen' in *Les Fleurs du mal*," Jakobson argued that the elements of this poem's title—"Spleen"—could be discerned in its lines, as the scattered parts of a concealed linguistic being that, after Saussure, he referred to as a "theme word" (*mot-thème*).[44] In his paper "Shakespeare's Verbal Art," he noted that "in a few of Shakespeare's sonnets (134–36) his name Will is inserted in a punning way and suggests the tentative question whether his signature is not anagrammatized in 129 so that the poet's remark—'every word doth almost tell my name' (Sonnet 76)—might be applied in its literal meaning to the poem under discussion."[45]

Yet Jakobson also argued that the texture of poetic language could be crucially determined by sound structures that summon no special words. Entire sections of the phonological systems of languages could be projected, in their associative relations, from the axis of selection to that of combination. They might involve elements of sound structure: vowels or consonants, for example, rendered functional by their appearance or even by their absence.[46] Similarly, Jakobson aimed in some readings to show that larger grammatical elements could in themselves become the material of poetic patterning. Parallelisms involving the disposition of articles in Yeats,[47] markers of gender in Baudelaire, "differences in tense, aspect and mood" in Sidney,[48] all suggested to him the existence of a "poetry of grammar" whose regularities were to be investigated by the new "grammar of poetry" that he proposed. One of its fundamental principles would be that "any noticeable reiteration of the same grammatical concept becomes an effective poetic device."[49] Strictly speaking, any grammatical unit whatsoever could become a unit of poetic patterning; it sufficed for it to become the element of syntagmatic recurrences. The linguistic study of literature, Jakobson wagered, demonstrated as much:

> Any unbiased, attentive, exhaustive, total description of the selection, distribution and interrelation of diverse morphological classes and syntactic constructions in a given poem surprises the examiner himself by unexpected, striking symmetries and asymmetries, balanced structures, efficient accumulation of equivalent forms and salient contrasts, finally by rigid restrictions in the repertory of morphological and syntactic constituents used in the poem, eliminations which, on the other hand, permit us to follow the masterly interplay of the actualized constituents.[50]

In treating sound play and anagrammatic play as of the same nature, and in refusing to grant Saussure's distinction between the level of merely metrical composition and that of suprametrical poetic "technique," Jakobson's theory of the poetic function effectively dissolved one distinction that had been fundamental to the system of the ninety-nine notebooks: the distinction, that is, between unconscious and conscious literary procedures. Poetic patterning, for Jakobson, remained a valid principle "whether the critic, on the one hand, and the versifier, on the other, wishes it or not."

Defending his readings of Baudelaire against critics who claimed that the French poet could not have conceived as subtle a set of grammatical parallelisms as he had uncovered, Jakobson recalled, for instance, Baudelaire's own claim in his "Poem of Hashish": "Grammar, barren grammar, itself become something akin to an evocative sorcery. Words come back to life, dressed in flesh and blood: the noun, in its substantial majesty; the adjective, with the transparent garment that clothes it and colors it like a glaze; and the verb, angel of movement, which causes the sentence to tremble."[51] Jakobson could also cite Poe, who likened the beauty of metric form to that of the crystal: "the equality of the sides pleases us; that of the angles doubles the pleasure. On bringing to view a second face in all respects similar to the first, this pleasure seems to be squared; on bringing to view a third it appears to be cubed, and so on."[52]

Yet Jakobson also held that poetic sequences might be operative even where speaking beings themselves consciously perceive no recurrences. He presented his argument most fully in an essay pointedly titled "Subliminal Verbal Patterning in Poetry," marshalling evidence in support of the claim that a host of popular and literary poetic forms can circulate unhindered by the nearly total lack of awareness of the equivalences that define their art:

> Phonology and grammar of oral poetry offer a system of complex and elaborate correspondences which come into being, take effect, and are handed down through generations without anyone's cognizance of the rules governing this intricate network. The immediate and spontaneous grasp of effects without rational elicitation of the processes by which they are produced is not confined to the oral tradition and its transmitters. Intuition may act as the main, or not seldom, even sole designer of the complicated phonological and grammatical structures in the writings of individual poets. Such structures, particularly powerful on the subliminal level, can function without any assistance of logical judgment and patent knowledge both in the poet's creative work and in its perception by the sensitive reader.[53]

Jakobson thus questioned one of the basic principles in the traditional study of meter, which held that the obligatory features of verse must be "in some way audible."[54] Formal structures, he argued, may be present without needing to be heard.[55] It would be an error, however, to infer that Jakobson therefore entertained the possibility that there might be no cause whatsoever of poetic regularities. "Verbal patterning," he maintained, excludes contingency. In every linguistic work, there is a "deliberate veto of any game of chance."[56] For Jakobson, as for Saussure before him, statistical regularity was therefore to be set aside. One might conclude that some subjective principle, for Jakobson, still motivates the poetic function. Yet the important point in his theory is that this principle may also remain indeterminate, in the sense that it does not matter whether patterning is voluntary or involuntary. One is tempted, indeed, to go still further and to maintain that this much *must* remain indeterminate.

Implicitly, Jakobson proceeded as if the neutralization of the difference between consciousness and its absence were the hallmark of poetics. In striking contrast to Saussure's notebooks, the "grammar of poetry" granted, in principle, the possibility that "a semblance of prosodic symmetries, sound repetitions, and a verbal substratum—*les mots sous les mots* (J. Starobinski's felicitous expression)—transpire without being supported by some speculative insight into the methods of the procedure involved."[57]

At the time he presented it, Jakobson's theory of the poetic function elicited considerable scholarly interest, becoming perhaps the most prominent example of the linguistic method that structuralist criticism seemed to promise. As such, it was once commented upon in detail.[58] There was much to discuss. Jakobson's essays, while always circumscribed in their linguistic objects, ranged over a poetic corpus seldom explored by a single critic. In addition to composing studies of Russian, Czech, Polish, French, and English poetry, Jakobson worked with colleagues to offer new perspectives on literature in Italian, Gallego-Portuguese, Norwegian, Japanese, and Chinese. As one might expect, specialists of these fields contested details of his readings. Yet literary scholars also raised certain basic questions concerning the principles that underlay Jakobson's conception of the poetic function.

These were fundamentally of two kinds. The first involved the potentially unlimited set of parallelisms that might be pertinent to "verbal art." Commenting on Jakobson's project to offer an "unbiased, attentive, exhaustive, total description of the selection, distribution and interrelation of diverse morphological classes and syntactic constructions in a given poem," Jonathan Culler argued that it could lead to any poetic analysis whatsoever:

> One can produce distributional categories almost *ad libitum*. One might, for example, begin by studying the distribution of substantives and distinguish between those which were objects of verbs and those which were subjects. Going one step further, one might distinguish between those which were objects of singular verbs and those which

were objects of plural verbs, and then one might subdivide each of these classes according to the tense of the verbs. This process of progressive differentiation can produce an almost unlimited number of distributional classes, and thus if one wishes to discover a pattern of symmetry in a text, one can always produce some class whose members will be appropriately arranged.[59]

Such patterns would be "'objectively' present in the poem," but "not for that reason of any importance."[60] That objection, in its conclusion, draws close to the second question raised against the theory of the "grammar of poetry," which was most famously formulated by Michel Riffaterre. In a review of the essay that Jakobson and Lévi-Strauss dedicated to Baudelaire's "Les chats," Riffaterre did not contest the linguistic validity of their analysis so much as the intrinsic literary significance that grammatical features, for the authors, possessed. "The method," he observed,

is based on the assumption that any structural system they are able to define in the poem is necessarily a poetic structure. Can we not suppose, on the contrary, that the poem may contain certain structures that play no part in its function and effect as a literary work of art, and that there may be no way for structural linguistics to distinguish between these unmarked structures and those that are literarily active?[61]

Jakobsonian poetics possesses the means to answer both objections. In response to the charge that the analysis of grammatical symmetries must be arbitrary, Paul Kiparsky has remarked that from the linguistic point of view, it is mistaken to suppose "that grammatical categories can be multiplied *ad libitum:*"

They are in fact a fixed set to be established within the theory of grammar. To be sure, there are open questions about *what* the correct theory of grammar is, including precisely how the set of categories should be delimited, but this much seems clear, that the pseudo-categories cited by Culler, such as objects of plural verbs, have no linguistically justifiable status whatever and therefore *should* not play any role in poetic patterning either.[62]

147

In the lengthy "Retrospect" that appears in the third volume of his *Selected Writings, Poetry of Grammar—Grammar of Poetry,* Jakobson dwelt at some length on Riffaterre's critique of his reading of Baudelaire. He confronted the question of the alleged need of a criterion by which to distinguish between merely grammatical recurrences and properly poetic features. Riffaterre argued that such a distinction could depend only on the "response" of individual readers. Aware that an individual reaction to a text would necessarily be partial, Riffaterre had sought to construct an imaginary reader through the postulate of a "special tool of analysis." Riffaterre baptized this tool the "superreader," explaining that he had constructed it by compiling a set of individual responses that he took to be pertinent for the study of Baudelaire's sonnet: statements made by the poet himself; remarks by two of his contemporaries; suggestions proposed by several translators and critics; and impressions gleaned, as the critic wrote, from "students of mine and other souls whom fate has thrown my way."[63] It is not difficult to discern the arbitrary element in the construction of such a "superreader." But it is equally clear that such a point of hermeneutic orientation, however anonymous, introduces a subjective principle of interpretation of the kind that Jakobsonian poetics excludes. Yet in the theory of the poetic function, there was, in any case, neither a need nor a place for the separation between "linguistic and poetic actualizations."[64] The reason is simple. Within the patterns of a poetic sequence, Jakobson maintained, the distinction between poetic and nonpoetic cannot be made. "If this organization of grammatical parallelisms and contrasts, a property characteristic of poetry, does not function as a poetic device," Jakobson asked, responding to the literary critics, "for what purpose is this framework introduced, scrupulously maintained, and remarkably diversified by poets?"

Before his work came to be discussed by historians and theorists of literature, Jakobson had, in any case, encountered this question. In his presentation of his theory of the poetic function, he recounted how, in 1919, the members of the Moscow Linguistic Circle had sought "to define and delimit the range" of poetic epithets. They met with an objection:

> The poet Majakovski rebuked us, saying that for him any adjective appearing in a poem was thereby a poetic epithet, even "great" in the *Great Bear* or "big" and "little" in such names of Moscow streets as *Bol'šaja* ("big") *Presnja* and *Malaja* ("little") *Presnja*. Cf. Majakovskij's poem of 1915, "I and Napoleon," which begins with the words *Ja živu na Bol'šoj Presne, /34, 32/*: "I live on the Big Presnja, 34, 42. Apparently it's not my business that somewhere in the stormy world people went and invented war." And the poem ends: "The war has killed one more, the poet from the Big Presnja" (*poèta s Bol'šoj Presni*). Briefly, poeticalness is not a supplementation of discourse with rhetorical adornment but a total reevaluation of the discourse and of all its components whatsoever.[65]

This "total reevaluation" does not admit the existence, in speech marked by the poetic function, of any opposition between the literary and the nonliterary. In the poem, not one, but every word possesses the capacity to be "felt as a word and not as mere representation of the object being named," for any element that can be grammatically defined may enter into a system of recurrences. Jakobson illustrated the poetic principle by means of an anecdote. "A missionary blamed his African flock for walking around with no clothes on. 'And what about yourself?' they pointed to his visage, 'are not you, too, somewhere naked?' 'Well, but that is my face.' 'Yet in us,' retorted the natives, 'everywhere is face.'"[66] Jakobson offered a gloss, referring the remark to the ineluctable consequence of positing the poetic function: "In poetry, any element is converted into a figure of poetic speech."

That statement clearly excludes the possibility that literary language be conceived as a domain in which only certain elements can play a poetic role. Yet it also casts an unexpected light on Jakobson's relation to Saussure's hypothesis of a technique dimly discernible in recurrent elements of sound. With respect to it, one might read Jakobson's dictum as imposing a law of disclosure. Where

"everywhere is face," where every "component"—metrical or phonic, stylistic or rhetorical—is as naked as the visage, nothing can be
hidden. There is no place in which to guard and transmit matters to
be kept "occult." Jakobson's opposition to Saussure's hypothesis, to
this degree, is principled. Yet such a presentation is only partial, for
Jakobson could also be said to set in place of Saussure's art an activity that is far more obscure. Against the idea of a literary technique
developed and passed on in secrecy, Jakobson advanced his theory
of a function whose rules can, in principle, elude the speakers who
appropriate and make use of them, clear and distinct awareness
being no requirement for "subliminal verbal patterning in poetry."
That suggestion amounts to the proposition of an intensely cryptic
thing. Jakobson's poetic function would have been concealed not
only from the public but also from the poets, not recently, or even in
the distant past, but from the beginning. Poetic patterning, in short,
would have always emerged and persisted, almost without notice, at
once familiar and unknown to all.

The secret of this patterning extends across space as well as
across time. Saussure had investigated a procedure detectable in
certain literary traditions, being instituted and transmitted in circumstances that, however opaque in themselves, could be clearly
delimited. He thus restricted his attention to Indo-European antiq-
uities. Jakobson's perspective, by contrast, is that of the general linguist. His object is a possibility given with the very ability to speak.
Since the elements of poetry are nothing but the units of grammar,
set in recurring relations of equivalence, they are implicit in all linguistic regularities. In this sense, too, poetry is no "supplementation
to discourse": nothing need be added to the grammatical system of
a language for verse to become possible in it. In every language, by
means of its structure, poetry remains, rather, potential. There is
no language in which, and of which, poetry's varied forms cannot
be made. There is none in which patterns of equivalence may not
somewhere begin to proliferate, as if distinctly willed, for reasons
clear or dark, although their rules may be impenetrable to those
who compose, transmit, and perceive them. "Poetry," in this sense,

may be composed each time anew, in a different idiom and setting, for the most diverse of reasons. The poetic function, by contrast, is one, being but a consequence of grammar. In the symmetries of sound and sense that extend to every part of every tongue, it remains discernible, if not discerned. It is the secret of no one that poems, in sound or silence, knowledge or ignorance, lay bare.

Tristan Tzara, Villon's Anagrams, TZR 698B (337) (courtesy of the Bibliothèque littéraire Jacques Doucet, Paris, France).

CHAPTER ELEVEN

Secrets of Tristan Tzara

On December 22, 1959, the French newspaper *Le Monde* ran an article bearing the striking, if tentative title: "New Findings about François Villon?"[1] A subtitle explained that enigmatic question in more certain terms: "Tristan Tzara Restores to the Poet of the *Testament* All the Lines Attributed to Jean Vaillant, Discovering 1600 Anagrams in Villon's Work, Increasing 'Master François's' Age by Two Years." The essay began by comparing Villon's famously tumultuous life to a dark forest that concealed within it not only trees but also "monks, archers, pickpockets, lawyers, poachers, ambushes, and enchantments." "For three years now," the article reported, "Tristan Tzara has been walking in this forest. He has left it dazzled, with the feeling of having grasped hold of something rare: a treasure, or a secret. In one month he will publish—or perhaps one should say, he will detonate, since it will be more like a bomb—a book on Villon, chock-full of explosive material."[2] The literary news quickly appeared elsewhere in the French press. Only a day later, on December 23, 1959, the French weekly *Les Lettres françaises* published an article by Charles Dobzynski whose title proclaimed: "Five Centuries after the *Testament*, Tristan Tzara Reveals *The Secret of François Villon*."[3]

"In a few weeks, Fasquelle will publish a surprising book," the article related, "a kind of challenge to the passing of time and the mystery that envelops certain poetic works, that draws away the depth of soul from attention to contemporary matters. The book is signed Tristan Tzara and is called *The Secret of François Villon*."[4] Lest the readers mistake the identity of the author, Dobzynski recalled that the Tzara who would soon unveil the unknown secret of the fifteenth-century poet was the same who had once founded Dada.

> Tristan Tzara is a man of surprises. Almost exactly half a century ago, with Dada, he invented a terrible weapon, a kind of destructive ray, that gave poets the right of life and death over language. Words were submitted to a strange fire that killed commonplaces and, at once, obliterated meanings that had been on the map for centuries. For four years now, in the quiet of his study, which is filled with mementos of Surrealism and Oceanic masks, all competing with the Phoenix of the unusual for perpetual rebirth, Tristan Tzara, like a scientist in his laboratory, has been preparing to reveal one of the most vertiginous literary surprises of the century. It will radically change our knowledge of the greatest poet of the end of the Middle Ages, François Villon, whose *Testament* is, in fact, the birth certificate of modern poetry. This time, therefore, Tristan Tzara has not confronted language in order to destroy it, but to discover within it, under the heavy ash of the centuries, the hidden sense, the fire that burned under the cold appearance of enigmatic allusions and cryptograms, encrusted in a text that has been studied a thousand times, interpreted, debated, in all its symbols.[5]

The Secret of Villon, however, was slow to be revealed to the public. The book did not appear in 1960, as the two articles from 1959 promised. At the time of Tzara's death in December 1963, the work had still not come to light. Christophe Tzara, the author's son, would later recall that his father had been "correcting the typed manuscript in his last moments."[6] Yet it was not printed in the immediate aftermath of his death. For further news of Tzara's final work, readers would have to wait till 1967, when Pierre Le Gentil, in a chapter of a monograph on Villon, related what he had found in studying the manuscript of Tzara's last book.[7] More information about *The Secret of Villon* was disclosed eight years later in an article by Jean Dufournet, "Tzara and Villon's Anagrams."[8] In the same journal in which Dufornet's essay appeared, Henri Béhar published a nine-page fragment from Tzara's book, titled "The Meaning of Anagrams."[9] He also contributed to the issue a critical essay of his own. Here he revealed that a complete edition of Tzara's work was underway and that, "at a later date," *The Secret of Villon* would appear in print, "so that the reader" could at last "form an exact and personal opinion" concerning the poet's "decidedly innovative thesis."[10] The "later date" turned out to belong to a future more distant than one might have anticipated. Only in 1991 did the sixth and final volume of Tzara's *Complete Works* appear, disclosing the aged but still new "New Findings" promised three decades earlier.

Tzara's interest in the medieval poet had long predated his last book. As early as 1949, he graced Pierre Savinel's edition of Villon's poems with a prefatory essay in which he stated that modern poetry, as a whole, "finds one of the elements of its functional mechanism in the poetry of Villon."[11] "Some have wished to see in Baudelaire the initiator of modern poetry," he wrote,

> because of his recognition of the real world from which he draws his poetry. In his sincerity, he represents a reaction against Romanticism. In the same way, Villon is at the source of an equally modern current in poetry: the one that, in reacting against the Romantic and later conventional love of the troubadours and against the unrealistic religious formalism of his time, announces the end of the Middle Ages. By this realistic position, and by moving from the elements of his life to reach a personal vision of the world, Villon bestows a new criterion on poetic criticism. The authenticity of poetry, from this point on, will be a quality residing in the variable and organic concordance between the apprehended fact and its expressed transposition. Poetry will be true if the sentiment that animates it has been intimately lived, not if it results from some received formula. It will be necessary, in short, for the poet to have lived it intensely enough for his poetic expression to be naturally adequate to it.[12]

In this sense, Tzara concluded, Villon's is not only a "poetry of circumstance" (*poésie de circonstance*), marked by a particular historical setting; it is, more fundamentally, "poetry of *the* circumstance" (*poésie de* la *circonstance*), which draws from the world the materials of an image uniquely faithful to the poet's encounter with it.[13]

In his preface, "The Modernity of Villon," Tzara made no mention of anything that the medieval poet might have sought to hide from his readership. The Villon of 1949, it seems, possessed no secret, or still kept it to himself. The revelation of *The Secret of Villon*, when made, would consist before all else in the disclosure of this one fact: that there existed a "secret of Villon" that had lain concealed for centuries. As the French press revealed, the cryptic thing in question consisted in an art of writing, which allowed Villon both to record and to conceal matters relating to the circumstances of his poetry: allusions, suggestions, accusations, and statements about contemporaries, signaled above all by the presence of proper names hidden in a web of anagrams.

Tzara began his book by recalling that Villon's *Lais* presents itself as a "romance" or "novel" (*roman*) of love that retells a major episode in the life of the poet and, more precisely, the reasons that "forced Villon to flee Paris." "While relating the continuation of his adventures, always in an ironic fashion, the *Testament* completes this first work and retrospectively explains the origins of his misfortunes."[14] Villon loved a woman and would have continued to do so, had he not suffered the combined blows of fate and poverty. The twenty-fifth stanza of the *Testament* could not be more explicit:

> Bien est verté que j'ay aimé
> Et amereoie voulentiers;
> Mais triste cuer, ventre affamé
> Qui n'est rassasié au tiers
> M'oste des amouereux sentiers.
> Au fort, quelqu'ung s'en recompence,
> Qui est ramply sur les chantiers!
> Car la dance vient de la pance.[15]

> It's very true I have loved
> And willingly would love again
> But a heavy heart and starved craw
> Never full by more than a third
> Drag me down from love's ways

By now someone else takes up the slack
Who's filled to the brim on the gantry
For the dance starts in the belly.[16]

Citing these lines, Tzara draws the reader's attention to the final couplet, which follows the poet's allusion to the "someone else" who, having taken "up the slack," is "filled to the brim on the gantry." "*Qui est ramply sur le chantier*," he notes, "is an expression of the period, meaning 'Who has eaten well and drunk well,' the *chantier* or *gantry*, the piece of wood supporting the barrel, being, by extension, the cellar. The line *Car la dance vient de la pance* [For the dance starts in the belly] paraphrases a known expression. Here *dance* has the erotic meaning implied by the context."[17] That commentary is supported by the scholarship on Villon's language, which Tzara knew well.[18] Quickly, however, Tzara passes from the poet's statement to a level of the text that lies beneath that of the words that compose it. He evokes a reading of the passage proposed by the early twentieth-century philologist and editor of Villon, Lucien Foulet.[19] The penultimate line of the stanza, Foulet suggested, contains four groups of sounds that, when combined, spell out the name of a contemporary of Villon's evoked in both the *Lais* and the *Testament*. It suffices to read "Qui est RAMplY sur les CHAN-TIERS" for the figure to appear, concealed in an extended anagram: "Itiers Marchant."[20] Foulet had drawn a simple conclusion from this unexpected fact: Itiers Marchant must be the rival "someone" whom Villon evokes, without explicitly naming, one line above.

Once noted in the line, the syllables of the name are difficult to deny. Being audible, their presence, however dislocated, is almost apparent. A note contained in Tzara's unpublished papers suggests that when he first encountered Foulet's remark, he was immediately persuaded of its validity. Yet he also sought to take a further step. He wondered whether there might not be other names hidden in such a form in the syllables of Villon's lines.

The anagram of Ythiers Marchant is perhaps not an isolated case. The analogy of certain lines of the *Lais* with the stanzas of the *Testament*, the nomenclature of the legatees, arranged according to category or order of importance, the correspondence of the nature of the inheritance left to his tutor and his mother, are in no way gratuitous. It is in this direction, it seems to me, that one should pursue investigations.[21]

By the time he composed *The Secret of Villon*, however, Tzara admitted that this first intuition had been mistaken. "Persuaded that there must be other revelations in the work of Villon," he recounts, "I looked for anagrams formed as indicated above—without the shadow of success."[22] Pierre Le Gentil later confirmed his conclusion. "Anagrams analogous to the one cited by Foulet," he asserted, albeit not unequivocally, "apparently exist nowhere else in lines by Villon."[23] Yet Tzara tells us that in time, his failure led to one major linguistic discovery. He found that in the line commented upon by Foulet, the name "Itiers Marchant" could also be represented as present in a form different from the one suggested by the philologist, according to anagrammatic rules more subtle, more exact, and more systematic than had ever been observed.

Tzara explains in his book that these rules, when conjoined, define a "procedure" that Villon adopted in the composition of a number of his poems, most notably the *Lais*. "The procedure consisted in including, in a line or in a portion of a line involving the anagram, a word or several words whose letters are systematically distributed with respect to a center, constituted by one or two alphabetic signs, the spaces between words counting as null."[24] Three points implicit in this summary are worth retaining. The first is that the anagrams detected by Tzara, unlike the cryptic figures that traditionally go by that name, cannot be restricted to the space of individual words, being in each case distributed across a single line of verse or one of its segments. The second point is that within such a textual extension, the white spaces between words can play no role. To recover the names hidden in Villon's lines, one must begin by counting only letters. Implicitly, Tzara reasons in this sense as did Mallarmé: for both, albeit in different ways, "from many expressions, the line makes a total, new word, foreign to language"

(*Le vers, qui de plusieurs vocables refait un mot total, neuf, étranger à la langue*).[25] Finally, within this new "word," a center may be discerned: an "axis," "constituted by one or two alphabetic signs," with respect to which the letters of the hidden word or words are distributed in strictly symmetrical positions to the left and to the right. For example, if a letter belonging to a secret expression can be discerned two positions to the left of the center, another will be legible two positions to its right; if, by contrast, no such component letter may be observed one position to the left of the center, none may be considered to lie one position to its right. Tzara adds that when the hidden word is composed of an even number of letters, "the center is constituted by one or two letters; in the latter case, the letters may or may not be used in the formation of the anagram." When the concealed expression, instead, possesses an odd number of letters, "the center will be represented by a single letter, which must inevitably count among those that are necessary for the formation of the anagram."[26]

For the poetic procedure to function fully, certain licenses are required. "While the numeric disposition of these anagrams is strictly observed," Tzara explains, "Villon takes liberties, which concern only the spelling of words."[27] Some reflect variations in orthography that are commonly to be found in medieval French manuscripts, not least those that transmit Villon's poems. For example, *pauvre* may be spelled as *povre*, *vieil* as *viel*, *vengeance* as *venjance*.[28] Yet Tzara insists that one also take into account other types of divergences in spelling. Scholarship on Villon's language, as it is recorded in manuscripts, suggested to him that the poet had taken as equivalent certain written signs that in Middle French were otherwise held to be distinct. Louis Thuasne noted, for instance, that in some cases, Villon adds to words a terminal *s* (or withholds it), without effecting any change in their meaning.[29] But Tzara argues that one must also admit further licenses in writing, many of which were, and remain today, generally unknown to specialists of Middle French scribal habits.

Tzara explains that, to grasp the words secretly scattered across Villon's lines, one must always keep in mind a complex system of orthographic imperatives: suppress a *t* at the end of a word ending in *-an* or *-en*, replacing it, if need be, by an *s*; erase any *s* before *t* inside a word; remove *l* before *x*; replace *l* by *z* or *x* or by *c* before *l*, *e*, or *a*; take *i*, *y*, and *j* to be equivalent (or replace a *y* with two *i*'s); exchange *j* and *g*; rewrite any double consonants as a single consonant or rewrite, instead, some single consonants by two consonants; treat any metrically elided or "mute" *e* as either possibly included in or excluded from the anagram; consider *o* to be equivalent to *a*; take *e* as interchangeable with *I*; write *ou* as *oe*, or *oue*; replace *c*, when necessary, with *g*; and take *m* to be equivalent with *n* and *n* as substitutable for *m*.[30] Such rules enable the reader to find certain words that, for the purposes of anagrammatic analysis, can be represented in a number of different shapes. The priest Sermoise, whom Villon is reported to have killed on June 5, 1455, for instance, appears in Tzara's readings in no fewer than twelve distinct forms: "Sarmoies," "Sarmoie," "Sarmoye," "Sermoye," "Sermoie," "Sermoies," "Cermoie," "Cermoye," "Cermoies," "Çarmoie," "Carmoie," and "Carmoies." Yet Tzara also admits that it is possible that his orthographic principles are imprecise, in the sense that "more general laws" concerning the proper spelling of Villon's manuscripts may still be found. "I do not claim," he observes, "to have exhausted the question."[31]

The Secret of Villon suggests a graphic method for the illustration of this procedure. It consists of tying individual letters on either side of the central axis to each other by means of "curves" drawn below the printed text.[32] The publishers of Tzara's final work include no images of this method of representation, of which Tzara offers an abbreviated description in his book. Yet one can find an example of its form in an article published in 1960 in which Louis Aragon announced that Tzara will soon unveil unseen anagrams in Villon's successor, Rabelais.[33]

The publishers of *The Secret of Villon* chose to present the anagrammatic procedure by more traditional typographic means, which are easily described. First, all the letters in a single line are set beside each other, without spaces, as if they formed an entire word. Then

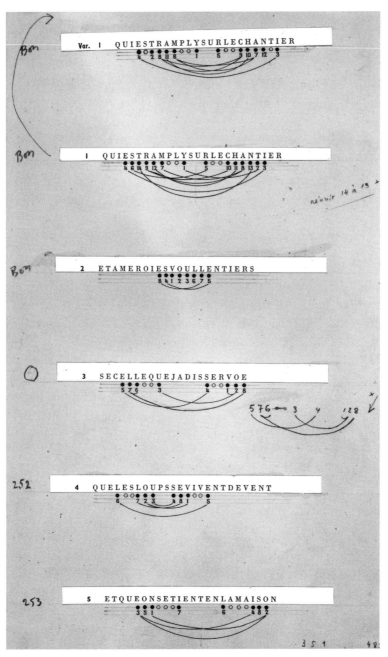

Tristan Tzara, Villon's Anagrams, TZR 718 (courtesy of the Bibliothèque littéraire Jacques Doucet, Paris, France).

on two successive lines below, two more sets of signs are printed. The first will indicate, by means of plus and zero signs, which letters play a role in the hidden word. On the second line beneath the text, the functional letters of the concealed expression will then be numbered according to the order of their appearance in the word or words that they evoke.

The first example printed in this form in *The Secret of Villon* is the line from the *Testament* analyzed by Foulet, which appears as follows:[34]

```
Q U I E S T R A M P L Y S U R L E C H A N T I E R
+ + + + + + o o +     + o o + + + + + +
4 6 14 9 12 7       1       5       10 11 8 13 2 3
```

Here Tzara recovers the same anagram as did Foulet—*Itiers Marchant*—without, however, admitting Foulet's implicit principle that the concealed name be present in the line through the rearrangement of its constituent syllables. Tzara reckons, in short, not in "anaphones," as did Saussure in his hidden notebooks on poetry but in *grammata* in the strict sense, letters distributed across each line. For him, the words concealed in Villon's verse are composed not from sound clusters but from graphic signs, which function as the indivisible elements of words. It follows that the hidden term ceases to be perceptible to the ear. The play of purely alphabetic units is too subtle, and too complex, to be heard as such. A syllabic decomposition of one of Villon's lines will issue in only eight or ten elements, depending on the verse form employed by the medieval poet. Admittedly, one may fashion more units by extracting the occasional phonemic part from a syllable, as Foulet does in drawing a *Y* from *ply* in *ramplY*. Yet as long as one counts in syllables, the set of functional units will remain small in number. If one reckons in letters, at least twice as many elements will appear. The possibilities of combination and recombination, accordingly, will increase.

Tzara knew this well. More than once in *The Secret of Villon*, he argues that several names can be found in the same words and phrases, being projected across a single metric space and written, so to speak, upon each other. Sometimes entire sentences may be recovered in the space of a line. In the conclusion to the book, for instance, Tzara gives a thorough analysis of Villon's "Ballade à s'amie," ending with an intense interpretation of its final address:

> Prince amoureux des amans le greigneur
> Vostre mal gré ne vouldroye encourir,
> Mais tout franc cuer doit, par Nostre Seigneur,
> Sans empirer, ung povre secourir.[35]

> Amorous prince and greatest lover
> I don't wish to call down your disfavor
> But every true heart must by the heavenly Father
> Save a poor man before he sinks under.[36]

Applying the rules of the procedure to the first line of this *envoi*, one discovers the hidden name of the "prince": Charles d'Orléans, Villon's friend and fellow poet. Yet one finds find six other names, which Villon has "ironically" written over his: "Noé Jolis," "Pardryers," "Denise," "Itiers," "Perinnet," and "Sarmoie."[37] In his analysis of the penultimate line of the same *envoi*, Tzara goes further, finding seven names, among them that of the knight Jehan le Cornu, that all point to the actors in the "drama" Villon cannot forget:[38]

```
MAISTOUTFRANCCUEURDOITPARNOSTRESEIGNEUR
   +oo+o+o+                          +o+o+oo+
   6   1 3 5                          8 7 4   2
=François
```

```
MAISTOUTFRANCCUEURDOITPARNOSTRESEIGNEUR
 +ooooo+ooooooo++o+o++oooooooo+ooooo+
 9     5       34 6 12          7       8
=Pardriers
```

```
MAI S TOUT F R A N C C U E U R D O I T P A R N O S T R E S E I G N E U R
            + o o + o +              + o + o o +
            6    1  4              3   5    2
```
=*Denise*

```
MA I S T O U T F R A N C C U E U R D O I T P A R N O S T R E S E I GN E U R
            + + o o o o + o o o o + +
            1 5        2        3 4
```
=*Cornu*

```
MA I S T O U T F R A N C C U E U R D O I T P A R N O S T R E S E I G N E U R
            + o + o o +              + o o + o +
            4   5   1              2    6   3
```
=*Itiers*

```
MA I S T O U T F R A N C C U E U R D O I T P A R N O S T R E S E I G N E U R
                        + o o + o o + + + o o + o o +
                        1   5   7 3 6   4      2
```
=*Perinet*

```
MA I S T O U T F R A N C C U E U R D O I T P A R N O S T R E S E I G N E U R
    + o o + o + o o o o + o o o o + o + o o +
    4   1 5      2      7  3    6
```
=*Sarmoie*

Having revealed all the members of this company, Tzara explains that Villon also encrypted in the line a "signature," "validating the authenticity of his anagrams." It consists of a sentence, its letters symmetrically placed as if in a single name:

```
MA I S T O U T F R A N C C U E U R D O I T P A R N O S T R E S E I G N E U R
    + + + + o o o + + o + o + +              + + o + o + + o o o + + + +
    9 1015 8      171  3  135              6 7  16  2 4      141812 11
```
=*François m'a escripte*, "François Wrote Me"

Personified, this final anagram writes of itself, commenting, in testamentary form, on the reasons for its persistence. It is the proof, Tzara writes, that Villon conceived the entire *Lais* as a continuous *roman à clef.* "One could even say *à double clé*," he adds, "if one keeps in mind that the key that serves to open the real domain of the drama and its characters is a function of the second key, which allows one to decipher the anagrams. Villon's rich and varied imagination is thus contained in the corset of a system of interpretation whose rigor and liberty reciprocally command each other."[39]

Learning of this late project, a reader familiar with the works of Tzara's youth might think of that other polyphonic poetic form, the *poème simultan*, which Tzara, together with Richard Huelsenbeck and Marcel Janco, famously performed in November 1916 before the public of the Cabaret Voltaire in Zurich. Read "in parallel" in French, German, and English, not successively, but in a single stretch of time, the poem "L'amiral cherche une maison à louer" consisted in the structural layering of three distinct texts upon one another.[40] In the explanatory "Note to the Bourgeois" that accompanied the original publication of this work, Tzara stated that it responded, in its composition, to a particular pictorial practice. The "transmutation of objects and colors" in "Picasso, Braque, Picabia, Duchamp-Villon, Delaunay" had prompted him to seek to "apply the same simultaneous principles in poetry." The resulting creation, as he wrote, was conceived in such a fashion as to permit any member of the public to link the disparate associations of the poem to the "elements characteristic of his own personality, mixing them, fragmenting them, etc., while remaining in the direction that the author channeled."[41] Despite its apparent cacophony, the *poème*, in this sense, was to be conducted, albeit in such a way as to suggest different executions to its diverse listeners. "A contrapuntal recitative," in Hugo Ball's words, it was to constitute a performance "in which three or more voices simultaneously speak, sing, whistle, or do something of the kind, such that their encounters constitute the elegiac, humorous, or bizarre shape of the matter."[42]

The simultaneity of text and anagram in *The Secret of Villon* is of another nature. In the Dadaist poem, three tongues coincide in a temporal extension, sharing a single acoustical form: each is read aloud. Every language is therefore equally perceptible, or imperceptible. Tzara presents Villon's poetry, by contrast, as animated by two formally distinct levels of enunciation, "superposed," like images, upon each other.[43] While the *poème simultan*, moreover, prompts those who hear it to "mix, fragment, etc." its elements in possibly incompatible ways, the two levels of the medieval work, for the late Tzara, necessarily compose an ordered and coherent whole. Villon's poetry "contains" its anagrams in every sense. Not only are the signs of the secret words literally present in those that compose its lines; what is concealed in them also reinforces, as if in a secondary role, what the text has openly said. "It will be observed," Tzara writes, "that the meaning of the anagrams is often inscribed in the line that contains it, although neighboring lines or parts of them may lend them a signification by implication."[44] Anagrams do not so much trouble the verse in which they can be discerned as offer them commentary: explanatory and revelatory notes for their interpretation. Tzara repeatedly calls them "signatures," which point to the reality from which the poems spring.[45] Over the syllables of Villon's songs and ballads, they sound softly, as "a kind of echo" or "a voice in mute" (*une voix en sourdine*).[46]

In several respects, the theory of this dark speech remains itself obscure. A first ambiguity involves the relation that is to obtain, for Tzara, between the medieval poet and his hermetic linguistic and literary procedure. *The Secret of Villon* suggests several possibilities. At times, Tzara argues that the poet's art of embedding words within words was never widely known. He reasons then that it allowed the poet to escape censure when inculpating his contemporaries, or when disclosing matters of an erotic nature, which medieval mores required him to keep concealed. The "secret," he suggests, was shared only with Villon's closest friends, Catherine and Noël Jolis, whom he "initiated" into the principle of his art.[47] This explains why "not one" of the medieval copyists who transcribed Villon's poems "seems to have had any knowledge of the treasure hidden inside the verbal matter of his verse," and why it is that to recover the buried gold, systematic orthographic adjustments must be made.[48]

At other times, however, Tzara suggests that the circle of those who knew of Villon's procedure was considerably wider than this summary would allow. Perhaps, he muses, Villon developed his technique with a view to the many friends who would be capable of detecting the recollections, thoughts, and reproaches encrypted in his verse. Tzara wonders even if Villon's misfortunes may not be, at least in part, attributable to the reactions of contemporaries, who could, and did, perceive the provocations that he had only faintly covered over in his poetry.[49]

Yet in the pages of Tzara's final work, one also encounters the possibility that the poet's concealed communications may, in truth, be "secrets" only for us. Tzara sought to show, in varying degrees of detail, that poets from the troubadours to Charles d'Orléans and Rabelais all employed the "procedure." At the limit, Villon's cryptographic method may have been transparent not to some but rather to all of his contemporaries. The content of the messages, then, would have been common knowledge. "If the anagrams give us revelations," Tzara writes, "we must nonetheless believe that in Villon's time, they were only ever 'open secrets' [secrets de Polichinelle]. He wrote the anagrams much more for the amusement of his friends than to unveil to them facts that they knew."[50]

The equivocation is of great consequence for Tzara's claims. Depending on the status of the "secret" revealed in the pages of his book, the procedure may, or may not, be employed as an historical and philological tool. Repeatedly, Tzara suggests that the presence or absence of anagrams in verse of Villon's epoch will be a positive criterion for the determination of authorship. One of the more provocative theses of his work, as the French press immediately grasped, was that all the poems attributed to the lesser fifteenth-century poet Jean Vaillant were, in fact, Villon's work. Part of Tzara's demonstration consisted in his proof that Villon's procedure could be detected in the poems of Vaillant: the names "François" and "Catherine," in particular, as he showed, are often scattered there. Yet if Villon's technique was a common one, the conclusion hardly holds, since any one of his contemporaries could have woven those names into his own lines. A similar ambiguity marks the substantial biographical assertions that Tzara sought to demonstrate by means of his anagrammatic decipherments. At some times, it seems that words found concealed in verse may be taken as biographical evidence of an almost documentary kind. The most striking example, in this regard, involves Tzara's treatment of Villon's alleged date of birth. On the basis of his recovery of hidden names, Tzara maintained that Villon must have been born two years earlier than had been thought.[51] At other times, Tzara defends the pertinence of the anagrams he has uncovered by anchoring them firmly in historical facts that he takes to be certain. In certain passages of his book, finally, Tzara suggests both possibilities simultaneously, as if unaware of the vicious circle that such a reasoning would imply. "One can only establish with certainty a point in the biography of Villon," Tzara then writes, "if the indications derived from the anagrams confirm the facts, and reciprocally."[52] Yet if the first proposition and its reciprocal are both true, neither, strictly speaking, holds.

Perhaps the most perplexing ambiguity in the argument of *The Secret of Villon* involves the status of those elements most often treated as secrets: names. It cannot be denied that Tzara's method of decipherment supposes that one know, before confronting Villon's poetry, which special words it may conceal. Unknown terms, as Tzara himself admits, cannot be recovered by this method. One must draw the name for which one searches, therefore, from Villon's own poetry, concealed names being all, in this sense, recurrences of apparent ones. Yet there is more. Even if one grants that the procedure consists in hiding what is known, so that it may, in time, be found anew, a troubling fact remains. It pertains to the identity of the secret names. On the surface, Tzara would seem to accept a common premise in research into anagrams, which holds that only forms with definite alphabetic shapes may be hidden and revealed in other expressions. Tzara can recover the distorted shapes of such names as

"Tabary" and "Perrinet," for example, since he knows the exact signs by which these names are written. Yet the principles of his method dictate that a name possess no single form. Just as "Sermoie" can be written as "Sermoye" or "Çarmoie," so "Tabary" can be spelled "Tabarye," "Tabarrie," or Tabaries," and Perrinet, as Tzara's own analyses demonstrate, may appear as "Parynet," "Perenet," "Parrinet," "Perynet," or "Parrenet." An intractable difficulty follows, for a simple reason: the very "liberties" that allow Tzara to recover certain names in Villon's work are those that forbid him from recognizing them with certainty. Inevitably, the crucial element in Villon's hermetic art of language—the secret of the secret—cannot but escape him.

In one of the earliest articles on Tzara's last project, Aragon wagered in 1960 that *The Secret of Villon* would, at a future date, provoke critical perplexity. "It will one day be a great subject of astonishment and study how it is that he who, almost half a century ago, founded the Dada Movement, has today become the researcher who, in Villon and Rabelais, takes pains to show that the obscurity of texts is essentially a result of our ignorance of both the social conditions and the biography of writers."[53] The exactitude of Aragon's prophecy is undeniable. Yet it also raises several questions. It is indeed remarkable that the author who once proclaimed that "there is a great destructive, negative task to accomplish" and who called, in his *Manifesto* of 1918, for the radical "sweeping away" of atrophied forms of artistic expression, should have later devoted such attention to the recovery of an ancient art of writing for which he must devote himself, over the course of almost a decade, to mastering the philology of medieval French.[54]

Beyond that formal observation, however, other differences are worth noting. Beginning with his earliest work, Tzara defined "spontaneity" as the supreme feature of future art.[55] In the "Lecture on Dada" that he gave in Weimar and Jena in 1922, he declared: "We have had enough of reflective movements that have dilated, beyond all measure, our credulity in the benefits of science. What we now want is *spontaneity*.... In art, Dada brings everything back to an initial, yet relative simplicity."[56] Again, the contrast with his later conception of Villon's metric lines of words upon words seems sharp. "They are the fruit of a meticulous assembly of disparate pieces, incessantly polished and polished anew so as to be able to follow each other," *The Secret of Villon* explains.[57] But it would be an error to infer that the late Tzara abandoned the literary quality he once extolled. "Granting that the term spontaneity has no meaning when referred to poetry," Tzara writes in his last book, "one must admit that Villon has succeeded in keeping intact the freshness of tone and the accents of his presence, despite the anagrams that lead their independent and swarming life on the inside of the lines that serve as their basis."[58]

The most profound tension between the projects of the early and the late Tzara, however, lies elsewhere. It involves a force that the Dadaists, as perhaps none before them, summoned in the fabric of their art: chance, or contingency.[59] In the "Dada Manifesto on Weak Love and Bitter Love," first read in Paris in 1920, Tzara offered this famous account of how "To Make a Dadaist Poem":

> Take a newspaper.
> Take a pair of scissors.
> From the newspaper, choose an article of the length you would like your poem to have.
> Cut out the article.
> Then cut out each of the words that compose the article and put them in a bag.
> Shake it softly.
> Then remove each cut-out, one after the other.
> Carefully copy them out
> In the order in which they left the bag.
> The poem will resemble you.
> And thus you will be an infinitely original writer of charming sensibility, although still unknown to the common crowd.[60]

These lines evoke a poetic practice in which the methodic destruction of a given text goes hand in hand with a partially random process of composition. The ultimate sequence of words in the "Dadaist poem" will be determined not only by the initial choice of an article, with its length and lexicon, but also by the "soft shaking" in a bag of its words, followed by the extraction of each cutout, "one after the other," in an order that the poet cannot anticipate. The experiment has been compared to practices of artists close to Tzara, not least the ones Hans Arp named in his "law of chance" (*Gesetz des Zufalls*).[61] As Hans Richter long ago remarked, of all the Dadaists, it was, however, Tzara who carried the principle of chance "to the most extreme point in literature."[62]

One might argue that Villon's procedure, as the late Tzara describes it, recalls to a certain degree the poetic method proposed in the *Manifesto* of 1920. A "meticulous assembly of disparate pieces, incessantly polished and polished anew so as to be able to follow each other," Villon's verse, which resembles him like no other, arises from the combination of minimal units, abstracted and "cut out," so to speak, from chains of signifying sequences. They are more minimal even than the elements that the *Manifesto* recommended as building blocks, being neither words nor even metric parts—syllables, rhymes, or vowels—but mere phonemes, transcribed, for the most part, in accordance with the graphic conventions of fifteenth-century France.

There, however, the similarities between the two literary practices end. The Tzara of *The Secret of Villon* insists that the sequence of names hidden in Villon's verse could be no mere fruit of chance. It must be willed. Like Saussure before him, Tzara could not, however, entirely exclude the possibility that certain stochastic processes might be at play in speech. The "keys" he had detected might partake somehow in random realizations of some possible combinations among others. "One cannot deny," he conceded in a fragment relating to his final work, "that chance plays a relatively important part in the formation of anagrams made of discontinuous letters. The question that arises is that of knowing whether Villon and the other anagrammatists, conscious of this chance, employed, amplified, or provoked it in intending to insert into their texts the greatest number of anagrams and, furthermore, to place them in the places that best suited them."[63]

Tzara had not been led to the "question that arises" entirely on its own. In July 1961, one M. Puisségur, teacher of mathematics in Nevers, happened, during his summer holidays, to read a newspaper article announcing an extraordinary cryptographic find: Tristan Tzara had discovered a forgotten method, once employed by poets, for embedding the letters of names in verse.[64] Few details of the technique were offered, yet the indications sufficed to arouse the scholar's curiosity. On the basis of the examples given, Puisségur began to devise a formal method for calculating, as best he could, the probability that names of a certain length might be present in lines of poetry, their letters distributed according to the symmetrical form that Tzara had identified. "Something" in the announcement, he would later recall, "had ruffled me."[65]

Once he completed his computations, Puisségur wrote to Tzara, through the intermediary of the paper, acquainting him with the results of his findings. They could be simply summarized: for the formation of discontinuous anagrams spelling out names in poetry, "chance," he concluded, "needs no help." In short, he took the postulate of a poetic procedure to be superfluous, because the laws of probability alone suffice for lines to contain within them the letters of certain names, distributed in strictly symmetrical patterns with respect to a central axis. In an essay published in the *Bulletin de l'Asssociation des professeurs de mathématiques de l'enseignement public* in 1971, eight years after Tzara's death, he summarized the formal reasoning that had led him to these conclusions. He also recounted how his first letter, years earlier, had met with a courteous reply. The famous poet invited the young mathematician to visit him at home. "Tzara received me in his rue de Lille apartment full of Picasso drawings and African masks," Puisségur recalled. He presented Tzara with his calculations. "I brought him no certitude," he would observe, "since to express a probability (unless it is equal to o or to 1) is to make a figured confession of ignorance."

I simply came to say to him, "This is what is due to chance. Let us decide." But faced with my figures, he responded with the conviction of a man who, having discovered a treasure, is told that some of his pieces, if not all, are counterfeit. To my doubts, he responded with his faith. It was difficult to separate the wheat from the chaff. But was there any wheat? He, too, must have asked himself this question, and I believe that for this charming, elderly man, I was the cause, that morning, of some pain.[66]

Tzara's papers suggest that he took the mathematician's arguments seriously, at least with respect to Rabelais, who, having been the subject of the newspaper article of 1961, was also their primary topic of conversation. "Employing most ingeniously the calculus of probability," we read in a posthumously published note, "M. Puisségur has obtained interesting results concerning the intrusion of chance in the formation of Rabelais's anagrams."[67] Yet Tzara maintained that such an "intrusion" could be curtailed—above all, with respect to Villon. The "authenticity" of the anagrams could be defended. "The proofs by which I have sought to demonstrate the authenticity of the anagrams in Villon's work are isolated and diverse, yet they are concordant."[68] Tzara distinguished, broadly speaking, between two types of demonstration. The first involved a hermeneutic principle: in each case, he held, what is hidden in verse responds semantically, in some form, to what is explicitly said in it. That such a rule rests on readings that would be difficult to verify is a point Tzara appears to have conceded: "One could object," he admits, "that these meanings all reflect a hypothetical interpretation that I give of the facts." Then he advanced his second proposition, whose implications far outstripped the interpretation of Villon, bearing on several centuries of literary history in the Romance languages. "The second phase in my demonstration has consisted in situating Villon's own activity in a historical movement in which the use of anagrams in poetry can be seen to stretch back to the twelfth century. Leaving aside the question of the origin and the history of anagrams, which I will, incidentally, take as a subject of study elsewhere," he continued, "I have found the prolongation of this activity, whose principles are immutable, even when the meaning given to anagrams and the means of employing them may differ from poet to poet, all the way up to the work of Rabelais, who is one of the last writers to have used it."[69] For Tzara, the two-part proof was sound. "It follows," he concluded, "that the doubts concerning the authenticity of the anagrams in the work of Villon must be definitely set aside."[70]

Yet the doubts were to return. In 1976, Lynn D. Stults published an article in the journal *Romania*, "A Study of Tristan Tzara's Theory Concerning the Poetry of Villon," in which she recalled that in 1959, it had been announced that a major literary-historical discovery would soon be revealed: "Apparently the celebrated Dadaist poet, Tristan Tzara, had been spending his late years developing a theory concerning the writings of Villon. Tzara had intended to publish his findings in a two-volume work about Villon, but he died before his plans could be realized."[71] Stults recalled that Puisségur, in an earlier article, had subjected the hypothesis of "the celebrated Dadaist poet" to linguistic scrutiny based on the principles of the mathematics of probability. Puisségur, she noted, devised a two-part formula to test Tzara's discoveries: "In the first part the number of possible symmetrical positions for an anagram of a given number of letters is calculated. In the second part the probability that the letters occupying those positions be identical with the letters of a particular name is calculated."[72] Although such reasoning is "mathematically sound," Stults wrote, "its application to French poetry is not." The reason is simple. Puisségur's formula accounts for the relative probability with which any letter will appear in the language (based, of course, on the statistical frequencies of modern, rather than medieval, French). The formula cannot, however, account for the probabilities dictated by the interdependence of letters in the language. One may, for example, calculate the relative probabilities that the letters F and R will appear in the language; but the relative probabilities that an F will appear after a R, or before it, or near it are another matter. The problem, Stults admitted, is not strictly mathematical. Linguistic research would need to provide crucial statistical data about the relations of letters in the language. Yet "the science of linguistics at its present stage is not equipped to construct a comprehensive system of the interdependence of letters in any natural language, let alone fifteenth-century French. Unfortunately such a system is a necessary component of any formula that could be used to predict accurately the number of symmetrical anagrams that can be expected to appear in a text by chance."[73]

Having renounced the possibility of determining the exact likelihood with which hidden names might be lodged in Villon's poetry, the scholar chose to evaluate Tzara's hypothesis by establishing a more modest literary fact: the frequency of anagrams contained in the corpus of Villon's verse when compared with those of two of his contemporaries. To this end, Stults availed herself of a computer program, specially designed by Robert Stults, named Vilgram, that would search for anagrams of forty-three names in Villon's *Lais*, Vaillant's *Le débat des deux soeurs*, and Charles d'Orléans' ballads.[74] Stults tabulated the findings reached by her computer, commenting that "from the breakdown of these results one fact clearly emerges: while all but six of the forty-three names searched for do appear in these six hundred lines of poetry, the majority of them do not appear significantly more frequently in the lines by Villon than in the lines by Charles d'Orléans."[75]

"One could perhaps argue," she conceded, "that Tzara's theory is strengthened by the rare occurrence of a long anagram, as for example in stanza 65 of l'*Embusche de Vaillant*, *leurs faitz ne sont point vicieux*":

```
L  E  U  R  S  F  A  I  T  Z  N  E  S  O  N  T  P  O  I  N  T  V  I  C  I  E  U  L  X
+  o  o  +  +  +  +  o  o  o  +  o  o  +  +  o  o  +  o  o  o  +  +  +  +  o  o  +  o
11       2  8  1  3           4        6  14       13          9  7  5  10       12
```

= *François Villon*

"On the other hand," she continued, "it would be rather unconvincing to follow the same logic and yet explain how the name of the Secretary of State of the United States crept into line 130 of *Le Lais*, *Regnier de Montigny trois chiens*":

R E G N I E R D E M O N T I G N Y T R O I S C H I E N S
+ + o o + + + o o o o + o + + o + o o o o + + + o o + +
4 2   7 13 14   3   10 12   5   8 6 1   11 9

= *Henry Kissinger* (c=k)[76]

Stults also noted a curious detail that Tzara seems not to have observed. "Often when the letters needed to form the anagram are present in a line, several symmetrical anagrams of the same name appear in the same line."[77] The name "Noé Jolis" thus appears not once but four times in the fifth line of the *Lais*, and Stults revealed the appearance of no fewer than "twenty Perrenets in line 285."

> It would be difficult to imagine that the appearances of all 20 symmetrical anagrams of the name Perrenet in line 285 of *Le Lais* was caused by the manipulations of the poet, and yet it would be equally difficult to determine which one of the twenty anagrams he intended to appear. It seems more reasonable to attribute these multiple anagrams to chance rather than to the efforts of the poet.[78]

Stults could only conclude that although Puisségur's demonstration was in part faulty, its conclusion was sound. "The results of my anagram search strongly suggest that Tzara's theory is invalid."[79]

One might have thought the secret of *The Secret of Villon* dissolved. More than fifteen years later, however, another scholar, Michel Bernard, reopened the dossier in an article, "*The Secret of Villon* Put to the Test of the Computer: Tzara and the Anagrams," published in the pages of the same journal.[80] Respectful of his predecessors in the mathematical study of linguistic regularities in poetry, he permitted himself nonetheless to restate Stults's criticisms of Puisségur. To it he now added that Stults's proof, too, was, from both a technical and a literary perspective, unsound. Although Stults's essay is "the more convincing of the two," he wrote, it "presents two failings that call her conclusions into question."[81] The first involved software: insufficient information had been given about the computer program, Vilgram, since the exact algorithm that had been employed had not been specified. Hence a troubling doubt: "Can one be certain that the program is truly capable of recovering all the symmetrical anagrams in a given verse?"[82] The second criticism was one of literary method. He recalled that Stults had compared the number of anagrams of selected names in Villon's poetry with those in the work of two of his medieval contemporaries, Charles d'Orléans and Jean Vaillant. Having proven that the quantities of hidden names were comparable in all three works, Stults judged it unlikely that Villon possessed an anagrammatic art of his own. Bernard pointed out that such a line of reasoning was weak.

> Charles d'Orléans is not only a contemporary but also a friend of Villon's, who could certainly have written under the name of the prince, or have entered into a contest of virtuosity with him, in the tradition of the *grands rhétoriqueurs*. The second corpus is even more problematic, since L.D. Stults studies the anagrams in *L'embusche Vaillant*, which Tzara, precisely, attributes to Villon! In theory, all three texts could therefore be written by the same author, and when L.D. Stults shows that there are even more anagrams in the works of Charles d'Orléans than in those of Villon, she does not necessarily demonstrate the falsehood of Tzara's theses.[83]

Bernard argued that a definitive refutation of Tzara's claims would need to involve poems unrelated to the literary culture of fifteenth-century France. This he set out to provide. Availing himself a computer program whose technical specifications he did not conceal, Bernard presented a thorough analysis of the combinatorial possibilities of a single line by the nineteenth-century poet Gérard de Nerval, "Je suis le Ténébreux—le Veuf—l'Inconsolé." He showed that in that alexandrine, one may detect, arranged according to the secret procedure identified by Tzara, a startlingly large set of distinguished authors: not least Breton, Corneille, Céline, Crevel, Ionesco, Roussel, and Villon.[84]

Yet Bernard also applied his program to the medieval corpus Tzara had studied. In the same 537 lines in which Tzara, by painstaking analysis, had recovered 1,235 anagrams, Bernard's program, working for twenty-four hours, found almost three times as many:

Béroul
JESUISLETENEBREUXLEVEUFLINCONSOLE
-------L------BR-------EU------O------

Breton
JESUISLETENEBREUXLEVEUFLINCONSOLE
---------T----BR--------------ON----E

Céline
JESUISLETENEBREUXLEVEUFLINCONSOLE
----I--E--N----------E--L--C-------

Corneille
JESUISLETENEBREUXLEVEUFLINCONSOLE
----I-L---N--R----E----L--C---O-E

Courteline
JESUISLETENEBREUXLEVEUFLINCONSOLE
--------ET-NE-R--------U-LI-CO------

Crevel
JESUISLETENEBREUXLEVEUFLINCONSOLE
-------L-------RE----EV-------C-------

Fénelon
JESUISLETENEBREUXLEVEUFLINCONSOLE
--------------------E----FL-N-ON----E

Fontenelle
JESUISLETENEBREUXLEVEUFLINCONSOLE
---------TE-E--E--L----F--N--N-OL-

Ionesco
JESUISLETENEBREUXLEVEUFLINCONSOLE
------------------------I-CONSO-E

Roussel
JESUISLETENEBREUXLEVEUFLINCONSOLE
------S-E------R---L---U------O-S---

Scève
JESUISLETENEBREUXLEVEUFLINCONSOLE
---S-------E----E----V-------C------

3,359 hidden names. "And not all Tzara's orthographic licenses," he added, "were even used."[85] Bernard had shown that the scholars who had sought to dismiss the theses of *The Secret of Villon* were in part mistaken in their methods and, at the limit, that they were unable to offer a firm foundation for their claims. Yet their intuitions were to be definitively confirmed when Tzara failed his last statistical test.

Despite the differences between these variously scholarly approaches to *The Secret of Villon*, certain critical elements in the discussion have remained constant. The question to be resolved, as Tzara himself, in the end, appears to have conceded, is not whether or not there are names hidden in the lines of the *Lais*, but to what degree it is linguistically probable that they are in fact present there. One may infer from the research that has been conducted on Villon's poetry that the precise likelihood of encountering the symmetrically placed letters of certain names in fifteenth-century manuscripts may remain unknown forever. What can be determined, however, is the approximate degree of probability that the letters of certain names may be distributed, according to the procedure, in octosyllabic and decasyllabic lines in the language.

It is here that one reaches what may be the most curious element in the mathematically informed refutation of Tristan Tzara's last work. Explicitly or implicitly, all the critics of *The Secret of Villon* orient their arguments with respect to one unstated axiom in Tzara's investigation: the axiom, namely, that it is unlikely that there will be names legible in Villon's verse as the procedure would dictate, or, positively stated, that the presence of such names, if established, will constitute an inherently improbable occurrence. Tzara means his unlikely hypothesis—that Villon embedded the letters of certain names in his lines, beyond the threshold of auditory or visual perception—to be supported by this unlikely fact: the names are truly there. The probability of an unlikely claim, in other words, is to be verified by an improbable but true proof. To refute Tzara, it suffices, then, to reject the validity of his evidence. If it is more likely than not that letters in a line, disjoined and placed in symmetrical positions, will spell out certain names, then the improbable claim will be revealed to be no more than what it appears to be: not only improbable, but, indeed, even arbitrary. Hence the curious form of disproof to which the critics ultimately submit Tzara's argument, which consists, in essence, in reasoning that the poet-scholar was mistaken to think that he had recovered some one thousand two hundred anagrams, because there are more than twice as many there that he did not see. He was more right, in other words, than he ever dared to hope. Therefore he was wrong.

Did the author of *The Approximate Man* anticipate such forms of reasoning? "It seems that it exists," he had declared in 1920, "more logical; very logical; too logical; less logical; illogical; truly logical; fairly logical."[86] By choice, by calling, or by chance, Tzara, at the end of his life, was still declining these various possibilities, while also suggesting a field in which they might be tested. Another element, however, also lies hidden in the revelation of Tzara's last work. A final mystery, so to speak, remains concealed, although from 1959 to this day, it has never ceased to lie in plain view. It consists in the simple fact that Tzara refused to consider the possibility that the poet's treasure might lie buried in the one place in which one might, in all likelihood, have expected to find it. Villon, by all accounts, wrote a series of poems in a form of speech meant to conceal certain matters. They are his so-called "Ballads in Jargon," which evoke the obscure idiom of the Coquillars, the bandits who plotted their unmentionable acts, as the authorities of fifteenth-century Dijon alleged, in "an exquisite language, which other people cannot understand" (*un langaige exquis, que aultres gens ne scevent entendre*). These ballads remain, to a significant degree, impenetrable to this day. Tzara, a learned reader of Villon and the scholarship devoted to him, knew them well. He had also read the critical essays published on their strange language, those by Marcel Schwob not least. Yet as Henri Béhar, Tzara's editor, observes, "curiously, none of his drafts shows any trace of an anagrammatic investigation carried out on the ballads in jargon."[87]

At the beginning of *The Secret of Villon*, Tzara appears to have anticipated that his book might well, for this reason, provoke some

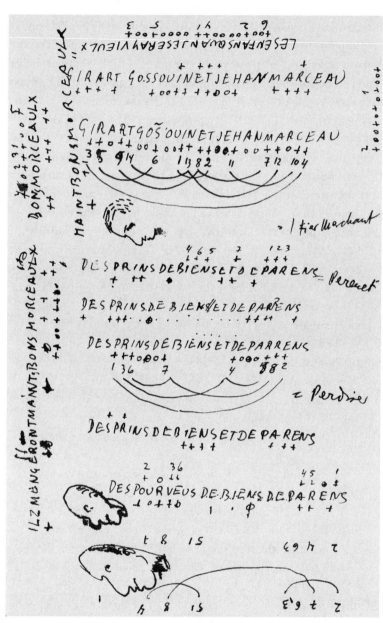

Tristan Tzara, Villon's Anagrams, TZR 701 (courtesy of the Bibliothèque littéraire Jacques Doucet, Paris, France).

surprise. As if to dispel the possibility of the reader's bewilderment or disappointment, he writes: "These inquiries do not cover the domain of *Jargon*. The presence of anagrams is all the more probable there, since this language, being in part recreated by Villon, must have rendered their formation easier."[88] His statement is worth pondering. It suggests, in truth, two propositions. The ballads, first, will not be considered as belonging to the corpus of poems containing anagrams; for anagrams, second, are most probably present there. It is difficult not to pose the question of the logical link that is to obtain between these statements. But Tzara offers another reason for the exclusion of jargon from his book. Raising the question of the opaque poems in a note that was to accompany an unfinished edition of Villon's work, he comments: "Despite the many more or less fantastical attempts that have been made at decipherment, one can only agree with Sainéan, the greatest specialist of jargon, that 'all things considered, most of the terms of the argot or *jobelin* will probably remain a closed book for us, and that, forever.'"[89]

The ballads in jargon, therefore, are probably hermetic and certainly obscure. In both cases, they can have no place in *The Secret of Villon*. The conclusion may seem sudden, but the truth is that it is far from arbitrary. One may even go so far as to define the object of Tzara's last book in punctual opposition to the two characteristics that, in these passing observations, he attributes to the poems composed in the bandits' cryptic tongue. In distinction from the obviously "closed book" of the ballads in jargon, the texts of the *Lais* appear to conceal no hidden message. Their obscurity, if one grants it, is uncertain in the extreme. Their secret, by that token, is unlikely. Faced with this fact, Tzara, in a sense, does no more than respect a principle that one might well wish to grant: were the treasure likely, were its appearance obvious, it would be none at all. He takes a further step when he effectively deduces the reality of a hidden thing from that of its unlikelihood, inferring that Villon's poems exhibit a secret procedure not despite but because of the improbability that such a possibility is real. The "explosive material" contained in this most vertiginous of literary finds ensues. The mystery,

Tzara will then implicitly maintain, lies in the brightest language of all, its darkness dimly discernible in the speech that would seem most crystalline. The true secret, like poetry for Breton, is there where one would least expect it.[90] In the light of evidence, in words manifestly free of the artifice of jargon, there are signs, names, and purposeful patterns, whispered in "a kind of echo" or by a "voice in mute," waiting quietly, below each line of verse, for their knowing reader. To take dictation from these unheard sources, to copy what had not been written, Tzara silenced the doubts that his interpretation provoked and that he himself lived, in part, to perceive. Diving ever deeper into the perilous waters of Villon's songs and ballads, he would not abandon the image of the treasure that he sought, even if it was to be at the risk that the language he discovered lay on the crystal's surface and that the secrets he uncovered were his own.

Notes

CHAPTER ONE: FORKINGS

1. Aristotle, *Politics* 1253a9.

2. See Johannes Lohmann, *Musiké und Logos: Aufsätze zur griechischen Philosophie und Musiktheorie.*

3. On this and other basic principles in the epistemology of linguistics, see Jean-Claude Milner, *Introduction à une science du langage*, esp. pp. 23–90.

4. Stéphane Mallarmé, "Crise de vers," in *Œuvres complètes*, pp. 363–64.

5. See Jürgen Werner, "Nichtgriechische Sprachen im Bewußtsein der antiken Griechen" and "Kenntnis und Bewertung fremder Sprachen bei den antiken Griechen I. Griechen und 'Barbaren': Zum Sprachbewußtsein und zum ethnischen Bewußtsein im frühgriechischen Epos"; Bruno Rochette, "Grecs et latins face aux langues étrangères: Contribution à l'étude de la diversité linguistique dans l'antiquité classique"; Vincenzo Rotolo, "La communicazione linguistica fra alloglotti nell'antichità classica"; Anna Morpurgo Davies, "The Greek Notion of Dialect."

6. See Homer, *Iliad* 2, 867; *Odyssey* 19, 172sq.

7. Herodotus, *Histories* 4.45. 2–5.

8. *Ibid.*, 2.50; for a discussion, see Richmond Lattimore, "Herodotus and the Names of Egyptian Gods."

9. See Diodorus 1.8.3, in Diels and Kranz (eds), *Die Fragmente der Vorsokratiker*, fragment B 5.

10. See Genesis 11:1–9.

11. Quintilian, *Institutio oratoria* 11.3.87.

12. See Rousseau, "Essai sur l'origine des langues," ch. 1.

13. Lucian, *De saltatione* 64.

14. Dante Alighieri, *De vulgari eloquentia*, 1.9.4, in *Opere minori*, p. 74.

CHAPTER TWO: COQUILLARS

1. Marcel Schwob, "Le jargon des Coquillars en 1455," in *Mémoires de la société linguistique de Paris* (June 1890), pp. 168–83 and 296–320, reprinted in Marcel Schwob, *Études sur l'argot français*, pp. 61–150 and 83.

2. Such a translation supposes that the word *coquillar* derives, as the legal dossier suggests, from the word *coquille*, "shell." It has also been suggested that the term derives from the word *coq*, "rooster," the bandits seizing their victims "with a powerful blow" like that by which roosters leap on chickens. See Pierre Guiraud, *Le jargon de Villon, ou Le gai savoir de la Coquille*, p. 8.

3. Schwob, *Études sur l'argot français*, p. 81.

4. *Ibid.*, pp. 81–82.

5. *Ibid.*, p. 82.

6. *Ibid.*, pp. 82–83.

7. *Ibid.*, pp. 83–84.

8. *Ibid.*, p. 91.

9. *Ibid.*, p. 92.

10. *Ibid.*, pp. 86–90.

11. *Ibid*, p. 61. Cf. Pierre Guiraud, *L'argot*, p. 49, who claims that the term is the first recorded word of jargon.

12. See, for example, Frédéric Godefroy, *Dictionnaire de l'ancienne langue française et tous ses dialectes du IXe au XVe siècle*, s.v. "jargon"; and Adolf Tobler and Erhard Lommatzsch, continued by Hans Helmut Christmann, *Altfranzösisches Wörterbuch*, s.v. "jargon." For a fuller and more recent treatment, see John Trumpner, "Slang and Jargons," esp. pp. 660–62.

13. Marie de France, *The Fables*, 46.55.13–14, pp. 132–33.

14. Cited in Godefroy, *Dictionnaire de l'ancienne langue française*, s.v. "jargon."

15. Tober-Lommatzsch (*Altfranzösisches Wörterbuch*, s.v. "jargon") gives as an example *Alexandre le Grand*, D 72, p. 198: "Quant sout par les esteilles la lour entencïon, / Un ris gitat de joie e dist une oreisun; Une charme en chaldeu, ne sai pas le jargoun."

16. See *Richard li biaus*, vv. 3334–53.

17. Georges Guieysse and Marcel Schwob, "Étude sur l'argot français," *Mémoires de la Société Linguistique de Paris* 7 (1889), pp. 5–28, reprinted in *Études*

sur l'argot français, pp. 7–60.

18. *Ibid.*, pp. 60–64.

19. *Ibid.*, p. 65.

20. Marcel Schwob, "François Villon," in *Œuvres*, vol. 1, p. 10.

21. See François Villon, *Poésies complètes*, p. 327.

22. Clément Marot, *Œuvres poétiques* vol. 2, p. 778. On Marot's relation to Villon, see Jacqueline Cerquiglini-Toulet, "Marot et Villon."

23. Geoffroy Tory, *Champ fleury, ou L'art et science de la proportion des lettres*, A VIII r°: "Quant Iargonneurs tiennent leurs Propos de leur malicieux Jargon & meschant langage, me semblent quilz ne se monstrent seullement ester dediez au Gibet, mais quil seroit bon quilz ne feussent oncques nez. Jaçoit que maistre François en son temps y aye este grandement ingenieux, si touteffois eust il myeulx faict d'avoir etendu a faire autre plus bonne chose."

24. Cited in Marcel Schwob, "François Villon et les compagnons de la Coquille," lecture presented to the Académie des Inscriptions, April 2, 1890, reprinted in Marcel Schwob, *François Villon*, p. 34. Cf. Lucien Schöne, *Le jargon et jobelin de Maistre François Villon, suivi de Jargon au théâtre*, p. 22.

25. Schwob, *François Villon*, pp. 29–30.

26. *Ibid.*, p. 34.

CHAPTER THREE: PRINCIPLES OF CANT

1. The *Oxford English Dictionary* relates that the term *cant*, while apparently derived from the Latin *cantus* and its neo-Latin forms (Provençal and Norman French *cant* and French *chant*), acquired its English sense by a derivation and development that remains unknown. The earliest attestation of the term dates to 1553. See *Oxford English Dictionary*, s.v. "cant."

2. Julie Coleman, *A History of Cant and Slang Dictionaries*, vol. 1: *1567–1784*, p. 4.

3. For Herodotus's remarks on the language of the Amazons, see *Histories* book 4, 117.

4. See John Trumper, "Romance Slangs and Jargons," p. 660.

5. On the argot in the *Jeu de saint Nicolas*, see Michel Dubois, "Sur un passage obscur du *Jeu de saint Nicolas*"; Francisque Michel, *Études de philologie comparée sur l'argot*, pp. viii–ix; Lazare Sainéan, *Les sources de l'argot ancien*, vol 1, p. 3.

6. *Richard li biaus*, vv. 3333–53, p. 92.

7. See Sainéan, *Les sources de l'argot ancien*, p. 3.

8. See Piero Camporesi, *Il libro dei vagabondi*, pp. 179–246. Camporesi dates the manuscript to 1484–86 (p. 13).

9. *Ibid.*, pp. 241–46.

10. For an English translation, see Anonymous, *The Book of Vagabonds and Beggars: With a Vocabulary of Their Language*.

11. *Ibid.*, p. 3.

12. *Ibid.*, pp. 4–5.

13. Thomas Harman, *Caveat or Warening for Common Cursetors*.

14. *Ibid.*, Epistle, A iii.v.

15. Lanthorne, ch. 1, B3r. cited in Coleman, *A History of Cant and Slang Dictionaries*, vol. 1, p. 31.

16. See the first two volumes of Coleman's *History of Cant and Slang Dictionaries*.

17. Henri Estienne, *Apologie pour Hérodote*, vol. 1, pp. 211–12.

18. See Pechon de Ruby, *La vive généreuse des Mercelots, Gueuz et Boesmiens, contenans leur façon de vivre, subtilitez & gergon*.

19. See Francisco Adolpho Coelho, *Os ciganhos de Portugal, com um estudo sobre o calão*.

20. The German word *Gauner* appears to derive from the Yiddish *ganef*, "thief." On the Yiddish term, see Uriel Weinrich, *Modern English-Yiddish, Yiddish-English Dictionary*, s.v. "ganef."

21. See Friedrich Christian Benedict Avé-Lallement, *Das deutsche Gaunertum in seiner sozialpolitischen, literarischen und linguistischen Ausbildung zu seinem heutigen Bestande*.

22. Alfredo Niceforo, *Il gergo nei normali, nei degenerati, e nei crimianli*.

23. M. A. K. Halliday, "Anti-Languages."

24. Marcel Cohen, "Note sur l'argot," p. 137.

25. See *ibid*, p. 139. Cohen also considers the related case of playful jargons, which are intended not to be secret, but may be so, in response to the "exigencies of a game."

26. See Jean-Claude Milner, *Introduction à une science du langage*, pp. 341–49.

27. Marcel Schwob, *Études sur l'argot français*, p. 22.

28. *Ibid.*, pp. 44–45.

29. On *verlan*, see Natalie J. Lefkowitz, "Talking Backwards in French."

30. There are other "dialects" of *javanais*. See Marc Plénat, "Le javanais: Concurrence et haplologie."

31. Raymond Queneau, *Exercices de style*, p. 123. On Queneau's *javanais* exercise, see Marc Plénat, "Morphologie d'un 'langage secret': Le javanais de Queneau, Description dans un cadre autosegmental."

32. Queneau, *Exercises in Style*, p. 158.

33. For the Queneau's exercise in *loucherbem* style, see *Exercices de style*, p. 122: "Un lourjingue vers lidimège sur la lateformeplic arrière d'un lobustotem, je gaffe un lypétinge avec un long loukem et un lapeauchard entouré d'un lalongif au lieu de lubanrogue." For an analysis of *loucherbème*, see Marc Plénat, "Morphologie du largonji des loucherbems."

34. In English, one may cite "pig Latin," discussed by Morris Halle, "Phonology in Generative Grammar," pp. 62–63. Cf. the case of the "pa-language of Mayalam," described and analyzed by Karuvannur Puthanveettil Mohnan, "Lexical Phonology," pp. 141–43. The bibliography on secret languages is abundant.

35. Pierre Guiraud, *L'argot*, p. 59.

36. See Guiraud's analysis in *ibid.*, p. 50.

37. See John Ayto, *Oxford Dictionary of Rhyming Slang*, p. 175.

38. *Ibid.*, p. 213, where the rhyme appears in its entire form.

39. On rhyming slang in general, see Leonard R. N. Ashley, "Rhyme and Reason: The Methods and Meanings of Cockney Rhyming Slang"; D. W. Maurer and Sidney J. Baker, "Australian Rhyming Argot in the American Underworld,"; St. Vincent Troubridge, "Some Notes on Rhyming Argot"; and Ayto, *Oxford Dictionary of Rhyming Slang*. On the history of the study of rhyming slang, see Julie Coleman, *A History of Cant and Slang Dictionaries*, vol. 3, pp. 91–96.

40. For Shklovsky's programmatic statement, see "Isskustvo, kak priyom"; English in "Art as Technique."

41. Paul Valéry, "Rhumbs," in *Œuvres*, vol. 2, p. 637. Roman Jakobson long ago drew attention to the "realistic and scientific" aspect of this definition. See his *Selected Writings*, vol. 3, p. 38.

CHAPTER FOUR: SIGNS

1. See Hans-Robert Jauss, *Die Alterität und Modernität der mittelalterichen Literatur: Gesammelte Aufsätze 1956–1976.*

2. Paul Zumthor, *Langue et techniques poétiques à l'époque romane (XIe–XIIIe siècles)*, p. 208.

3. Alfred Pillet, "Grundlagen, Aufgaben und Leistungen der

Troubadours-Forschung," p. 342, reprinted in *Der provenzalische Minnesang: Ein Querschnitt durch die neuere Forschungsdiskussion*, p. 56.

4. See István Frank, *Repertoire métrique de la poésie des troubadours*, vol. 1, p. xvi.

5. See Frank, *Repertoire métrique*; P. G. Beltrami, *Rimario trobadorico provenzale*; Giovanna Santini, *Rimario dei trovatori*.

6. On the expression *trobar clus*, see Ulrich Mölk, *Trobar clus, Trobar leu: Studien zur Dichtungstheorie der Trobadors*; cf. Aurelio Roncaglia, "Trobar clus: Discussione aperta."

7. Glynnis M. Cropp, *Le vocabulaire des troubadours de l'époque classique*, p. 17.

8. See *ibid.*, pp. 17–47.

9. André Moret, *Anthologie du Minnesang*, p. 34, commented in Jacques Lacan, *L'éthique de la psychanalyse, 1959–1960*, pp. 189–90.

10. For an enumeration of the troubadours who give their name in their poems, see F. M. Chambers, *Proper Names in the Lyrics of the Troubadours*.

11. *Purgatorio* 26.117.

12. For Guinizelli's identification of Arnaut, see *Pugratorio* 26.117. For an early reading of the enigmatic phrase, see Jean Boutière and Alexander Herman Schulz, *Biographies des troubadours: Textes provençaux des XIIIe et XIVe siècles*, 10.43–45, p. 15. Arnaut names himself in thirteen of his seventeen lyric poems. This signature appears in "En cest sonet coind'e leri."

13. For an exact account of the relative frequency of such invocations in the concluding stanza of the troubadour lyric, see Eduardo Vallet, "Il *senhal* nella lirica trobadorica," p. 154.

14. On *Addressentornaden*, see *Bernart de Ventadorn: Seine Lieder mit Einleitung und Glossar*, p. XCIX.

15. Alfred Christlieb Kalischer, *Observationes in poesim romanensem provicialibus in primis respectis*, pp. 25–26.

16. See Pasero (ed.), *Poesie di Guglielmo IX*, *Mon Esteve*, VII.47; *Mon Bel Vezi*, X.26.

17. See Vallet, "Il *senhal* nella lirica trobadorica," p. 114. For the continuation and conclusion of Vallet's study, see his "Il *senhal nella lirica trobadorica* (con alcune note su *Bel / Bon Esper* in Gaucelm Faidit)."

18. See Alfred Jeanroy, *La poésie lyrique des troubadours*, vol. 1, pp. 317–18.

19. See the lexicographic analysis in Vallet, "Il *senhal* nella lirica trobadorica (con alcune note su *Bel / Bon Esper* in Gaucelm Faidit)," pp. 283–85.

20. In Adolphe Félix Gatien-Arnoult (ed.), *La flors del gay saber, estier dichas Las leys d'Amors,*vol. 1, p. 338. Cf. the explanation of the *senhal* in the verse version of the *Les leys d'dmours*, ed. Joseph Anglade, vol. 2, p. 176.

21. Jean Boutière and Alexander Herman Schulz, *Biographies des troubadours*, LXXXIV, p. 267, 12–15.

22. *Ibid.*, XIV C, p. 28, 1–2.

23. *Ibid.*, XCIV B, p. 323, 23–25.

24. *Ibid.*, XC A, p. 310, 20–21.

25. *Ibid.*, LXXXIII, p. 264, 2–10.

26. *Ibid.*, XVII A, p. 35, 8–10.

27. See Ernest Hoepffner, "Le *Castiat* du troubadour Peire Vidal."

28. Stanislaw Strónski (ed.), *Le troubadour Folquet de Marseille*, p. 33.

29. Boutière and Schulz, *Biographies des troubadours*, XLVII, p. 151, 23–24.

30. See Bertran de Born, *The Poems of the Troubadour Bertran de Born*, p. 55.

31. Isabel de Riquer, "*Linhaure*: Cent ans d'études sur un *senhal*," p. 63.

32. Alfred Jeanroy, *La poésie lyrique des troubadours*, vol. 1, p. 317.

33. V. De Bartholomaeis, "Du rôle et des origines de la tornade," p. 462.

34. See Martín de Riquer, *Los trovadores: Historia literaria y textos* (Barcelona: Planeta, 1975), vol. 1, pp. 95–96.

35. Alois Richard Nykl, *Hispanio-Arabic Poetry and Its Relations with the Old Provençal Troubadours*, p. 271.

36. Riquer, *Los trovatores*, vol. 1, pp. 95–96.

37. See *Bernart de Ventadorn* 20.21–22.

38. Gérard Gourian, *L'amour et la guerre: L'oeuvre de Bertran de Born*, p. LXV; Luciano Formisano, *La lirica*, p. 69.

39. Na Castelloza, "Ja de chantar no dreg'aver talen," in Oskar Schultz-Gora (ed.), *Die provenzalische Dichterinnen: Biographien und Texte*, 8.59, p. 24. See Marianne Shapiro, "The Trobairitz and the Limits of Courtly Love," p. 571.

CHAPTER FIVE: KNOWINGS

1. The expression is Henry Adams Bellows's. See Bellows (ed. and trans.), *The Poetic Edda*, p. xii. For a more recent appraisal, see Klaus von See, Beatrice La Farge, Eve Picard, Ilona Priebe, and Katja Schulz, *Kommentar zu den Liedern der Edda*.

2. They have also been called the *Edda Sæmundar*. For translations, see Bellows,

The Poetic Edda; Ursula Dronke, *The Poetic Edda*; Carolyne Larrington, *The Poetic Edda*; Andy Orchard, *The Elder Edda: A Book of Viking Lore*.

3. E. V. Gordon, *An Introduction to Old Norse*, p. xxxix.

4. On the formal structure of the *dróttkvætt* stanza, see Roberta Frank, *Old Norse Court Poetry: The Dróttkvætt Stanza*; Hans Kuhn, *Das Dróttkvætt*; Kari Ellen Gade, *The Structure of Old Norse Dróttkvætt Poetry*.

5. For the Old Norse text, see Snorri Sturluson, *Edda: Skáldskaparmál*, ed. Anthony Faulkes, vol. 1; for translations, see Snorri Sturluson, *Edda*, ed. and trans. Anthony Faulkes and *The Prose Edda*, trans. Arthur Gilchrist Brodeur.

6. Snorri Sturluson, *Skáldskaparmál* 58, in Faulkes, *Edda*, vol. 1, p. 5; English in Faulkes, *Edda*, p. 64.

7. *Ibid*.

8. See the account in Heinrich Lausberg, *Handbuch der literarischen Rhetorik: Eine Grundlagung der Literaturwissenschaft*, § 589–98.

9. Snorri Sturluson, *Skáldskaparmál* 1, in Faulkes, *Edda*, vol. 1, p. 5.17–18; English in Faulkes, *Edda*, p. 64.

10. The meaning of Snorri's use of *fornǫfn* has been much discussed. See Faulke's comments in *Edda*, vol. 1, pp. xxix–xxx. Cf. Faulkes's glossary, *Edda*, vol. 2, pp. 277–78; Snorri devotes a longer discussion to *fornǫfn* in ch. 67 of the *Skáldskaparmál*. Cf. Arthur G. Brodeur, "The Meaning of Snorri's Catgeories"; Margaret Clunines Ross, *Skáldskaparmál: Snorri Sturluson's ars poetica and Medieval Theories of Language*, pp. 64–79.

11. Roberta Frank, s.v. "kenning," *Dictionary of the Middle Ages*.

12. *An Icelandic-English dictionary*, s.v. "kenna."

13. Snorri Sturluson, *Skáldskaparmál* 1, in Faulkes, *Edda*, vol. 1, p. 5.25–28; English in Faulkes, *Edda*, p. 64.

14. Snorri Sturluson, *Skáldskaparmál* 1, in Faulkes, *Edda*, vol. 1, p. 5.17–21; English in Faulkes, *Edda*, p. 64. Translation slightly modified.

15. For the kennings of Odin, see *Skáldskaparmál* 2; for the kennings of Freyja, see *Skáldskaparmál* 20.

16. Snorri Sturluson, *Skáldskaparmál* 69, in Faulkes, *Edda*, vol. 1, p. 108.6–8; English in Faulkes, *Edda*, p. 153.

17. Snorri Sturluson, *Skáldskaparmál* 25, in Faulkes, *Edda*, vol. 1, p. 36.24–29; English in Faulkes, *Edda*, p. 91.

18. Frank, "Kenning," p. 230.

19. *Ibid.*

20. Frank, *Old Norse Court Poetry*, p. 46.

21. *Ibid.*, p. 47.

22. *Ibid.*, p. 46.

23. Rudolf Meissner, *Die Kenningar der Skalden: Ein Beitrag zur skaldischen Poetik*, p. 2.

24. See Eyvindr Finnsson Skáldaspillir, *Die Dichtung des Eyvindr skáldaspillir: Edition-Kommentar-Untersuchungen*, pp. 274–76.

25. Sturla Þórðarson, 3, in Kari Ellen Gade, *Poetry from the Kings' Sagas*, vol. 2, *From c.1035 to 1300*, pp. 731–32.

26. On Anglo-Saxon kennings, see Wilhelm Bode, *Die Kenningar in der angelsächsischen Dichtung*; James Walter Rankin, "A Study of the Kennings in Anglo-Saxon Poetry"; Hendrik van der Merwe Scholz, *The Kenning in Anglo-Saxon and Old Norse Poetry*; and Thomas Gardner, "The Old English Kenning: A Characteristic Feature of Germanic Poetical Diction?"

27. Andreas Heusler, *Altgermanische Dichtung*, p. 136.

28. *Ibid.*, p. 137.

29. To the play of metaphor, which substitutes one term for another by "denotation," the kenning thus adds a play of metonymy, which functions by "connotation," thus joining paradigmatic and syntagmatic processes. See Bjarne Fidjestøl, "The Kenning System: An Attempt at a Linguistic Analysis," esp. p. 22.

30. See Gardiner, "The Old English Kenning."

31. Frank, *Old Norse Court Poetry*, p. 42.

32. *Ibid.*, p. 45.

33. Snorri Sturluson, *Edda: Hátttal*, ed. Anthony Faulkes, 2, p. 5.11; English in Faulkes, *Edda*, p. 168.

34. *Ibid.*

35. Gordon, *An Introduction to Old Norse*, p. xl.

36. Jorge Luis Borges, "Las Kenningar," pp. 42, 35, 53.

37. Frank, *Old Norse Court Poetry*, p. 28.

38. Borges, "Las Kenningar," p. 50.

39. Gordon, *An Introduction to Old Norse*, p. xi. Cf. Frederic Amory, "Towards A Grammatical Classification of Kennings as Compounds," which builds in large part on this hypothesis.

40. On the literary system of the kennings, see Edith Marold, *Kenningkunst:*

Ein Beitrag zu einer Poetik der Skaldendichtung. For an analysis of the kennings as forming a linguistic system, see Fidjestøl, "The Kenning System: An Attempt at a Linguistic Analysis." Cf. the synthetic perspective offered by Gary Holland, "Kennings, Metaphors, and Semantic Formulae in Norse *dróttkvætt.*"

41. Snorri Sturluson, *Skáldskaparmál* 57, in Faulkes, *Edda*, vol. 1, p. 3.5–8; English in Faulkes, *Edda*, p. 61.

42. *Ibid.* The phrase "í runum" could also mean "in writing." On *rûn*, see Jan de Vries, Altnordisches etymologisches Wörterbuch, pp. 453–54.

CHAPTER SIX: RIDDLES

1. See *Oxford English Dictionary*, s.v. "secret."

2. Archer Taylor, "The Riddle," p. 141.

3. John C. Messenger, Jr., "Anang Proverb-Riddles," p. 226.

4. John Blacking, "The Social Value of Venda Riddles," p. 5.

5. Lyndon Harries, "The Riddle in Africa," pp. 379–80.

6. For Plato's definition of the riddle, see Plato, *Charmides*, 161c–d; cf. Aristotle, *Poetics* 1458a26–30. On the rhetoric of the enigma, see Eleanor Cook, *Enigmas and Riddles in Literature*, esp. pp. 27–63.

7. Taylor, "The Riddle," p. 129.

8. For the riddle, see Archer Taylor, *English Riddles from Oral Tradition*, 277a; for the commentary, see Robert A. Georges and Alan Dundes, "Towards a Structural Definition of the Riddle," p. 112.

9. George and Dundes, "Towards a Structural Definition of the Riddle," p. 113.

10. See, for example, Charles T. Scott, *Persian and Arabic Riddles: A Language-Centered Approach to Genre Definition*, p. 8.

11. For Frege's distinction, see Gottlob Frege, "Über Sinn und Bedeutung," *Zeitschrift für Philosophie und philosophische Kritik*, pp. 25–50; reprinted in Gottlob Frege, *Funktion, Begriff, Bedeutung*, pp. 40–65.

12. *Rig Veda* 1.164. In Wendy Doniger's edition and translation, *The Rig Veda*, it is called the "Riddle of the Sacrifice." See pp. 71–83. On the "Riddle Hymn," see Walter Porzig, "Das Rätsel im Rigveda: Ein Beitrag zum Kapitel Sondersprache"; and Jan E. M. Houben, "Ritual Pragmatics of a Vedic Hymn: The 'Riddle Hymn' and the Pravargya Ritual."

13. Porzig, "Das Rätsel im Rigveda," p. 654.

14. *Ibid.*, p. 655.

15. *Rig Veda* 1.164.45. Text and translation in George Thompson, "The Brahmodya and Vedic Discourse," p. 15; for a different English translation, see Doniger, *The Rig Veda*, p. 80.

16. Porzig, "Das Rätsel im Rigveda," p. 654.

17. *Ibid.*, p. 656.

18. Andreas Heusler, *Das Altgermanische Dichtung*, pp. 131–32.

19. John Lindow, "Riddles, Kennings, and the Complexity of Skaldic Poetry," p. 312.

20. Hugo Gering, cited in Henry Adams Bellows, *The Poetic Edda*, p. 183.

21. *Alvíssmál*, 9–10, in Finnur Jónsson, *De gamle Eddadigte*, p. 133.

22. Andy Orchard (trans.), *The Elder Edda: A Book of Viking Lore*, p. 109.

23. Several hypotheses have been advanced for the reasons of the transformation. See Paul Acker, "Dwarf Love in Alvíssmál," in Paul Acker and Carolyne Larrington, (eds.), *The Poetic Edda: Essays on Old Norse Mythology.*

24. On the principles that govern this identity, see the illuminating paper by Lennart Moberg, "The Languages of Alvíssmál." Cf. Rudolf Meissner, "Die Sprache der götter, riesend und zwerge in den Alvissmal."

25. Jónsson, *De gamle Eddadigte*, p. 55.

26. *Vafþrúðnismál*, 11–12, in Orchard, trans., *The Elder Edda*, p. 41.

27. Christopher Tolkien (trans.), *Saga Heiðreks konungs ins vitra: The Saga of King Heidrek the Wise*, (58), pp. 38–39.

28. See Carolyne Larrington, "Vafþrúðnismál and Grímnismál: Cosmic History, Cosmic Geography," p. 63.

29. Anders Hultgård, "The Wisdom Contest in the *Vafþrúðnismál*," pp. 536–38.

30. On the *brahomdya*, see Ernest Renou and Lilian Silburn, "Sur la notion de *bráhman*"; Thompson, "The Brahmodya and Vedic Discourse"; and Tat'jana Jakovlevna Elizarenkova and Vladimir Nikolaevič Toporov, "Zum vedischen Rätsel des Typs Brahmodya," in Eismann, and Grzybek (eds.), *Semiotische Studien zum Rätsel: Simple Forms Reconsidered II*, pp. 39–73. On Sanskrit riddles more generally, see Ludwik Sternbach, *Indian Riddles: A Forgotten Chapter in the History of Sanskrit Literature.*

31. Thompson, "The Brahmodya and Vedic Discourse," p. 14; cf. Renou, "Sur la notion du *bráhman*," p. 97.

32. Thompson, "The Brahmodya and Vedic Discourse," p. 17.

33. *Vajasaneyi Samhita* 23.61–62 (a quotation of *Rig Veda* 164.34–46), cited in

Thompson, "The Brahmodya and Vedic Discourse," p. 17.

34. Tolkien (trans.), *Saga Heiðreks konungs ins vitra*, p. 44. The same question appears at the end of the *Vafþrúðnismál* (54), suggesting, as many scholars have pointed out, a link between the two literary contests in wisdom.

35. *Ibid.*

36. See W. J. Pepicello and Thomas A. Green, *The Language of Riddles: New Perspectives*, who distinguish systematically, in similar terms, between the "metaphorical" and the "grammatical."

37. Archer, *English Riddles*, 587 B, discussed in Pepicello and Green, *The Language of Riddles*, p. 215.

38. See the helpful treatment in Pepicello and Green, *The Language of Riddles*, p. 27.

39. *Ibid.*, p. 37.

40. *Ibid.*, p. 38.

41. *Ibid.*, p. 35.

42. *Ibid.*, p. 45.

43. *Ibid.*, p. 34.

44. Miguel de Cervantes Saavedra, *La Galatea*, p. 245.

45. See Dan Pagis, *'Al sod ḥatum: Le-toldot ha-ḥidah ha-'Ivrit be-Iṭalyah uve-Holand*, p. 248.

46. Dan Pagis, "Towards a Theory of the Literary Riddle," p. 87.

47. *Ibid.*, pp. 87–90.

48. *Ibid.*, p. 88.

49. So, too, the similarly formed "Me lo dico, me lo ripeto, me lo torno a dir di nuovo, e se non lo capirò, testa d'asino sarò; indovina che cos'è?" (*il melo*), "Te lo dico, te lo provo, te Lo torno a dir di nuovo, e se tu non lo capirai, testa d'asino sarai; indovina che cos'è?" (*il telo*).

50. Osip Maksimovich Brik, "Zvukovye povtory," in *Two Essays on Poetic Language*, p. 131; Roman Jakobson, "Subliminal Verbal Patterning in Poetry," in *Selected Writings*, vol. 3, pp. 140–43; Aleksandr Iosivič Gerbstman, "O zvukovom stroenii naradnoj zagadki."

51. Tzvetan Todorov, *Les genres du discours*, p. 245.

52. Elizarenkova and Toporov, "Zum vedischen Rätsel des Typs Brahmodya"; Vladimir Milicic, "Subliminal Structures in Folklore: Anagrammatized Answers to Riddles," pp. 63–76. The term "anagrammatic," while commonly employed,

may be misleading; it suggests letters (*grammata*), while many of the traditions in question developed in the absence of systems of writing. On "anagrammatic riddles," see also Vladimir Nikolaevič Toporov, "Das Anagramm im Rätsel," in Eismann and Grzybek (eds.), *Semiotische Studien zum Rätsel: Simple Forms Reconsidered* II, pp. 181–90.

53. Milicic, p. 75. Milicic gives eleven examples, which, as he indicates, he culls from the set of thirty-four riddles published by David Evans in his "Riddling and the Structure of Context."

CHAPTER SEVEN: NOMINA DIVINA

1. For a helpful summary of the corpus, see M. L. West, commentary to 831, in *Hesiod*, pp. 368–88. On the Greek language of the gods, see Hermann Güntert, *Von der Sprache der Götter und Geister: Bedeutungsgeschichtliche Untersuchungen zur homerischen und eddischen Göttersprache*; Alfred Heubeck, "Die homerische Göttersprache"; Calvert Watkins, "Language of Gods and Language of Men: Remarks on Some Indo-European Metalinguistic Traditions"; Romano Lazzeroni, "Lingua degli dei e lingua degli uomini"; José Calderéon Felices, "Lengua de los dioses / Lengua de los hombres"; Ann Suter, "Language of Gods and Language of Men: The Case of Paris / Alexandros"; and Françoise Bader, *La langue des dieux ou l'hermetisme des poètes indo-européens*.

2. Bader, *La langue des dieux*, p. 191.

3. Homer, *Iliad* 1.403–404.

4. *Ibid.*, 2.813–14.

5. *Ibid.*, 14.290–91.

6. *Ibid.*, 20.72–74.

7. Homer, *Odyssey* 10.305–306.

8. *Ibid.*, 12.61.

9. Eusthatius 1658.53, cited in Jenny Clay, "The Planktai and Moly: Divine Naming and Knowing in Homer," p. 128.

10. *Ibid.*

11. Plato, *Cratylus* 391d4.

12. On the passage, see among others, John E. Joseph, *Limiting the Arbitrary: Linguistic Naturalism and Its Opposites in Plato's* Cratylus *and Modern Theories of Language*, pp. 39–58.

13. J. van Leeuwen, "Homerica XVI: De lingua deorum."

14. H. Jacobsohn, "Aeolische Doppelconsonanz: Zur Sprache und Verstechnik des Homerischen Epos," pp. 81–84.

15. Paul Kretschmer, review of Güntert, *Von der Sprache der Götter und Geister.*

16. Antoine Meillet, review of Hermann Güntert, *Von der Sprache der Götter und Geister,* p. 56.

17. Romano Lazzeroni, "Lingua degli dei e lingua degli uomini," pp. 14–15.

18. Jakob Grimm, *Deutsche Mythologie,* vol. 1, p. 275.

19. *Ibid.,* p. 276. For special studies of the languages of the *Alvíssmál,* see Lennart Moberg, "The Languages of *Alvíssmál,*" and Rudolf Meissner, "Die Sprache der götter, riesend und zwerge in den Alvissmal."

20. Güntert, *Von der Sprache der Götter und Geister.*

21. *Ibid.,* pp. 110–11; cf. p. 153.

22. *Ibid.,* p. 170.

23. *Ibid.* pp. 157–58.

24. *Ibid.,* p. 158.

25. *Rig Veda* 1.164.45.

26. M. L. West, *Indo-European Poetry and Myth,* p. 161.

27. *Ibid.*

28. *Śatapatha Brāhmaṇa* 1.1.4.4. For a translation, see West, *Indo-European Poetry and Myth,* p. 161.

29. Calvert Watkins, *How to Kill a Dragon: Aspects of Indo-European Poetics,* p. 265. On the Aśvamedha, see *ibid.,* "The Aśvamedha or Horse Sacrifice: An Indo-European Liturgical Form," pp. 265–76.

30. *Śatapatha-Brāhmaṇa* 10.6.4.1. See Vladimir N. Toporov, "Die indoeuropäische Poetik und ihre Ursprünge," p. 204. See also Bader, *La langue des dieux,* pp. 248–49.

31. West, *Indo-European Poetry and Myth,* p. 161.

32. See Watkins, "Language of Gods and Language of Men," pp. 5–6; Güntert, *Von der Sprachen der Götter und der Geister,* p. 132; Toporov, "Die indoeuropäische Poetik und ihre Ursprünge," pp. 204–205; Bader, *La langue des dieux,* pp. 248–49.

33. E. Laroche, "Hattic Deities and their Epithets," p. 188.

34. Johannes Friedrich, "Göttersprache und Menschensprache im hethitischen Schriftum," p. 139. Cf. Lazzeroni, "La lingua degli dei," pp. 18–23; Watkins, "Language of Gods and Language of Men," pp. 7–8; Bader, *La langue des dieux,* pp. 244–45.

35. See Hermann Güntert, *Über die ahurischen und daēvischen Ausdrücke im Awesta: Eine semasiologische Studie*, as well as the critical remarks in Émile Benveniste, "Une différenciation de vocabulaire dans l'Avesta." Cf. Bader, *La langue des dieux*, pp. 246–47.

36. See George Calder (ed.), *Auraicept na N-Éces: The Scholar's Primer, Being the Texts of the Ogham Tract from the Book of Ballymote and the Yellow Book of Lecan, and the Text of the Trefhocul from the Book of Leinster.*

37. Watkins, "Language of Gods and Language of Men," p. 9, which cites the long version of the *Yellow Book of Lecan* (4554–56).

38. Watkins, *How to Kill a Dragon*, p. 181.

39. See West, *Indo-European Poetry and Myth*, p. 160.

40. Bader, *La langue des dieux*, p. 248.

41. That there are elaborate non–Indo-European traditions of the "language of gods" may also be worth recalling. See the comparative study, Marcel Detienne and Gilbert Hamonic, et al. (eds.), *La déesse parole: Quatre figures de la langue des dieux.*

42. Watkins, "Language of the Gods and Language of Men," p. 2.

43. See Roman Jakobson's influential formulation, "Signe zéro," in *Selected Writings*, vol. 2, pp. 211–19, which rests, as Jakobson makes clear, on Saussure's famous principle that language can content itself with the opposition of something and nothing (*Cours de linguistique générale*, p. 124).

44. Watkins, "Language of the Gods and Language of Men," p. 7.

45. *Ibid.*, p. 11.

46. Walter Porzig, "Die Rätsel im Rigveda," p. 656.

CHAPTER EIGHT: NOMINA SACRA

1. C. Suetonius Tranquillus, *De vitae caeserum*, *Divus Julius*, 56.6; English in *The Lives of the Twelve Caesars*, p. 80.

2. C. Suetonius Tranquillus, *De vitae caeserum*, *Divus Augustus*, 88.3; *The Lives of the Twelve Caesars*, p. 257. On the two Caesars' "ciphers," see Albert C. Leighton, "Secret Communication among the Greeks and Romans," pp. 152–53.

3. For *Shesakh* in place of *Bavel*, see Jeremiah 25:26 and 51:41. Perplexed by the reasons for the procedure, Wilhelm Gesenius already raised doubts about its existence in the prophetic text: "Assuming, but not conceding, that this secret language is really so old, one can still see no reason why in 51, 41 Babylon should

be called once by its true name and the other time by a concealed name." See his *Hebräisches und chaldäisches Handwörterbuch über das Alte Testament*, s.v. "ššk." For a more recent discussion that argues in support of the antiquity of atbash, see Richard C. Steiner, "The Two Sons of Neriah and the Two Editions of Jeremiah in the Light of Two Atbash Code-Words for Babylon," pp. 81–84. On related practices in the ancient world, see Aaron Demsky, "A Proto-Canaanite Abecedary Dating from the Period of the Judges and Its Implications for the History of the Alphabet," pp. 19–20.

4. Virgilius Maro, *Epitomae* 10.4–9, in *Virgilius Maro Grammaticus: Opera omnia*, p. 213. For a discussion of Virgilius's teachings on the subject, see Vivian Law, *Wisdom, Authority and Grammar in the Seventh Century*, pp. 84–88.

5. See Charles Malamoud, *Cuire le monde: Rite et pensée dans l'Inde ancienne*, p. 242.

6. See *ibid.*, p. 243.

7. Jan Gonda, *Notes on Names and the Name of God in Ancient India*, p. 81.

8. Malamoud, *Cuire le monde*, p. 243.

9. *Ibid.*

10. *Ibid.*, p. 244. *Aitareya-Āraṇyaka* 2.4.3; *Aitareya-Upaniṣad* 3.13ff.

11. *Ibid.* Text in *Śatapatha-Brāhmaṇa*, 6.1.1.11.

12. *Ibid.*, p. 245.

13. *Ibid.*, p. 246. *Aitareya-Brāhmaṇa* 3.33, English p. 219.

14. Malamoud, *Cuire le monde*, p. 246.

15. *Ibid.*, p. 248.

16. Charles Malamoud, *Le jumeau solaire*, p. 131. On writing and speech in classical India more generally, see *ibid.*, pp. 127–49; Charles Malamoud, *Féminité de la parole: Études sur l'Inde classique*, pp. 61–91.

17. *Gopatha-Brāhmaṇa*, 1.31. Cited in Malamoud, *Le jumeau solaire*, p. 142.

18. Kumārila, *Tantravārtikka* ad *Jaimini-Sūdra*, 1.3.7. Cited in Malamoud, *Le jumeau solaire*, p. 142.

19. Malamoud, *Féminité de la parole*, p. 63.

20. Strabo 15.1.53; English in *The Geography of Strabo*, vol. 7, pp. 87–89.

21. See the analytic commentary on Megasthenes *apud* Strabo in Harry Falk, *Schrift im alten Indien: Ein Forschungsbericht mit Anmerkungen*, pp. 291–93. On the history of writing in ancient India more generally, see Gérard Fussman, "Histoire du monde indien: Les premiers systèmes d'écriture en Inde." On the status of

books in classical India, see Malamoud, *Le jumeau solaire*, p. 128.

22. Edward C. Sachau, *Alberuni's India: An Account of the Religion, Philosophy, Literature, Geography, Chronology, Astronomy, Customs, Laws and Astrology of India about A.D. 1030*, vol. 1, pp. 125–26.

23. Julius Caesar, *De bello gallico*, 6.13; English in *Commentaries on the Gallic and Civil Wars, with the Supplementary Books Attributed to Hirtius, Including the Alexandrian, African and Spanish Wars.*

24. *Ibid.*, 6.14.

25. *Ibid.*

26. See, for instance, Georges Dumézil, "La tradition druidique et l'écriture," pp. 125–33.

27. Tacitus, *Germania* 10.1, in *Cornelii Taciti De Germania*, ed. Henry Furneaux; English in *The Complete Works of Tacitus*, p. 713.

28. On the semantic field of Old English *run* and its cognates, see R. I. Page, *An Introduction to English Runes*, pp. 106–107.

29. *Ibid.*; for a less skeptical position, see R. W. V. Elliott, *Runes*, pp. 65–66. On runes and magic, see Karl Martin Nielsen, "Runen und Magie: Ein forschungsgeschichtliche Überblick"; and, for Anglo-Saxon runes in particular, I. A. Page, "Anglo-Saxon Runes and Magic."

30. René Derolez, *Runica manuscripta: The English Tradition*, pp. 354–55.

31. Robert DiNapoli, "Odd Characters: Runes in Old English Poetry," p. 148.

32. Riddle 58, lines 14–15, in Craig Williamson (ed.), *The Old English Riddles of the Exeter Book*, p. 102.

33. The solution would appear to be *radrod*, "well sweep," a tool for drawing water. See Williamson, *The Old English Riddles of the Exeter Book*, p. 312; cf. John D. Niles, *Old English Enigmatic Poems and the Play of the Texts*, pp. 89–92.

34. Patrick J. Murphy, *Unriddling the Exeter Riddles*, p. 65. On the use of runes in the Exeter riddles, see also Dieter Bitterli, *Say What I Am Called: The Old English Riddles of the Exeter Book and the Anglo-Latin Riddle Tradition*, esp. pp. 84–97.

35. Ludwig Traube, *Nomina sacra: Versuch einer Geschichte der christlichen Kürzung.*

36. *Ibid.*, p. 24.

37. W. M. Lindsay, "Traube's Nomina Sacra and Posthumous Works," p. 133.

38. Traube, *Nomina sacra*, p. 33. The manuscript is Primasius, Oxford Douce 140.

39. *Ibid.*, p. 284.

40. Antoine Meillet, "Quelques hypothèses sur des interdictions de vocabulaire dans les langues indo-européennes," in *Linguistique historique et linguistique générale*, p. 281.

41. *Ibid.*

42. Émile Benveniste, "La blasphémie et l'euphémie," in *Problèmes de linguisique générale*, vol. 2, p. 257. The article first appeared in 1969. Cf. his "Euphémismes anciens et modernes," in *Problèmes de linguistique générale*, vol. 1, pp. 308–14.

43. Benveniste, "La blasphémie et l'euphémie," p. 257.

44. H. L. Mencken, "American Profanity," p. 243. The examples (*ibid.*, pp. 242–43) are drawn from M. L. Walter's *Dictionary of Profanity and Its Substitutes*, which Mencken consulted in a special collection of the Princeton University Library.

CHAPTER NINE: ANAPHONES

1. Ferdinand de Saussure, Letter of January 10, 1906, to Antoine Meillet, in Émile Benveniste, "Lettres de Ferdinand de Saussure à Antoine Meillet," p. 105.

2. Ferdinand de Saussure, Letter of January 23, 1906, to Antoine Meillet in Benveniste, "Lettres de Ferdinand de Saussure," p. 106.

3. For more recent work on the Saturnian, see Thomas Cole, "The Saturnian Verse"; and Jed Parsons, "A New Approach to the Saturnian Verse and Its Relation to Latin Prosody."

4. Horace, *Epistles* 2.1.157.

5. For a summary of the debate, see Frank Frost Abbott, "The Accent in Vulgar and Formal Latin."

6. Saussure, Letter of September 23, 1907 to Meillet, in Benveniste, "Lettres de Ferdinand de Saussure," p. 109.

7. Peter Wunderli, "Ferdinand de Saussure, *1er cahier à lire préliminairement*: Ein Basistext seiner Anagrammstudien," p. 204.

8. Ferdinand de Saussure, Letter of July 5, 1906, in Aldo L. Prosdocimi and Anna Marinetti, "Saussure e il saturnio: Tra scienza, biografia e storiografia," p. 43.

9. *Ibid.*

10. Ferdinand de Saussure, Letter of July 17, 1906, in Prosdocimi and Marinenetti, "Saussure e il saturnio," pp. 45–46.

11. *Ibid.*, p. 51.

12. *Ibid.*, p. 52.

13. Ferdinand de Saussure, Ms. 3962.7.20 v, reproduced in Prosdocimi and Marinetti, "Saussure e il saturnio," p. 56.

14. For Saussure's self-diagnosed "graphophobia," see Paola Villani, "Documenti saussuriani conservati a Lipsia e a Berlino," p. 26. Elsewhere, Saussure evokes his "horror of writing" (*ibid.*, p. 24).

15. The *Course* now exists in several forms. For a critical edition of the 1916 text, see Ferdinand de Saussure, *Cours de linguistique générale*. On the textual composition of the *Course*, see Robert Godel, *Les sources manuscrites du Cours de linguistique générale de F. de Saussure*. Cf. the critical edition by Robert Engler, Saussure, *Édition critique du Cours de linguistique générale de Ferdinand de Saussure*, with the supplementary view provided by Eisuke Komatsu and George Wolf (eds.), in Saussure, *Saussure's First Course of Lectures in General Linguistics*; *Saussure's Second Course of Lectures in General Linguistics*; and *Saussure's Third Course of Lectures in General Linguistics*.

16. Jean Starobinski, *Les mots sous les mots: Les anagrammes de Ferdinand Saussure*. Robert Godel was the first to evoke 99 anagram notebooks: see his "Inventaire des manuscrits de F. de Saussure remis à la Bibliothèque publique et universitaire de Genève," p. 11. Michel Dupuis, in his account of the Geneva manuscripts, puts the number of anagram notebooks at 117: Dupuis, "À propos des anagrammes saussuriennes," pp. 11–12. W. Terrence Gordon and Henry G. Schogt count 134 notebooks: "Ferdinand de Saussure: The Anagrams and the *Cours*," p. 140.

17. William Camden, *Remaines concerning Britaine: But especially England, and the Inhabitants thereof*, p. 168.

18. See Christine Luz, *Technopaignia: Formspiele in der griechischen Dichtung*, pp. 147–78.

19. *Ibid.*, p. 150.

20. Ferdinand de Saussure, Letter of July 14, 1906, in Starobinski, *Les mots sous les mots*, p. 21.

21. *Ibid.*

22. *Ibid.* p. 22.

23. Ferdinand de Saussure, Lettter of September 23, 1907, in Benveniste, "Lettres de Ferdinand de Saussure," p. 110.

24. *Ibid.* Livius Andronicus 18.1–2.

25. Saussure, Letter of September 23, 1907, in Benveniste, "Lettres de Ferdinand de Saussure," pp. 110–11.

26. Saussure, Letter of July 14, 1906, in Starobinski, *Les mots sous les mots*, p. 21.

27. Saussure, Letter of September 23, 1907, in Benveniste, "Lettres de Ferdinand de Saussure," p. 111.

28. Saussure, Letter of July 17, 1906, in Prosdocimi and Marinetti, "Saussure e il saturnio," pp. 52–53.

29. Starobinski, *Les mots sous les mots*, pp. 134 and 133.

30. *Ibid.*, p. 36.

31. Ferdinand de Saussure, Letter to Meillet of September 27, 1907, in Benveniste, "Lettres de Ferdinand de Saussure," p. 114.

32. On metathesis, see Peter Wunderli, *Ferdinand de Saussure und die Anagramme: Linguistik und Literatur*, p. 38.

33. Starobinski, *Les mots sous les mots*, p. 47.

34. *Ibid.*, p. 47.

35. This diagram is drawn from Peter Wunderli, "Saussure's Anagrams and the Analysis of Literary Texts," p. 177.

36. Saussure, Letter of September 23, 1907, in Benveniste, "Lettres de Ferdinand de Saussure," p. 110.

37. See Wunderli, *Ferdinand de Saussure und die Anagramme*, pp. 20–21.

38. Starobinski, *Les mots sous les mots*, p. 50.

39. See *ibid.*, pp. 50–55.

40. *Ibid.*, p. 51.

41. Saussure, Letter of September 23, 1907, in Benveniste, "Lettres de Ferdinand de Saussure," p. 113.

42. Starobinski, *Les mots sous les mots*, p. 37. On Saussure's notebooks on Vedic hymns, see David Shepheard, "Saussure's Vedic Anagrams," pp. 513–23.

43. See Starobinski, *Les mots sous les mots*, pp. 79–100; on Saussure's work on Lucretius, see Francis Gandon, *De dangereux édifices: Saussure lecteur de Lucrèce, Les cahiers d'anagrammes consacrés au De rerum natura*.

44. Starobinski, *Les mots sous les mots*, p. 27.

45. On the hypogram, see Wunderli, *Ferdinand de Saussure und die Anagramme*, pp. 46–51.

46. For Saussure's terms, see Wunderli, *Ferdinand de Saussure und die Anagramme*, pp. 42–54; cf. Gandon's glossary in *De sangereux édifices*, pp. 381–93.

47. Starobinski, *Les mots sous les mots*, pp. 69 and 78; see also the manuscript (*ms. fr.* 3964) cited in Wunderli, *Ferdinand de Saussure und die Anagramme*, p. 51. Gandon (*De dangereux édifices*, p. 16) holds that "cryogram" is synonymous with "anagram."

48. Ferdinand de Saussure, Letter of August 7, 1906, "Correspondance Bally-Saussure," Cahiers Ferdinand de Saussure 48 (1994), p. 115.

49. Gandon, *De dangereux édifices*, p. 116.

50. Starobinski, *Les mots sous les mots*, pp. 100–107.

51. Wunderli, "Ferdinand de Saussure, *1er cahier à lire préliminairement*," p. 212.

52. Starobinski, *Les mots sous les mots*, p. 60.

53. *Ibid.*, p. 125.

54. Wunderli, *Ferdinand de Saussure und die Anagramme*, p. 15.

55. Starobinski, *Les mots sous les mots*, p. 59.

56. On the distinction between the synchronic (or "idiosynchronic") and the "diachronic," see Saussure, *Cours de linguistique générale*, pp. 114–40.

57. Starobinski, *Les mots sous les mots*, p. 133.

58. On the status of the sign in the *Course*, see, among others, Jean-Claude Milner, *Le périple structural: Figures et paradigme*, pp. 15–44; Françoise Gadet, *Saussure: Une science de la langue*, pp. 29–48; Simon Bouquet, *Introduction à la lecture de Ferdinand de Saussure*, pp. 279–91. Cf. the materials collected in Ferdinand de Saussure, *Écrits de linguistique générale* and Saussure, *Ferdinand de Saussure: Linguistik und Semiologie: Notizen aus dem Nachlaß, Texte Briefe und Dokumente*.

59. Jean-Claude Milner, *L'amour de la langue*, pp. 85–97.

60. *Ibid.*, p. 89.

61. On Saussure's principle of linearity, see Wunderli, *Ferdinand de Saussure und die Anagramme*, pp. 178–85; and Wunderli, "Zur Geltung des Linearitätsprinzips bei Saussure." The principle has been questioned. For a critical appraisal, see Jean-Claude Milner, *Introduction à une science du langage*, pp. 385–95.

62. Saussure, *Cours de linguistique générale*, p. 103.

63. *Ibid.*, p. 170.

64. Starobinski, *Les mots sous les mots*, p. 47.

65. Saussure, Letter of September 23, 1907, in Benveniste, "Lettres de Ferdinand de Saussure," p. 113; Letter to Bally, July 17, 1906, in Prosdocimi and Marinetti, "Saussure e il saturnio," p. 53.

66. Ferdinand de Saussure Letter to Meillet, January 8, 1908, in Benveniste,

"Lettres de Ferdinand de Saussure," p. 118.

67. See Gandon, *De dangereux édifices*, p. 18.

68. For the "furor of phonic play," see Saussure, Letter to Meillet, January 8, 1908, in Benveniste, "Lettres de Ferdinand de Saussure," p. 118.

69. See Starobinski, *Les mots sous les mots*, pp. 146–48. Saussure mistakenly believed Thompson lived within a generation of his own time.

70. Milner, *L'amour de la langue*, p. 88.

71. See Starobinski, *Les mots sous les mots*, pp. 115–20.

72. *Ibid.*, p. 154. For the correspondence with Pascoli, see also Giuseppe Nava, "Lettres de Ferdinand de Saussure à Giovanni Pascoli."

73. Starobinski, *Les mots sous les mots*, p. 151.

74. *Ibid.*, pp. 133 and 128.

75. Saussure alludes at several points to a calculus of probabilities: see Starobinski, *Les mots sous les mots*, pp. 50, 128–32, 133; and Saussure, Letter of September 23, 1907, in Benveniste, "Lettres de Ferdinand de Saussure," p. 112.

76. "The Two Saussures" was the title of a special issue of *Recherches* devoted to the anagram notebooks in 1975, edited by Sylvère Lotringer. See his introduction, "Flagrant délire."

77. Starobinski, *Les mots sous les mots*, p. 154.

78. For "madness," see Michel Deguy, "La folie de Saussure"; for "dementia," see Jean-Jacques Lecercle, *The Violence of Language*, p. 30; for "schizophrenia," see Luce Iragaray, "Le schizophrène et la question du signe." Recently, Gandon (*De dangereux édifices*, p. 69) has evoked "obsession."

79. For an annotated bibliography, see Ivan Callus, "A Chronological and Annotated Bibliography of Works Referring to Ferdinand de Saussure's Anagram Notebooks," Cahiers Ferdinand de Saussure 55 (2002), pp. 269–95.

80. John E. Joseph, *Saussure*, p. 488. For a different account of the importance of the anagram research in the development of Saussure's linguistic theory, see Bouquet, *Introduction à une lecture de Ferdinand de Saussure*, pp. 79–80 n. 5.

81. Roman Jakobson and Linda Waugh, assisted by Martha Taylor, *The Sound Shape of Language*, p. 221.

82. Elizarenkova, *Language and Style of the Vedic Ṛṣis*, p. 124.

83. See in particular, Vladimir Toporov, "Die indoeuropäische Poetik und ihre Ursprünge," pp. 189–251; Françoise Bader, *Anagrammes et allitérations*; Ranko Matasović, *A Theory of Textual Reconstruction in Indo-European Linguistics*, pp.

114–28; and Joshua T. Katz, "Wordplay" and "Saussure's Anaphonie."

84. Jean Starobinski, "Lettres et syllabes mobiles: Complément à la lecture des *Cahiers* d'anagrammes de Ferdinand de Saussure," p. 8.

85. Starobinski, *Les mots sous les mots*, p. 135.

86. *Ibid.*

87. See *ibid.*, p. 133.

88. *Ibid.*, p. 135.

CHAPTER TEN: PATTERNS

1. Robert Godel, "Inventaire des manuscrits de F. de Saussure remis à la Bibliothèque publique et universitaire de Genève," p. 11.

2. Jean Starobinski, "Les anagrammes de Ferdinand de Saussure."

3. Jean Starobinski, "Les mots sous les mots."

4. Roman Jakobson, "La première Lettre de Ferdinand de Saussure sur les anagrammes."

5. *Ibid.*, p. 21.

6. Roman Jakobson, "Retrospect," in *Selected Writings*, vol. 4, p. 685.

7. Jakobson, "La première Lettre de Ferdinand de Saussure," p. 21.

8. *Ibid.*

9. *Ibid.* Jakobson's reference is to Starobinski, "Les anagrammes de Ferdinand de Saussure," p. 256.

10. Jakobson, "La première Lettre de Ferdinand de Saussure," p. 22.

11. See Starobinski, "Le mots sous les mots," p. 1907.

12. Roman Jakobson, "Retrospect," in *Selected Writings*, vol. 5, p. 570.

13. See Jakobson's account in his retrospective "Vers une science de l'art poétique," in *Selected Writings*, vol. 5, pp. 241–44.

14. Roman Jakobson, "What is Poetry?," in *Selected* Writings, vol. 3, p. 750.

15. Roman Jakobson, "Linguistics and Poetics," first published in Thomas A. Sebeok (ed.), *Style and Language*; it appears in *Selected Writings*, vol. 3, pp. 18–51.

16. See *ibid.*, pp. 21–22.

17. *Ibid.*, p. 24.

18. *Ibid.*, p. 25.

19. *Ibid.*, p. 27.

20. See Ferdinand de Saussure, *Cours de linguistique générale*, pt. 2, ch. 5, pp. 170–76.

21. *Ibid.* p. 171.

22. Jakobson, "Linguistics and Poetics," in *Selected Writings*, vol. 3, p. 27.

23. *Ibid.*

24. *Ibid.*

25. Edgar Allan Poe, "The Rationale of Verse," in *Essays and Reviews*, p. 33.

26. Jakobson, "Linguistics and Poetics," in *Selected Writings*, vol. 3, p. 39.

27. Gerard Manley Hopkins, *Journals and Papers*, p. 85, cited by Jakobson in "Linguistics and Poetics," *Selected Writings*, vol. 3, p. 39.

28. Letter of July 14, 1906, in Jean Starobinski, *Les mots sous les mots*, p. 21.

29. Roman Jakobson and Linda Waugh, *The Sound Shape of Language*, p. 221. The reference is to Starobinski, *Les mots sous les mots*, pp. 21–23 and 33.

30. Perhaps for this reason, Jakobson could go so far as to suggest that arithmetical regularities could, in themselves, play a functional role in verse. See, for example, Roman Jakobson, "Shakespeare's Verbal Art in Th'Expense of Spirit," in *Selected Writings*, vol. 3, pp. 284–303. Of course, if one reasons in modern terms, incommensurable quantities may also be considered to fall within the domain of arithmetic. Yet Jakobson appears not to have considered the possibility that quantities of this kind could play a role in verse.

31. Starobinski, *Les mots sous les mots*, p. 47.

32. Roman Jakobson, *Six Lectures on Sound and Meaning*, in *Selected Writings*, vol. 8, pp. 378–79.

33. Saussure, *Cours de linguistique générale*, pt. 2, ch. 5, p. 170.

34. See, Jakobson, *Six Lectures on Sound and Meaning*, in *Selected Writings*, vol. 8, pp. 378–79; for a later presentation, see *The Sound Shape of Language*, pp. 122–76.

35. In this sense, Jakobson's theory of the phoneme constitutes an example of the structuralist procedure. It may be even its clearest illustration. See Jean-Claude Milner, *Le périple structural: Figures et paradigme*.

36. Jakobson, *Six Lectures on Sound and Meaning*, in *Selected Writings*, vol. 8, p. 380.

37. For a summary presentation, see John J. McCarthy, "Nonlinear Phonology."

38. Jakobson, "Language in Operation," in *Selected Writings*, vol. 3, p. 11. Jakobson refers to Roland G. Kent, "Assimilation and Dissimilation."

39. Jakobson, "Retrospect," in *Selected Writings*, vol. 3, p. 775.

40. Edgar Allan Poe, "The Philosophy of Composition," in *Essays and Reviews*, p. 18.

41. Jakobson, "Linguistics and Poetics," in *Selected Writings*, vol. 3, p. 43. Cf. the more extended discussion in Jakobson, "Language in Operation," *ibid.*, pp. 7–17.

42. Poe, "The Philosophy of Composition," *Essays and Reviews*, p. 18.

43. Roman Jakobson, "Subliminal Verbal Patterning in Poetry," in *Selected Writings*, vol. 3, p. 138.

44. Roman See Jakobson, "Une Microscopie du dernier 'Spleen' dans *Les fleurs du Mal*," in *Selected Writings*, vol. 3, pp. 465–81.

45. Roman Jakobson, "Shakespeare's Verbal Art," in *Selected Writings*, vol. 3, p. 300.

46. See, for example, Jakobson and Lévi-Strauss's suggestion that the unvoiced fricative /ch/ plays a remarkable role in its near absence from Baudelaire's sonnet: "*Les Chats* de Charles Baudelaire," *L'Homme* 2.1 (1962), pp. 5–21, in *Selected Writings*, vol. 3, pp. 447–64. Cf. Jakobson, "'Si Nostre Vie: Observations sur la *composition & structure de motz* dans un sonnet de Joachim du Bellay," in *Selected Writings*, vol. 3, pp. 239–74, esp. pp. 266–68.

47. Roman Jakobson, with S. Rudy, "Yeats' 'Sorrow for Love' through the Years," in *Selected Writings*, vol. 3, pp. 613–14.

48. See Roman Jakobson, "The Grammatical Texture of a Sonnet from Sir Philip Sidney's *Arcadia*," in *Selected Writings*, vol. 3, pp. 275–83, esp. p. 278.

49. Roman Jakobson, "Poetry of Grammar and Grammar of Poetry," in *Selected Writings*, vol. 3, p. 92.

50. *Ibid.*, pp. 92–93.

51. "La grammaire, l'aride grammaire elle-même, devient quelque chose comme une sorcellerie évocatoire; les mots ressuscitent revêtus de chair et d'os, le substantif, dans sa majesté substantielle, l'adjectif, vêtement transparent qui l'habille et le colore comme un glacis, et le verbe, ange du mouvement, qui donne le branle à la phrase." Charles Baudelaire, *Œuvres complètes*, vol. 1, p. 431; cited in Roman Jakobson, "Retrospect," in *Selected Writings*, vol. 3, p. 769.

52. Poe, "The Rationale of Verse," *Essays and Reviews*, p. 33.

53. Jakobson, "Subliminal Verbal Patterning in Poetry," in *Selected Writings*, vol. 3, p. 147.

54. Roman Jakobson, "On the So-Called Vowel Alliteration in Germanic Verse," in *Selected Writings*, vol. 5, p. 195. Jakobson cites E. H. Sturtevant: "we may take it for granted that an obligatory feature of versification must be in some way

audible." See E. H. Sturtevant, "The Doctrine of Caesura, a Philological Ghost," p. 337.

55. Paul Kiparsky has suggested that linguistics must go further, recognizing "that even linguistic features which *must* remain latent play a role in verse." Kiparsky, "Roman Jakobson and the Grammar of Poetry," p. 34.

56. Jakobson, "Retrospect," in *Selected Writings*, vol. 3, p. 769.

57. Jakobson, "Subliminal Verbal Patterning in Poetry," in *Selected Writings*, vol. 3, p. 142.

58. See, among others, Tzvetan Todorov, "Roman Jakobson poéticien"; Leo Bersani, "Is There a Science of Literature?"; James A. Boon, *From Symbolism to Structuralism: Lévi-Strauss in a Literary Tradition*, pp. 38–61; Jonathan Culler, *Structuralist Poetics: Structuralism, Linguistics, and the Study of Literature*, pp. 55–74; Paul Werth, "Roman Jakobson's Verbal Analysis of Poetry"; Linda R. Waugh, "The Poetic Function in the Theory of Roman Jakobson"; and Jean-Claude Milner, "À Roman Jakobson, ou le bonheur par la symétrie," in *Le périple structural*, pp. 131–40.

59. Culler, *Structuralist Poetics*, p. 57.

60. *Ibid.*, p. 58.

61. Michel Riffaterre, "Describing Poetic Structures: Two Approaches to Baudelaire's Les Chats," p. 202.

62. Kiparsky, "Roman Jakobson and the Grammar of Poetry," p. 33.

63. Riffaterre, "Describing Poetic Structures," p. 215.

64. The term "linguistic and poetic actualizations" is Riffaterre's; see *ibid.* p. 213.

65. Jakobson, "Linguistics and Poetics," in *Selected Writings*, vol. 3, p. 50.

66. *Ibid.*

CHAPTER ELEVEN: SECRETS OF TRISTAN TZARA

1. Jean Couvreur, "Du nouveau sur François Villon?," p. 9.

2. *Ibid.*

3. Charles Dobzynski, "Le Secret de François Villon," pp. 1–4.

4. *Ibid.*, p. 1.

5. *Ibid.*

6. Henri Béhar, "À mots découverts," p. 96.

7. Pierre Le Gentil, *Villon*, pp. 21–30.

8. Jean Dufournet, "Tzara et les anagrammes de Villon"; cf. the later version of the essay by the same title that appears in Dufournet, *Nouvelles recherches sur Villon*, pp. 249–73.

9. Tristan Tzara, "La signification des anagrammes."

10. Béhar, "À mots découverts," p. 96.

11. Tristan Tzara, "L'Actualité de Villon," in *Oeuvres complètes*, vol. 5, pp. 115–24, p. 119.

12. *Ibid.*

13. *Ibid.*

14. Tristan Tzara, *Le Secret de Villon*, in *Oeuvres complètes*, vol. 6, p. 9.

15. *Ibid.* The Middle French text cited here appears in the format given by Tzara. For a more recent edition of Villon's text, see François Villon, *Poésies complètes*, p. 107.

16. François Villon, *The Testament*, in *The Poems of François Villon*, p. 38.

17. Tzara, *Le secret de Villon*, in *Œuvres complètes*, vol. 6, p. 10.

18. See, most recently, Claude Thiry's remarks in Villon, *Poésies completes*, p. 106.

19. See Villon, *Œuvres de Villon*, p. 158. Before being noted by Foulet, they were already observed by Jean Acher in a contribution that Foulet most likely read: Acher, review of Lognon, p. 22. See Béhar's notes, *Œuvres complètes*, vol. VI, p. 539. The passage appears as folio 124.

20. François Villon, *Lais* 81 (stanza XI), in *Poésies complètes*, p. 67; *Testament* 970 (stanza XCIV), p. 169.

21. Tzara, *Œuvres complètes*, vol. 6, p. 539.

22. Tzara, *Le secret de Villon*, in *Œuvres complètes*, vol. 6, p. 10.

23. Le Gentil, *Villon*, p. 22.

24. Tzara, *Le secret de Villon*, in *Œuvres complètes*, vol. 6, pp. 10–11.

25. Stéphane Mallarmé, "Crise de vers," in *Œuvres complète*, p. 368.

26. Tzara, *Le secret de Villon*, in *Œuvres complètes*, vol. 6, p. 11.

27. *Ibid.*, p. 12.

28. See Dufournet, *Nouvelles recherches sur Villon*, p. 251.

29. Tzara refers (*Le secret de Villon*, in *Œuvres complètes*, vol. 6, pp. 292–95) to Louis Thuasne's "La rime chez Villon," in Thuasne, *Villon et Rabelais: Notes et commentaires*, pp. 369–418.

30. See Tzara, *Le secret de Villon*, in *Œuvres complètes*, vol. 6, pp. 13–16. Cf.

Dufournet, *Nouvelles recherches sur Villon*, p. 251.

31. Tzara, *Le secret de Villon*, in Œuvres complètes, vol. 6, p. 16.

32. *Ibid.*, p. 11.

33. Louis Aragon, "Tristan Tzara découvre une oeuvre nouvelle de Rabelais," p. 7.

34. Tzara, *Le secret de Villon*, in Œuvres complètes, vol. 6, p. 11.

35. Villon, *Testament* 966–969 (stanza CXIII), in Villon, *Poésies complètes*, p. 167; for Tzara's analysis, see *Le secret de Villon*, in Œuvres complètes, vol. 6, pp. 278–82.

36. Kinnell, *The Poems of François Villon*, p. 87.

37. For the name Charles d'Orléans, see Tzara, *Le secret de Villon*, in Œuvres complètes, vol. 6, p. 254; for the "ironic" names, see *ibid.*, pp. 278–79.

38. See Tzara, *Le secret de Villon*, in Œuvres complètes, vol. 6, pp. 280–81.

39. *Ibid.*, p. 282.

40. For Tzara's "simultaneous poems," see Tzara, *Œuvres complètes*, vol. 1, pp. 492–500.

41. See the statement accompanying the poem, *ibid.*, pp. 492–93.

42. Hugo Ball, cited in Hans Richter, *Dada, Kunst und Anti-Kunst: Der Beitrag Dadas zur Kust des 20. Jahrhunderts*, p. 28.

43. Tzara uses the term "superposition" at various points. See, for example, *Le secret de Villon*, in Œuvres complètes, vol. 6, p. 18.

44. *Ibid.*, p. 17.

45. *Ibid.*, p. 519.

46. *Ibid.*, p. 91.

47. *Ibid.*, p. 91.

48. *Ibid.*, p. 16.

49. *Ibid.*, p. 89.

50. *Ibid.*, p. 17.

51. For a discussion, see Dufournet, *Nouvelles recherches sur Villon*, p. 264.

52. Tzara, *Le secret de Villon*, in Œuvres complètes, vol. 6, p. 215.

53. Aragon, "Tristan Tzara découvre une oeuvre nouvelle de Rabelais," p. 7.

54. Tristan Tzara, "Manifeste Dada," in Œuvres complètes, vol. 1, p. 366.

55. *Ibid.*, 364–67.

56. Tristan Tzara, "Conférence sur Dada," in Œuvres complètes, vol. 1, p. 421.

57. Tzara, *Le secret de Villon*, in Œuvres complètes, vol. 6, p. 219.

58. *Ibid.*, p. 220.

59. See Harrett Ann Watts, *Chance: A Perspective on Dada.*

60. Tristan Tzara, "Dada manifeste sur l'amour faible et l'amour amer," in *Œuvres complètes*, vol. 1, p. 382.

61. See Richter, *Dada, Kunst und Anti-Kunst*, pp. 51–65; and Watt, *Chance*, pp. 51–136.

62. Richter, *Dada, Kunst und Anti-Kunst*, p. 54.

63. Tristan Tzara, *Œuvres complètes*, vol. 6, p. 525.

64. Jean-Loup Debardie, *Candide*, July 26, 1961.

65. M. Puisségur, "Rabelais, Dada, et les probabilités," p. 10.

66. *Ibid.*, p. 23.

67. Tristan Tzara, *Œuvres complètes*, vol. 6, p. 526.

68. *Ibid.*, p. 525.

69. *Ibid.*

70. *Ibid.*, p. 530.

71. Lynn D. Stults, "A Study of Tristan Tzara's Theory Concerning the Poetry of Villon," p. 433.

72. *Ibid.*, p. 453.

73. *Ibid.*, pp. 453–54.

74. *Ibid.*, pp. 445–46.

75. *Ibid.*, p. 451.

76. *Ibid.*, p. 454.

77. *Ibid.*, p. 455.

78. *Ibid.*, pp. 457–58.

79. *Ibid.*, p. 458.

80. Michel Bernard, "*Le Secret de Villon* à l'épreuve de l'ordinateur: Tzara et les anagrammes."

81. *Ibid.*, p. 245.

82. *Ibid.*

83. *Ibid.*, pp. 245–46.

84. See *ibid.*, p. 249.

85. *Ibid.*, p. 248.

86. Tzara, "Dada manifeste sur l'amour faible et l'amour amer," *Œuvres complètes*, vol. 1, p. 381.

87. Henri Béhar, in Tzara, *Œuvres complètes*, vol. 6, p. 550 n. 4.

88. Tzara, *Le secret de Villon*, in *Œuvres complètes*, vol. 6, p. 17.

89. *Ibid.*, 550.

90. Roger Vitrac, "André Breton n'écrira plus," *Le Journal du Peuple*, April 7, 1923, reprinted in André Breton, *Œuvres complètes*, vol. 1, p. 1215.

Bibliography

Abbott, Frank Frost, "The Accent in Vulgar and Formal Latin," *Classical Philology* 2.4 (1907), pp. 444–60.

Acher, Jean, review of Lognon, *Œuvres de Villon*, *Zeitschrift für frazösische Sprache und Literatur* 38.2 (1911), pp. 18–25.

Acker, Paul, and Carolyne Larrington (eds.), *The Poetic Edda: Essays on Old Norse Mythology* (New York: Routledge, 2002).

Akehurst, F. R. P., and Judith M. Davis, *A Handbook of the Troubadours* (Berkeley: University of California Press, 1995).

Amory, Frederic, "Towards A Grammatical Classification of Kennings as Compounds," *Archiv för nordisk filologi* 97 (1982), pp. 67–80.

Anglade, Joseph (ed.), *Les leys d'amours*, 4 vols. (Toulouse: E. Privat, 1919–1920).

Anonymous, *The Book of Vagabonds and Beggars: With a Vocabulary of Their Language*, ed. Martin Luther, trans. James Camden Hotten (London: James Camden Hotten, 1860).

Aragon, Louis, "Tristan Tzara découvre une oeuvre nouvelle de Rabelais," *Lettres françaises* 1000, October 24, 1963, p. 7.

Ashley, Leonard R. N., "Rhyme and Reason: The Methods and Meanings of Cockney Rhyming Slang, *Names* 25.3 (1977), pp. 124–54.

Avé-Lallement, Friedrich Christian Benedict, *Das deutsche Gaunertum in seiner sozialpolitischen, literarischen und linguistischen Ausbildung zu seinem heutigen Bestande* (Leipzig: Brodhaus, 1872).

Ayto, John, *Oxford Dictionary of Rhyming Slang* (Oxford: Oxford University Press, 2002).

Bader, Françoise, *La langue des dieux ou l'hermetisme des poètes indo-européens* (Pisa: Giardini, 1989).

215

——, *Anagrammes et allitérations* (Louvain: Peeters, 1993).

Bartholomaeis, V. De, "Du rôle et des origines de la tornade," *Annales du Midi* 19 (1907), pp. 448–64.

Baudelaire, Charles, *Œuvres complètes*, ed. Claude Pichois, 2 vols. (Paris: Gallimard-La Pléiade, 1975).

Béhar, Henri, "À mots découverts," *Europe* 53.555–556 (1975), pp. 95–112.

Bellows, Henry Adams (ed. and trans.), *The Poetic Edda* (New York: American-Scandinavian Foundation, 1926).

Beltrami, P. G., *Rimario trobadorico provenzale*, 2 vols. (Pisa: Pacini, 1988).

Benveniste, Émile, "Une différenciation de vocabulaire dans l'Avesta," *Studia Indo-Iranica: Ehrengabe für Wilhelm Geiger* (Leipzig: Harrassowitz, 1931), pp. 219–26.

——, "Lettres de Ferdinand de Saussure à Antoine Meillet," *Cahiers Ferdinand de Saussure* 21 (1964), pp. 93–130.

——, *Problèmes de linguisique générale*, 2 vols. (Paris: Gallimard, 1966–1974).

Bernard, Michel, "*Le Secret de Villon* à l'épreuve de l'ordinateur: Tzara et les anagrammes," *Romania* 113 (1992–1995), pp. 242–52.

Bernart de Ventadorn, *Bernart de Ventadorn: Seine Lieder mit Einleitung und Glossar*, ed. Carl Appel (Halle: Niemeyer, 1915).

Bersani, Leo, "Is There a Science of Literature?," *Partisan Review* 39 (1972), pp. 535–63.

Bertran de Born, *The Poems of the Troubadour Bertran de Born*, ed. William Paden, Tilde Sankovitch, and Patricia H. Stäblein (Berkeley: University of California Press, 1986).

Bitterli, Dieter, *Say What I Am Called: The Old English Riddles of the Exeter Book and the Anglo-Latin Riddle Tradition* (Toronto: University of Toronto Press, 2009).

Blacking, John, "The Social Value of Venda Riddles," *African Studies* 20.1 (1961). pp. 1–32.

Bode, Wilhelm, *Die Kenningar in der angelsächsischen Dichtung* (Darmstadt: Zernin, 1886).

Boon, James A., *From Symbolism to Structuralism: Lévi-Strauss in a Literary Tradition* (New York: Blackwell, 1972).

Borges, Jorge Luis, "Las Kenningar," in *Historia de la eternidad* (Buenos Aires: Viau y Zona, 1936), pp. 35–56.

Bouquet, Simon, *Introduction à la lecture de Ferdinand de Saussure* (Paris: Payot, 1997).

Boutière Jean, and Alexander Herman Schulz, *Biographies des troubadours: Textes provençaux des XIIIe et XIVe siècles* (Paris: Nizet, 1964).

Breton, André, *Œuvres complètes*, ed. Marguerite Bonnet et al., 4 vols. (Paris: Gallimard-La Pléiade, 1988–2008).

Brik, Osip Maksimovich, *Two Essays on Poetic Language*, preface by Roman Jakobson (Ann Arbor: University of Michigan Press, 1964).

Brodeur, Arthur G., "The Meaning of Snorri's Catgeories," *University of California Publications in Modern Philology* 36.4 (1952), pp. 1–13.

Calder, George (ed.), *Auraicept na N-Éces: The Scholar's Primer, Being the Texts of the Ogham Tract from the Book of Ballymote and the Yellow Book of Lecan, and the Text of the Trefhocul from the Book of Leinster* (Edinburgh: J. Grant, 1917).

Callus, Ivan, "A Chronological and Annotated Bibliography of Works Referring to Ferdinand de Saussure's Anagram Notebooks," *Cahiers Ferdinand de Saussure* 55 (2002), pp. 269–95.

Camden, William, *Remaines concerning Britaine: But especially England, and the Inhabitants thereof* (London: Simon Waterson, 1614).

Camporesi, Piero, *Il libro dei vagabondi*, preface by Franco Cardini (Milan: Garzani, 2003).

Cerquiglini-Toulet, Jacqueline, "Marot et Villon," in *Villon et ses lecteurs: Actes du colloque international des 13–14 décembre 2000* (Paris: Champion, 2005), pp. 19–31.

Cervants, Miguel de, Saavedra, *La Galatea*, ed. Juan Bautista Avalle-Arce (Madrid: Espasa-Calpe, 1985).

Chambers, F. M., *Proper Names in the Lyrics of the Troubadours* (Chapel Hill: University of North Carolina Press, 1971).

Clay, Jenny, "The Planktai and Moly: Divine Naming and Knowing in Homer," *Hermes* 100.2 (1972), pp. 127–31.

Cleasby, Richard, *An Icelandic-English Dictionary*, subsequently revised, enlarged, and completed by Gudbrand Vigfusson, 2nd ed. (Oxford: Oxford University Press, 1957).

Coelho, Francisco Adolpho, *Os ciganhos de Portugal, com um estudo sobre o calão* (Lisbon: Imprensa nacional, 1892).

Cohen, Marcel, "Note sur l'argot," *Bulletin de la Société Linguistique de Paris* 21.67 (1919), pp. 132–47.

Cole, Thomas, "The Saturnian Verse," in *Studies in Latin Poetry*, ed. Thomas Cole and Christopher Dawson (Cambridge: Cambridge University Press, 1969), pp. 3–74.

Coleman, Julie, *A History of Cant and Slang Dictionaries*, 4 vols. (Oxford University Press: 2004–2010).

Cook, Eleanor, *Enigmas and Riddles in Literature* (Cambridge: Cambridge University Press, 2006).

Couvreur, Jean, "Du nouveau sur François Villon?" *Le Monde*, December 22, 1959, p. 9.

Cropp, Glynnis M., *Le vocabulaire des troubadours de l'époque classique* (Geneva: Droz, 1975).

Culler, Jonathan, *Structuralist Poetics: Structuralism, Linguistics, and the Study of Literature* (Ithaca: Cornell University Press, 1975).

Dante Alighieri, *Opere minori*, vol. 3, pt. 2: *De vulgari eloquentia e Monarchia*, ed. Pier Vincenzo Mengaldo and Bruno Nardi (Milan: Ricciardi Editore, 1999).

Davies, Anna Morpurgo, "The Greek Notion of Dialect," *Verbum* 10 (1987), pp. 7–28.

Debardie, Jean-Loup, *Candide*, July 26, 1961.

Deguy, Michel, "La folie de Saussure," *Critique* 25 (1969), pp. 20–26.

Delaplace, Denis, *Le Jargon des Coquillars à Dijon au milieu du XVe siècle selon Marcel Schwob (1892)* (Paris: Classiques Garnier, 2011).

Demsky, Aaron, "A Proto-Canaanite Abecedary Dating from the Period of the Judges and Its Implications for the History of the Alphabet," *Tel Aviv* 4 (1977), pp. 14–27.

Derolez, René, *Runica manuscripta: The English Tradition* (Brugge: De Tempel, 1954).

Detienne, Marcel, and Gilbert Hamonic (eds.), with the participation of Georges Charachidzé, Marcel Detienne, Gilbert Hamonic, Charles Malamoud, and Carlo Severi, *La déesse parole: Quatre figures de la langue des dieux* (Paris: Flammarion, 1995).

Diels, Hermann (ed.), *Die Fragmente der Vorsokratiker: Griechisch und Deutsch,* 6th ed., edited by Walther Kranz, 3 vols. (Berlin: Weidmann, 1951).

DiNapoli, Robert, "Odd Characters: Runes in Old English Poetry," in *Verbal Encounters: Anglo-Saxon and Old Norse Studies for Roberta Frank*, ed. Antonina Harbus and Russell Poole (Toronto: University of Toronto Press, 2005), pp. 146–61.

Dobzynski, Charles, "Le Secret de François Villon," *Lettres françaises* 803, December 17–23, 1959, pp. 1–4.

Dronke, Ursula, *The Poetic Edda*, 3 vols. (Oxford University Press, 1969–2011).

Dubois, Michel, "Sur un passage obscur du *Jeu de saint Nicolas*," *Romania* 40 (1929), pp. 256–58.

Dufournet, Jean, "Tzara et les anagrammes de Villon," *Europe* 555–56 (1975), pp. 113–34.

——, "Tzara et les anagrammes de Villon," *Nouvelles recherches sur Villon* (Paris: Champion, 1980), pp. 249–73.

Dumézil, Georges, "La tradition druidique et l'écriture," *Revue de l'histoire des religions* 122 (1940), pp. 125–33.

Dupuis, Michel, "À propos des anagrammes saussuriennes," *Cahiers d'analyse textuelle* 19 (1977), pp. 7–24.

Eismann, Wolfgang, and Peter Grzybek (eds.), *Semiotische Studien zum Rätsel: Simple Forms Reconsidered II* (Bochum: N. Brockmeyer, 1987).

Elizarenkova, Tat'jana Jakovlevna, *Language and Style of the Vedic R̥ṣis*, ed. with an intro. Wendy Doniger (Albany: State University of New York Press, 1995).

Estienne, Henri, *Apologie pour Hérodote*, ed. Paul Ristelhuber, 2 vols. (Paris: Isidore Liseux, 1879).

Elliott, R. W. V., *Runes* (Manchester: Manchester University Press, 1959).

Evans, David, "Riddling and the Structure of Context," *Journal of American Folklore* 89.352 (1976), pp. 166–88.

Eyvindr Finnsson Skáldaspillir, *Die Dichtung: Edition-Kommentar-Untersuchungen*, ed. Arnulf Krause (Leverkusen: Literaturverlag Norden Mark Reinhardt, 1990).

Falk, Harry, *Schrift im alten Indien: Ein Forschungsbericht mit Anmerkungen* (Tübingen: Günter Narr, 1993).

Felices, José Calderéon, "Lengua de los dioses / Lengua de los hombres," *Faventia* 4.1 (1982), pp. 5–33.

Fidjestøl, Bjarne, "The Kenning System: An Attempt at a Linguistic Analysis," in *Selected Papers*, ed. Odd Einar Haugen and Else Mundal, trans. Peter Foote (Odense University press, 1997), pp. 16–67.

Formisano, Luciano, *La lirica* (Bologna: Il Mulino, 1990).

Frank, István, *Repertoire métrique de la poésie des troubadours*, 2 vols. (Paris: Champion, 1966).

Frank, Roberta, *Old Norse Court Poetry: The Dróttkvætt Stanza* (Ithaca: Cornell University Press, 1978).

———, s.v. "kenning," in *Dictionary of the Middle Ages*, ed. Joseph Strayer, 13 vols. (New York: Scribner, 1982–1989).

Frege, Gottlob, *Funktion, Begriff, Bedeutung*, ed. Günther Patzig, 6th ed. (Göttingen: Vandenhoeck und Ruprecht, 1986).

Friedrich, Johannes, "Göttersprache und Menschensprache im hethitischen Schrifttum," in *Sprachgeschichten und Wortbildung: Festschrift A. Debrunner* (Bern: Francke, 1954), pp. 135–39.

Fussman, Gérard, "Histoire du monde indien: Les premiers systèmes d'écriture en Inde," *Annuaire du Collège de France* 89 (1988–1989), pp. 507–14.

Gade, Kari Ellen, *The Structure of Old Norse Dróttkvætt Poetry* (Ithaca: Cornell University Press, 1995).

———, *Poetry from the Kings' Sagas*, vol. 2, *From c. 1035 to 1300* (Turnhout: Brepols, 2009).

Gadet, Françoise, *Saussure: Une science de la langue* (Paris: Presses universitaires de France, 1987).

Gandon, Francis, *De dangereux édifices: Saussure lecteur de Lucrèce, Les cahiers d'anagrammes consacrés au De rerum natura* (Louvain: Peeters, 2002).

Gardner, Thomas, "The Old English Kenning: A Characteristic Feature of Germanic Poetical Diction?," *Modern Philology* 67.2 (1969), pp. 109–17.

Gatien-Arnoult, Adolphe Félix (ed.), *La flors del gay saber, estier dichas Las leys d'Amors*, 3 vols. (Toulouse: J.-B. Paya, 1841).

Georges, Robert A., and Alan Dundes, "Towards a Structural Definition of the Riddle," *Journal of American Folklore* 76.300 (1963), pp. 111–18.

Gerbstman, Aleksandr Iosivič, "O zvukovom stroenii naradnoj zagadki," *Russkij folklor* 11 (1968), pp. 185–97.

Gesenius, Wilhelm, *Hebräisches und chaldäisches Handwörterbuch über das Alte Testament*, 2nd ed. (Leipzig: F. W. C Vogel, 1823).

Godefroy, Frédéric, *Dictionnaire de l'ancienne langue française et tous ses dialectes du IXe au XVe siècle*, 10 vols. (Paris: F. Viewig, 1881–1902).

Godel, Robert *Les sources manuscrites du Cours de linguistique générale de F. de Saussure* (Geneva: Droz, 1957).

———, "Inventaire des manuscrits de F. de Saussure remis à la Bibliothèque publique et universitaire de Genève," *Cahiers Ferdinand de Saussure* 17 (1960), pp.

5-11.

Gonda, Jan, *Notes on Names and the Name of God in Ancient India* (Amsterdam: North Holland, 1970).

Gordon, E. V., *An Introduction to Old Norse* (2nd rev. ed., A. R. Taylor (Oxford: Oxford University Press,1957).

Gordon, W. Terrence, and Henry G. Schogt, "Ferdinand de Saussure: The Anagrams and the *Cours*," in *The Emergence of the Modern Language Sciences: Studies on the Transition from Historical-Comparative to Structural Linguistics in Honour of E. F. K. Koerner*, vol. 1, *Historiographical Perspectives*, ed. Sheila Embleton, John E. Joseph, and Hans-Joseph Niederehe (Philadelphia: John Benjamins, 1999), pp. 139-50.

Gourian, Gérard, *L'amour et la guerre: L'oeuvre de Bertran de Born* (Aix-en-Provence: Université de Provence, 1985).

Grimm, Jakob, *Deutsche Mythologie*, 4th ed., 3 vols. (Berlin: F. Dümmler, 1875).

Guiraud, Pierre, *L'argot* (Paris: Presses Universitaires de France, 1956).

——, *Le jargon de Villon, ou Le gai savoir de la Coquille* (Paris, Gallimard, 1968).

Güntert, Hermann, *Über die ahurischen und daēvischen Ausdrücke im Awesta: Eine semasiologische Studie* (Heidelberg: C. Winter, 1914).

——, *Von der Sprache der Götter und Geister: Bedeutungsgeschichtliche Untersuchungen zur homerischen und eddischen Göttersprache* (Halle: Niemeyer, 1921).

Halle, Morris, "Phonology in Generative Grammar," *Word* 18 (1962), pp. 54-72.

Halliday, M. A. K., "Anti-Languages," in *Language as a Social Semiotic: The Social Interpretation of Language and Meaning* (Baltimore: University Park Press, 1978), pp. 164-82.

Harman, Thomas, *Caveat or Warening for Common Cursetors* (London: William Griffith, 1567).

Harries, Lyndon, "The Riddle in Africa," *Journal of American Folklore* 84.334 (1971), pp. 377-93.

Hesiod, *Theogony*, with prolegomena and commentary by M. L. West (Oxford: Clarendon Press, 1966).

Heubeck, Alfred, "Die homerische Göttersprache," *Würzburger Jahrbücher für die Altertumswissenschatf* 4.2 (1949-1950), pp. 197-219.

Heusler, Andreas, *Altgermanische Dichtung*, 2nd ed. (1923; Darmstadt: Hermann Gentner, 1943).

Hoepffner, Ernest, "Le *Castiat* du troubadour Peire Vidal," in *Mélanges de philologie et d'histoire offerts à M. Antoine Thomas* (Paris: Champion, 1927), pp. 211–20.

Holland, Gary, "Kennings, Metaphors, and Semantic Formulae in Norse *dróttkvætt*," *Arkiv för nordisk filologi* 120 (2005), pp. 123–47.

Hollander, Lee M. (trans.), *The Poetic Edda* (Austin: University of Texas Press, 1962).

Homer, *Iliad*, trans. A.T. Murray (Cambridge, MA: Harvard University Press, 1924).

——, *Odyssey*, trans. A.T. Murray (Cambridge, MA: Harvard University Press, 1924).

Hopkins, Gerard Manley, *The Journals and Papers*, ed. Humphrey House, completed by Graham Storey (Oxford: Oxford University Press, 1959).

Houben, Jan E.M., "Ritual Pragmatics of a Vedic Hymn: The 'Riddle Hymn' and the Pravargya Ritual," *Journal of the American Oriental Society* 120.4 (2000), pp. 499–36.

Hultgård, Anders, "The Wisdom Contest in the *Vafþrúðnismál*," *Analecta Septentrionalia* 65 (2009), pp. 531–39.

Iragaray, Luce, "Le schizophrène et la question du signe," *Recherches* 16 (1975), pp. 31–42.

Jacobsohn, H., "Aeolische Doppelconsonanz: Zur Sprache und Verstechnik des Homerischen Epos," *Hermes* 45.1 (1910), pp. 67–124.

Jakobson, Roman, "La première Lettre de Ferdinand de Saussure sur les anagrammes," *L'Homme* 11.2 (1971), pp. 15–24.

——, *Selected Writings*, 8 vols. (The Hague: Mouton, 1962–1988).

Jakobson, Roman and Linda Waugh, assisted by Martha Taylor, *The Sound Shape of Language* (Bloomington: Indiana University Press, 1979).

Jauss, Hans-Robert, *Die Alterität und Modernität der mittelalterichen Literatur: Gesammelte Aufsätze 1956–1976* (Munich: W. Fink, 1977).

Jeanroy, Alfred, *La poésie lyrique des troubadours*, 2. vols. (Paris: Didier, 1934)

Jónsson, Finnur, *De gamle Eddadigte* (Copenhagen: G.E.C. Gads Forlag, 1932).

Joseph, John E., *Limiting the Arbitrary: Linguistic Naturalism and Its Opposites in Plato's* Cratylus *and Modern Theories of Language* (Amsterdam: John Benjamins, 2000).

——, *Saussure* (Oxford University Press, 2012).

Julius Caesar, *Commentaries on the Gallic and Civil Wars, with the Supplementary Books Attributed to Hirtius, Including the Alexandrian, African and Spanish Wars,* trans. William Alexander McDevitte and W. S. Bohn (New York: Harpers, 1870).

Kalischer, Alfred Christlieb, *Observationes in poesim romanensem provicialibus in primis respectis* (Berlin: Duemmler, 1866).

Katz, Joshua T., "Saussure's Anaphonie," in *The Other Senses: Antiquity beyond the Visual Paradigm*, ed. Shane Butler and Alex Purves (Durham: Acumen, forthcoming).

——, "Wordplay," in *Proceedings of the 20th Annual UCLA Indo-European Conference*, ed. Stephanie W. Jamison, H. Craig Melchert, and Brent Vine (Bremen: Hempen Verlag, 2009), pp. 79–114.

Kent, Roland G., "Assimilation and Dissimilation," *Language* 12.4 (1936), pp. 245–58.

Kiparsky, Paul, "Roman Jakobson and the Grammar of Poetry," in *A Tribute to Roman Jakobson, 1896–1982* (Berlin: Mouton, 1983), pp. 27–39.

Kretschmer, Paul, review of Herann Güntert, *Von der Sprache der Götter und Geister*, *Glotta* 13 (1924), pp. 266–67.

Kuhn, Hans, *Das Dróttkvætt* (Heidelberg: Winter, 1983).

Lacan, Jacques, *L'Éthique de la psychanalyse, 1959–1960* (Paris: Seuil, 1986).

Laroche, E., "Hattic Deities and their Epithets," *Journal of Cuneiform Studies* 1.3 (1947), pp. 187–216.

Larrington, Carolyne, *The Poetic Edda* (Oxford: Oxford University Press, 1996).

——, "Vafþrúðnismál and Grímnismál: Cosmic History, Cosmic Geography," in Acker and Larrington, (eds.), *The Poetic Edda: Essays on Old Norse Mythology* (New York: Routledge, 2002).

Lattimore, Richmond, "Herodotus and the Names of Egyptian Gods," *Classical Philology* 34.4 (1939), pp. 357–65.

Law, Vivian, *Wisdom, Authority and Grammar in the Seventh Century* (Cambridge: Cambridge University Press, 1995).

Lausberg, Heinrich, *Handbuch der literarischen Rhetorik: Eine Grundlagung der Literaturwissenschaft*, 2nd ed. (Munich: Max Hüber, 1973).

Lazzeroni, Romano, "Lingua degli dei e lingua degli uomini," *Annali della Scuola Normale di Pisa* 26 (1957), pp. 1–25.

Lecercle, Jean-Jacques, *The Violence of Language* (London: Routledge, 1990).

Leeuwen, J. van, "Homerica XVI: De lingua deorum," *Mnemosyne* n.s. 20 (1892), pp. 127–40.

Lefkowitz, Natalie J., "Talking Backwards in French," *The French Review* 63.2 (1989), pp. 312–22.

Le Gentil, Pierre, *Villon* (Paris: Hatier, 1967).

Leighton, Albert C., "Secret Communication among the Greeks and Romans," *Technology and Culture* 10.2 (1969), pp. 139–54.

Lindow, John, "Riddles, Kennings, and the Complexity of Skaldic Poetry," *Scandinavian Studies* 47,3 (1975), pp. 311–27.

Lindsay, W. M., "Traube's Nomina Sacra and Posthumous Works," *Classical Quarterly* 3.2 (1909), pp. 132–36.

Lohmann, Johannes, *Musiké und Logos: Aufsätze zur griechischen Philosophie und Musiktheorie*, ed. Anastasios Giannarás (Stuttgart: Musikwissenschaftliche Verlagsgesellschaft, 1970).

Lotringer, Sylvère, "Flagrant délire," *Recherches* 16 (1975), pp. 7–14.

Luz, Christine, *Technopaignia: Formspiele in der griechischen Dichtung* (Leiden: E. J. Brill, 2010).

Malamoud, Charles, *Cuire le monde: Rite et pensée dans l'Inde ancienne* (Paris: La Découverte, 1989).

——, *Féminité de la parole: Études sur l'Inde classique* (Paris: Albin Michel, 2005).

——, *Le jumeau solaire* (Paris: Éditions du Seuil, 2002).

Mallarmé, Stéphane, *Œuvres complètes*, ed. Henri Mondor (Paris: Gallimard, 1945).

Marie de France, *The Fables*, trans. Mary Lou Martin (Birmingham, AL: Summa Publications, 1984).

Marold, Edith, *Kenningkunst: Ein Beitrag zu einer Poetik der Skaldendichtung* (Berlin: De Gruyter, 1983).

Marot, Clément, *Œuvres poétiques,* ed. Gérard Defaux, 2 vols. (Paris: Classiques Garnier, 1990–1993).

Matasović, Ranko, *A Theory of Textual Reconstruction in Indo-European Linguistics* (Fankfurt am Main: Peter Lang, 1996).

Maurer, D. W., and Sidney J. Baker, "Australian Rhyming Argot in the American Underworld," *American Speech* (1944), pp. 183–95.

McCarthy, John J., s.v. "nonlinear phonology," in *International Encyclopedia of the Social and Behavioral Sciences*, ed. Neil J. Smelser and Paul B. Baltes (Oxford: Pergamon, 2001), pp. 11392–95.

Meillet, Antoine, *Linguistique historique et linguistique générale* (Paris: Champion, 1921).

———, review of Hermann Güntert, *Von der Sprache der Götter und Geister, Bulletin de la Société linguistqiue de Paris* 23.2 (1922), pp. 56–57.

Meissner, Rudolf, *Die Kenningar der Skalden: Ein Beitrag zur skaldischen Poetik* (Leipzig: Schroeder, 1921).

———, "Die Sprache der götter, riesend und zwerge in den Alvissmal," *Zeitschrift für deutsches Altertum und deutsche Literatur* 61.2–3 (1924), pp. 128–40.

Mencken, H. L., "American Profanity," *American Speech* 19.4 (1944). pp. 241–49.

Messenger, John C., Jr., "Anang Proverb-Riddles," *Journal of American Folklore* 73,289 (1960), pp. 225–35.

Michel, Francisque, *Études de philologie comparée sur l'argot* (Paris: Firmin Didot, 1856).

Milicic, Vladimir, "Subliminal Structures in Folklore: Anagrammatized Answers to Riddles," *Slavic and East European Journal* 26.1 (1982), pp. 63–76.

Milner, Jean-Claude, *L'amour de la langue* (Paris: Seuil, 1978).

———, *Introduction à une science du langage* (Paris: Seuil, 1986).

———, *Le périple structural: Figures et paradigme* (Paris: Seuil, 2002).

Mohnan, Karuvannur Puthanveettil, "Lexical Phonology," Ph.D. dissertation, Massachusetts Institute of Technology, 1981.

Mölk, Ulrich, *Trobar clus, Trobar leu: Studien zur Dichtungstheorie der Trobadors* (Munich: Fink, 1968).

Moberg, Lennart, "The Languages of *Alvíssmál*," *Saga-Book* 18.4 (1973), pp. 299–323.

Moret, André, *Anthologie du Minnesang* (Paris: Aubier, 1949).

Murphy, Patrick J., *Unriddling the Exeter Riddles* (Philadelphia: Pennsylvania University Press, 2011).

Nava, Giuseppe, "Lettres de Ferdinand de Saussure à Giovanni Pascoli," *Cahiers Ferdinand de Saussure* 24 (1968), pp. 73–81.

Niceforo, Alfredo, *Il gergo nei normali, nei degenerati, e nei crimianli* (Turin, Fratelli Bocca, 1897).

Nielsen, Karl Martin, "Runen und Magie: Ein forschungsgeschichtliche Überblick," *Frühmittelalterliche Studien* 19 (1985), pp. 75–97.

Niles, John D., *Old English Enigmatic Poems and the Play of the Texts* (Turnhout: Brepols, 2006).

Nykl, Alois Richard, *Hispanio-Arabic Poetry and Its Relations with the Old Provençal Troubadours* (Baltimore: n.p., 1946).

Orchard, Andy, *The Elder Edda: A Book of Viking Lore* (London: Penguin Books, 2011).

Oxford English Dictionary, 2nd ed., 20 vols. (Oxford: Oxford University Press, 1989).

Page, R.I., "Anglo-Saxon Runes and Magic," in *Runes and Runic Inscriptions: Collected Essays on Anglo-Saxon and Voking Runes*, ed. David Parsons (Rochester: The Boydell Press, 1995), pp. 105–25.

——, *An Introduction to English Runes*, 2nd ed. (Suffolk: Boydell & Brewer, 1999).

Pagis, Dan, *'Al sod ḥatum: Le-toldot ha-ḥidah ha-'Ivrit be-Iṭalyah uve-Holand* (Jerusalem: Y.L. Magnes, 1986).

——, "Towards a Theory of the Literary Riddle," in *Untying the Knot: On Riddles and Other Enigmatic Modes*, ed. Galit Hasan-Rokem and David Shulman (New York: Oxford University Press, 1996), pp. 81–108.

Parsons, Jed, "A New Approach to the Saturnian Verse and Its Relation to Latin Prosody," *Transactions of the American Philological Association* 129 (1999), pp. 117–37.

Pasero, Nicolò, ed., *Poesie di Guglielmo IX* (Modena: S.T.E.M., 1973).

Pepicello, W.J., and Thomas A. Green, *The Language of Riddles: New Perspectives* (Columbus: Ohio State University Press, 1984).

Pillet, Alfred, "Grundlagen, Aufgaben und Leistungen der Troubadours-Forschung," *Zeitschrift für romanische Philologie* 47 (1927), pp. 316–38, rpt. in *Der provenzalische Minnesang: Ein Querschnitt durch die neuere Forschungsdiskussion* (Darmstadt: Wissenschaftliche Buchgesellschaft, 1967), pp. 20–65.

Plénat, Marc, "Le javanais: Concurrence et haplologie," *Langages* 25.101 (1991), pp. 96–117.

——, "Morphologie d'un 'langage secret': Le javanais de Queneau. Description dans un cadre autosegmental," *Cahiers de grammaire* 6 (1983), pp. 150–94.

——, "Morphologie du largonji des loucherbems," *Langages* 20.78 (1985), pp. 73–95.

Poe, Edgar Allan, *Essays and Reviews*, ed. Gary Richard Thompson (New York: Library of America, 1984).

Pollock, Sheldon, *The Language of the Gods in the World of Men: Sanskrit, Culture and Power in Premodern India* (Berkeley: University of California Press, 2006).

Porzig, Walter, "Das Rätsel im Rigveda: Ein Beitrag zum Kapitel Sondersprache," in *Germanica: Eduard Sievers zum 75. Geburtstage 25. November 1925* (Halle: Max

Niemeyer, 1925), pp. 646–60.

Prosdocimi, Aldo L., and Anna Marinetti, "Saussure e il saturnio: Tra scienza, biografia e storiografia," *Cahiers Ferdinand de Saussure* 44 (1990), pp. 37–71.

Puisségur, M., "Rabelais, Dada, et les probabilités," *Bulletin de l'Association des professeurs de mathématiques de l'enseignement public* 277 (1971), pp. 9–23.

Queneau, Raymond, *Excercises de style* (Paris: Gallimard, 1947).

—— *Exercises in Style*, trans. Barbara Wright (New York: New Directions, 1981).

Rankin, James Walter, "A Study of the Kennings in Anglo-Saxon Poetry," *Journal of Germanic Philology* 8.3 (1909), pp. 357–422 and *Journal of Germanic Philology* 9.1 (1910), pp. 49–84.

Renou, Ernest, and Lilian Silburn, "Sur la notion de *bráhman*," *Journal asiatique* 237 (1949), pp. 83–166.

Richard li Biaus, ed. Wendelin Foerster (Vienna: Alfred Hölder, 1874).

Richter, Hans, *Dada, Kunst und Anti-Kunst: Der Beitrag Dadas zur Kust des 20. Jahrhunderts* (Cologne: DuMont Schauberg, 1964).

Riffaterre, Michel, "Describing Poetic Structures: Two Approaches to Baudelaire's Les Chats," *Yale French Studies* 36–37 (1966), pp. 200–42.

Rig Veda, The, ed. and trans. Wendy Doniger (New York: Penguin, 1981).

Riquer, Martín de, *Los trovadores: Historia literaria y textos*, 3 vols. (Barcelona: Planeta, 1975).

Riquer, Isabel de, "*Linhaure*: Cent ans d'études sur un *senhal*," *Revue des langues romanes* 96.1 (1992), pp. 41–67.

Rochette, Bruno, "Grecs et latins face aux langues étrangères: Contribution à l'étude de la diversité linguistique dans l'antiquité classique," *Revue belge de philologie et d'histoire* 73.1 (1995), pp. 5–16.

Roncaglia, Aurelio, "Trobar clus: Discussione aperta," *Cultura neolatina* 39.1–2 (1969), pp. 5–55.

Ross, Margaret Clunines, *Skáldskaparmál: Snorri Sturluson's ars poetica and Medieval Theories of Language* (Odense: Odense University Press, 1987).

Rotolo, Vincenzo, "La communicazione linguistica fra alloglotti nell'antichità classica," in *Studi classici in onore di Quintino Cataudella*, vol. 1 (Catania: Università di Catania, 1972), pp. 395–414.

Ruby, Pechon de, *La vive généreuse des Mercelots, Gueuz et Boesmiens, contenans leur façon de vivre, subtilitez & gergon*, ed. Denis Delaplace (Paris: Champion, 2007).

Sachau, Edward C., *Alberuni's India: An Account of the Religion, Philosophy, Literature,*

Geography, Chronology, Astronomy, Customs, Laws and Astrology of India about A.D. 1030, 2 vols. (London: Kegan Paul, Trench, Trübner & co., 1910).

Sainéan, Lazare, *Les sources de l'argot ancien*, 2 vols (Paris: Champion, 1912).

Santini, Giovanna, *Rimario dei trovatori* (Rome: Nuova Cultura, 2010).

Saussure, Ferdinand de, *Écrits de linguistique générale*, ed. Simon Bouquet and Rudolf Engler (Paris: Gallimard, 2002).

——, *Cours de linguistique générale*, ed. Tullio de Mauro (Paris: Payot, 1974).

——, *Édition critique du cours de linguistique générale de Ferdinand de Saussure*, ed. Robert Engler, 3 vols. (Wiesbaden: Harrassowitz, 1967–1974).

——, *Linguistik und Semiologie: Notizen aus dem Nachlaß, Texte Briefe und Dokumente*, ed. Johannes Fehr (Frankfurt am Main: Suhrkamp, 1997).

——, *Saussure's First Course of Lectures in General Linguistics*, ed. Eisuke Komatsu and George Wolf (London: Pergamon, 1996).

——, *Saussure's Second Course of Lectures in General Linguistics*, ed. Eisuke and George Wolf (Oxford: Pergamon, 1997).

——, *Saussure's Third Course of Lectures in General Linguistics*, ed. Eisuke Komatsu and George Wolf (Oxford: Pergamon, 1993).

Savinel, Pierre, *Poésies de François Villon*, preface by Tristan Tzara (Paris: Audin, 1949).

Scott, Charles T., *Persian and Arabic Riddles: A Language-Centered Approach to Genre Definition* (Bloomington: Indiana University Press, 1965).

Schöne, Lucien, *Le jargon et jobelin de Maistre François Villon, suivi de Jargon au théâtre* (Paris: Alphonse Lemerre, 1888).

Schultz-Gora, Oskar (ed.), *Die provenzalische Dichterinnen: Biographien und Texte* (Leipzig: Gustav Fock, 1888).

Schwob, Marcel, *Études sur l'argot français* (Paris: Éditions Allia, 2004).

——, *François Villon* (Paris: Éditions Allia, 2008).

——, *Œuvres*, 2 vols. (Paris: Mercure de France, 1921).

Sebeok, Tomas A., *Style in Language* (Cambridge, MA: Technology Press of the Massachusetts Institute of Technology, 1960).

See, Klaus von, Beatrice La Farge, Eve Picard, Ilona Priebe, and Katja Schulz, multiple volumes, *Kommentar zu den Liedern der Edda* (Heidelberg: C. Winter, 1997–).

Shapiro, Marianne, "The Trobairitz and the Limits of Courtly Love," *Signs* 3.3 (1978), pp. 560–71.

Shepheard, David, "Saussure's Vedic Anagrams," *Modern Language Review* 77.3 (1982), pp. 513–23.

Shklovsky, Victor, "Art as Technique," in *Russian Formalist Criticism: Four Essays*, trans. and ed. Lee T. Lemon and Marion J. Reis (Lincoln: University of Nebraska Press, 1965), pp. 3–24.

——, "Isskustvo, kak priyom," *Sborniki* 2 (1917), pp. 3–14.

Starobinski, Jean, "Les anagrammes de Ferdinand de Saussure," *Mercure de France* (1964), pp. 243–62.

——, "Lettres et syllabes mobiles: Complément à la lecture des *Cahiers* d'anagrammes de Ferdinand de Saussure," *Littérature* 99 (1995), pp. 7–18.

——, *Les mots sous les mots: Les anagrammes de Ferdinand Saussure* (Paris: Gallimard, 1971).

——, "Les mots sous les mots," in *To Honor Roman Jakobson: Essays on the Occasion of his Seventieth Birthday*, vol. 3 (The Hague: Mouton, 1967), pp. 1906–17.

Steiner, Richard C., "The Two Sons of Neriah and the Two Editions of Jeremiah in the Light of Two Atbash Code-Words for Babylon," *Vetus Testamentum* 46.1 (1996), pp. 74–84.

Sternbach, Ludwik, *Indian Riddles: A Forgotten Chapter in the History of Sanskrit Literature* (Hoshiapur: Vishveshvaranand Vedic Research Institute, 1975).

Strabo, *Geography*, trans. Horace Leonard Jones, 9 vols. (Cambridge, MA: Harvard University Press, 1932).

Strónski, Stanislaw (ed.), *Le troubadour Folquet de Marseille* (Cracow: Académie des Sciences, 1910).

Stults, Lynn D., "A Study of Tristan Tzara's Theory Concerning the Poetry of Villon," *Romania* 96 (1975), pp. 433–58.

Sturluson, Snorri, *Edda*, ed. and trans. Anthony Faulkes (London: Dent, 1987).

——, *Edda: Hátttal*, ed. Anthony Faulkes (London: Viking Society for Northern Research, University College London, 2007).

——, *Edda: Skáldskaparmál*, ed. Anthony Faulkes, 2 vols. (London: Viking Society for Northern Research, University College London, 1998).

——, *The Prose Edda*, trans. Arthur Gilchrist Brodeur (New York: The American-Scandinavian Foundation, 1923).

Sturtevant, E. H., "The Doctrine of Caesura, a Philological Ghost," *American Journal of Philology* 45 (1924), pp. 329–50.

Suetonius, C. Tranquillus, *The Lives of the Twelve Caesars*, trans. Alexander

Thomson, revised and corrected by T. Forester (Cambridge, MA: Harvard University Press, 1913).

——, *De vitae caeserum*, ed. Maximiliam Ihm (Leipzig: Teubner, 1908).

Suter, Ann, "Language of Gods and Language of Men: The Case of Paris / Alexandros," *Lexis* 7–8 (1991), pp. 13–25.

Tacitus, Cornelius, *The Complete Works of Tacitus*, trans. Alfred John Church and William Jackson Brodribb (New York: Modern Library, 1942).

——, *De Germania*, ed. Henry Furneaux (Oxford: Oxford University Press, 1894).

Taylor, Archer, *English Riddles from Oral Tradition* (Berkeley: University of California Press, 1951).

——, "The Riddle," *California Folklore Quarterly* 2.2 (1943), pp. 129–47.

Thompson, George, "The Brahmodya and Vedic Discourse," *Journal of the American Oriental Society* 117.1 (1997), pp. 13–37.

Thuasne, Louis, *Villon et Rabelais: Notes et commentaires* (Paris: Fischbacher, 1911).

Tobler, Adolf, and Erhard Lommatzsch, continued by Hans Helmut Christmann, *Altfranzösisches Wörterbuch*, 11 vols. (Wiesbaden: Franz Steiner, 1960).

Todorov, Tzvetan, *Les genres du discours* (Paris: Éditions du Seuil, 1978).

——, "Roman Jakobson poéticien," *Poétique* 7 (1971), pp. 275–86.

Tolkien, Christopher (trans.), *Saga Heiðreks konungs ins vitra: The Saga of King Heidrek the Wise* (London: Thomas Nelsons & Sons, 1960).

Toporov, Vladimir N., "Die indoeuropäische Poetik und ihre Ursprünge," *Poetica* 13 (1981), pp. 181–251.

Tory, Geoffroy, *Champ fleury, ou L'art et science de la proportions des lettres* (Paris: Charles Bosse, 1931).

Traube, Ludwig, *Nomina sacra: Versuch einer Geschichte der christlichen Kürzung* (Munich: C. H. Beck'sche Verlagsbuchhandlung, Oskar Beck, 1907).

Troubridge, St. Vincent, "Some Notes on Rhyming Argot," *American Speech* 21.1 (1946), pp. 45–47.

Trumper, John, "Slang and Jargons," in *The Cambridge History of the Romance Languages*, vol. 1, *Structures*, ed. Martin Maiden and John Charles Smith (Cambridge, MA: Cambridge University Press, 2011), pp. 660–81.

Tzara, Tristan, *Œuvres complètes*, ed. Henri Béhar, 6 vols. (Paris: Flammarion, 1975–1991).

——, "La signification des anagrammes," *Europe* 53.555–556 (1975), pp. 86–95.

Valéry, Paul, *Œuvres*, ed. Jean Hytier, 2 vols. (Paris: Gallimard, 1960).

Vallet, Eduardo, "Il *senhal* nella lirica trobadorica," *Studi testuali* 5 (2003), pp. 111–59.

———, "Il *senhal nella lirica trobadorica* (con alcune note su *Bel / Bon Esper* in Gaucelm Faidit)," *Rivista di studi testuali* 6–7 (2004–2005), pp. 281–325.

Villani, Paola, "Documenti saussuriani conservati a Lipsia e a Berlino," *Cahiers Ferdinand de Saussure* 44 (1990), pp. 3–33.

Villon, François, *Œuvres*, ed. A. Lognon, revised by Lucien Foulet (Paris: G. Crès, 1919).

———, *The Poems of François Villon*, trans. Galway Kinnell (Hanover: Houghton Mifflin, 1965).

———, *Poésies complètes*, ed. Claude Thiry (Paris: Librairie Générale française, 1991).

Virgilius Maro Grammaticus, *Opera omnia*, ed. Bengt Löfstedt (Leipzig: Teubner, 2003).

Vries, Jan de, *Altnordisches etymologisches Wörterbuch* (Leiden: Brill, 1961).

Watkins, Calvert, *How to Kill a Dragon: Aspects of Indo-European Poetics* (Oxford: Oxford University Press, 1995).

———, "Language of Gods and Language of Men: Remarks on Some Indo-European Metalinguistic Traditions," in *Myth and Law Among the Indo-Europeans: Studies in Indo-European Comparative Mythology*, ed. Jaan Puhvel (Berkeley: University of California Press, 1970), pp. 1–17.

Watts, Harriett Ann, *Chance: A Perspective on Dada* (Ann Arbor: UMI Research Press, 1980).

Waugh, Linda R., "The Poetic Function in the Theory of Roman Jakobson," *Poetics Today* 2.1a (1980), pp. 57–82.

Weinrich, Uriel, *Modern English-Yiddish, Yiddish-English Dictionary* (New York: YIVO Books, 1968).

Werner, Jürgen, "Kenntnis und Bewertung fremder Sprachen bei den antiken Griechen I. Griechen und 'Barbaren': Zum Sprachbewußtein und zum ethnischen Bewußtsein im frühgriechischen Epos," *Philologus* 133.2 (1989), pp. 169–76.

———, "Nichtgriechische Sprachen im Bewußtsein der antiken Griechen," in *Festschrift für Robert Muth*, ed. Paul Händel and Wolfgang Meid (Innsbruck: Innsbrucker Beiträge zur Kultuwissenschaft, 1983), pp. 583–95.

Werth, Paul, "Roman Jakobson's Verbal Analysis of Poetry," *Journal of Linguistics*

12.1 (1976), pp. 21–73.

West, M. L., *Indo-European Poetry and Myth* (Oxford: Oxford University Press, 2007).

Williamson, Craig (ed.), *The Old English Riddles of the Exeter Book* (Chapel Hill: University of North Carolina Press, 1977).

Wunderli, Peter, *Ferdinand de Saussure und die Anagramme: Linguistik und Literatur* (Tübingen: Niemeyer, 1972).

——, "Ferdinand de Saussure, *1er cahier à lire préliminairement*: Ein Basistext seiner Anagrammstudien," *Zeitschrift für französische Sprache und Literatur* 82.3 (1972), pp. 193–216.

——, "Zur Geltung des Linearitätsprinzips bei Saussure," *Vox romanica* 31 (1972). pp. 225–52.

——, "Saussure's Anagrams and the Analysis of Literary Texts," in *The Cambridge Companion to Saussure*, ed. Carol Sanders (Cambridge: Cambridge University Press, 2004), pp. 174–85.

Zumthor, Paul, *Langue et techniques poétiques à l'époque romane (XIe–XIIIe siècles)* (Paris: Klincksieck, 1963).

Index

Dekker, Thomas, 34–35.
Democritus, 12.
DiNapoli, Robert, 102.
Diodorus, 12.
Divine language, 84–94, 98–99.
Dobzynski, Charles, 153–54.
Donats proensals, 32.
Druids, 100–101.
Dufournet, Jean, 154.

EDDAS, 55–57, 62, 71.
Elizarenkova, Tatyana, 81, 128.
Enigmas. *See* Riddles.
Encomium, 129.
Epitomae, 96.
Etienne, Henri, 35.
Euphemism, 105–107.
Eustathius of Thessaloniki, 86.
Exeter Book, 102.

FABLIAUX, 33.
Finnsson Skáldaspillir, Eyvindr, 60.
Foulet, Lucien, 157–58, 162, 211 n.19.
France, Marie de, 24.
Frank, Roberta, 59–60, 63.
Frege, Gottlob, 68.
Friedrich, Johannes, 90.

GALLIC WARS, 100.
Garnier, Joseph, 19.
Genesis. See The Bible.
Genre, 45, 80, 129.
Gentil, Pierre Le, 154, 158.
Georges, Robert A., 67–68.
Gerbstman, Alexander, 81.
Gergons, 24, 32.
Germanic Mythology, 87.
Godel, Robert, 131.
Gonda, Jan, 97.
Gordon, E. V., 56, 62–63, 64.
Grimm, Jakob, 87.
Guilhem de Petieus. *See* William of
   Aquitaine.
Guiraud, Pierre, 41, 186 n.2.
Guieyesse, Georges, 38, 39.
Güntert, Hermann, 87–89.

HANDBOOK OF THE LEARNED, THE.
   See Scholar's Primer, The.

Harman, Thomas, 34.
Head, Richard, *30*, 35.
Herodotus, 12, 32.
Heusler, Andreas, 60–62, 71.
Hittite, 90–91.
Hoepffner, Ernest, 51.
Homer, 11, 84–89, 116.
Homonymous substitution, 23, 41.
Homophony, 41, 79–81.
Hopkins, Gerard Manley, 138.
Horace, 110.
Hypograms. *See* Anaphones.

JACOBSOHN, H., 86.
Jakobson, Roman, 127–28, 131–50, 199
   n.43, 208 n.30.
Jargon, 20–28, 31, 37–38, 94; compared
   with cant, 32.
*Jargon among the Normal, the Degenerate,
   and the Criminal*, 36.
Javanais, 40.
Jeanroy, Alfred, 52.
Jeu de saint Nicolas, Le, 32.
Joseph, John E., 127, 206 n.80.
Journals and Papers, 138.

KALISCHER, ALFRED, 48.
Kandragupta, King, 99.
Kenning, 57–64, 193 n. 29.
Khlebnikov, Velimir, 143.
Kiparsky, Paul, 147, 210 n.55.
Kretschmer, Paul, 86.

LANGUAGES, DIVERSITY OF, 12–15.
Largonji de loucherbème, 40.
Laws of Love, The, 49.
Lazzeroni, Romano, 87.
Leewen, J. van, 86.
Letters, 95–99, 101–105, 119, 139,
   159–60. *See also* Anagrams.
Levet, Pierre, 26.
Lindow, John, 61, 71.
Lindsay, W. M., 104.
Logos, 9–13, 68.
Lucian, 16.
Lucretius, 119–21, 120.
Luther, Martin, 33–34.
Lycophron, 113.

MALAMOUD, CHARLES, 97–99.
Mallarmé, 10, 158–59.
Marot, Clément, 27.
Meillet, Antoine, 87, 105–106.
Meissner, Rudolf, 60–61.
Mémoires de la Société Linguistique de Paris, 19, 25.
Memory, 99–102.
Mencken, H. L., 106.
Messenger, John, 66.
Metaphor, 24, 39–40, 61, 64, 67, 70–71.
Metathesis, 117.
Metonymy, 23–24, 39, 70–71 78–79, 143.
Michel, Francisque, 19.
Milicic, Vladimir, 81.
Milner, Jean-Claude, 39, 123, 125.
Moret, André, 47.

NERVAL, GÉRARD DE, 177.
Niceforo, Alfredo, 36.
Noms de métier, 22–23.
Nykl, A. R., 52.

ON THE LANGUAGE OF THE GODS AND THE LANGUAGE OF SPIRITS, 87–89.
OPOJAZ, 134.
d'Orléans, Charles, 24, 175–77.

PAGIS, DAN, 80.
Pantomime, 16.
Parallelism, 115, 141–48.
Pascoli, Giovanni, 126.
Peire Vidal, 51.
People of the Shell. *See* Coquillars.
Philology, 13, 28, 33, 35, 51, 104; Divine speech and, 86–94.
Phonology, 40, 79, 81, 114–15, 140–41.
Phonetics, 16, 84, 110–11.
Phonic imitation. *See* Anaphones.
Pillet, Alfred, 46.
Pini of Urbino, Teseo, 33.
Plato, 11, 67, 86.
Poe, Edgar Allan, 138, 141–42, 144.
Poetic function, 121, 134–51.
Poetic theology, 93–94.
Poeticity. *See* Poetic function.
Politics, 9.
Porzig, Walter, 69–70, 78, 94.
Probability, 172–79.

Prostitutes, 36, 40, 42.
Proto-Indo-European, 13.
Puisségur, M., 172–74, 176.
Puns, 41.

QUENEAU, RAYMOND, 40, 189 n.33.
Quintilian, 16.

RABELAIS, FRANÇOIS, 173–74.
Rabustel, Jean, 21, 22, 24, 26.
Raimbaut d'Aurenga, 50, 51–52.
Raimbaut de Vacquerias, 50, 51.
Remains concerning Britaine, 113.
Renou, Ernest, 75.
Rhyming slang, 41–42, 189 n.39.
Richard li biaus, 25, 32.
Richter, Hans, 171.
Riddles, 65–82, 94, 102–103, 196 n.52; Precedent and Sequent in, 66–69, 76, 79–81.
"Riddle Hymn," 69–70, 89.
Riffaterre, Michel, 147–48.
Riquer, Martín de, 52.
Riquier, Isabel de, 51.
Ritual, 75–76, 89–90. *See also* Sacrifice.
Rogues, 19–28, 31–38.
Rousseau, Jean-Jacques, 16.
Runes, 101–103.

SACRIFICE, 74–75, 89–90, 100.
Saturnian, 109–18, 121–23, 125–26, 138–39.
Saussure, Ferdinand de, 109–50.
Savinel, Pierre, 155.
Scholar's Primer, The, 90–91.
Schöne, Lucien, 27.
Schwob, Marcel, 19–20, 25–29, 38, 39.
"Scramblings," 95–96.
Scribes, 102, 104–105, 166–67.
Secret of Villon, The, 153–83, 158–82.
Selected Writings, Poetry of Grammar—Grammar of Poetry, 148.
Shklovsky, Viktor, 42.
Six Lectures on Sound and Meaning, 139–40.
Simultaneous poem, 165–66.
Signifiers, 123–24, 139–40.
Skeggjason, Markús, 59.
Skalds, 55–64, 71–72.

Zone Books series design by Bruce Mau
Typesetting by Meighan Gale
Image placement and production by Julie Fry
Printed and bound by Maple Press